THE LAE

# POPULAR DOGS BREED SERIES

# THE LABRADOR
# RETRIEVER

## LORNA, COUNTESS HOWE AND
## GEOFFREY WARING

**POPULAR DOGS**
London Melbourne Sydney Auckland Johannesburg

Popular Dogs Publishing Co. Ltd

An imprint of the Hutchinson Publishing Group

17–21 Conway Street, London W1P 6JD

Hutchinson Publishing Group (Australia) Pty Ltd
16–22 Church Street, Hawthorn, Melbourne, Victoria 3122

Hutchinson Group (NZ) Ltd
32–34 View Road, PO Box 40–086, Glenfield, Auckland 10

Hutchinson Group (SA) Pty Ltd
PO Box 337, Bergvlei 2012, South Africa

First published as *The Popular Labrador Retriever*
by Lorna Countess Howe 1957
Revised 1959, 1961, 1964
Reissued as *The Labrador Retriever* 1975
Revised 1978, 1981,1985

© Executors of the estate of Lorna, Countess Howe
and © Geoffrey Waring 1975, 1978, 1981, 1985

Line drawings © Popular Dogs Publishing Co. Ltd 1975

Set in Baskerville by BookEns, Saffron Walden, Essex

Printed and bound in Great Britain by Anchor Brendon Ltd,
Tiptree, Essex

ISBN 0 09 153031 8

# CONTENTS

# ILLUSTRATIONS

Ch. Cookridge Tango
*Owned by Mrs M. Y. Pauling*
Ch. Cornlands My Fair Lady
*Owned by Mrs D. P. Rae*
Ch. Ruler of Blaircourt
*Owned by Mr and Mrs Grant Cairns*
F.T. Ch. Zelstone Moss
*Owned by Mrs Audrey Radclyffe*
Ch. Braeduke Joyful
*Owned by Mrs Ann Wynyard*
Ch. Kinley Skipper
*Owned by Mr Fred Wrigley*

*Between pages 96 and 97*

Aust. Ch. Ramah Royal Archer UDX, CDX and Danish Int. Ch. Ramah Raisin
*Royal Archer owned by Lt-Col Redvers Dunbar*
*Raisin owned by Mr Dan Dissing Madson*
Aust. Dual Ch. Ellenarta Garnet CM, CD; Aust. Dual Ch. Baldorra Jewel CM; and Aust. Ret. Trial Ch. Ellenarta Tahitian Pearl
*All owned by Major and Mrs A. G. Everingham*
Aust. Ch. Karnmore Ruler
*Owned by Mr Ray Clarke*
Aust. Ch. Ramah Royal Archer
*Owned by Lt-Col Redvers Dunbar*
Aust. Ch. Duffton Glen Angus
*Owned by Mr and Mrs A. E. Sutch*
Aust. Dual Ch. Baldorra Belle
*Owned by Mr and Mrs Heidtman*
AFC, FC and Nat. Amateur Ret. FC Super Chief
*Owned by Mr August Belmont*
NFC, AFC, CFC Cork of Oakwood Lane
*Owned by Dr A. Harold Mork*
Am. Ch. Whygin Gold Bullion
*Owned by Mrs F. B. Gimnel*

## IN THE TEXT

## LORNA HOWE'S INTRODUCTION
## TO THE FIRST EDITION

I have been asked to write this book and it has given me great pleasure to write anything which may be of use to those who love the Labrador Retriever as much as I do. I have always loved dogs and horses from my earliest days. My most severe punishment as a child was to have, on account of some crime, my riding activities, curtailed, or my dog taken away, and so it has gone on all through my life. I should be utterly miserable without dogs.

It was in 1913 that I first had much to do with Labradors. In 1914 I, so to speak, 'flung my bonnet over the mill' and decided to take up the breed seriously. From then until this present year I have whenever possible run dogs at field trials and shown them on the bench. Now I have given up running dogs at trials and showing Labradors. I shall never show another one. I have had a wonderful time with all breeds of gundog at trials and have had such generous help from so many, now alas dead, who were so kind in teaching me how to train and handle dogs at trials – people like the late Mr Charles Alington, Captain A. E. Butter, Mr J. H. Hulme, the Hon. W. J. Hewitt, the Hon. Arthur Holland Hibbert, later Third Viscount Knutsford, Major Maurice Portal, and many others.

I cannot be sufficiently grateful to T. Gaunt, who has been my kennel manager for over thirty years and is, I am thankful to say, still with me. I think he is generally acknowledged to be probably the greatest handler not only of Labradors but Pointers, Setters and Spaniels that there has ever been. What I owe to him I cannot express.

Whilst I am writing about training and teaching to train I cannot leave out my Dual Ch. Banchory Bolo. I think it is only fair to such a great Labrador that he should be paid tribute to and be made known as a dog who could train and handle human beings, because through my intimate knowledge and personal devotion to him I certainly learnt more from him than he did from me.

In writing this foreword I feel I should thank all those who have so very kindly given me help. I am more than grateful to the present Lord Knutsford, who lent me his father's record of his Labradors; to the Duke of Buccleuch, who lent me the wonderful account of the Labrador written by Lord George Scott; to Mr Holland Buckley, who has helped me so much with matters I wished to verify at the Kennel Club; to Mr and Mrs Taylor, the hon. secretaries of the Midland Labrador Club; to Mrs Wormald, the hon. secretary of the Yellow Labrador Club; to Mrs Manson, who gave me much information from the Labrador Club of Scotland; to the Secretary of the Northumberland and Durham Labrador Retriever Club; to Mr J. G. Severn, and to Mrs Thomas Fall for his infinite trouble in reproducing the photographs from Lord Knutsford's book, and other sources.

Very great help I have found in the Labrador Retriever Club's Stud Book and record of Retrievers and trials compiled by the late Mr C. Mackay Sanderson. This book is indeed a mine of information and a really wonderful work. I must also thank Mr H. S. Lloyd, who has given me great assistance in writing a chapter on Labradors as policemen. To all these I am indeed grateful and can say a really heartfelt 'Thank you'. I have always been far more interested in training, working and running dogs than I have in shows, though I love those too.

When I broke my hip for the second time I had to realize that I could no longer handle a Labrador at trials or even at shows. It was a bitter blow, but I knew I must have some breed of dog at least to show so I took up Pugs. They are very like Labradors in many ways, especially in their fidelity and sagacity, but of course their tails cannot be called otter-like. However, I am grateful to them for the many happier hours they have given me.

I am indeed fortunate to have had such generous help from so many who have such an infinity of knowledge of the Labrador. I cannot sufficiently express my gratitude.

I have purposely refrained, as far as possible, from mentioning many of the well-known breeders and owners of the present time. There are so many that it would be hard to differentiate; therefore, with few exceptions, I have refrained from mentioning many of the post-war Labradors. I have picked out certain dogs which I consider outstanding examples of their breed; amongst these I must include three bitches, one yellow Ch. Landyke Sheba, now dead, which was owned by Mr J. Hart, the black Ch. Ballyduff Whatstandwell Rowena, the property of Dr and Mrs Acheson, and the lovely Judith Aikshaw – all quite outstanding.

The opinions expressed in all I have written are my own – I do not expect them to be the opinions of many; it would indeed be a dull world if we all thought alike, and showing would become very monotonous and probably cease. What I have tried to stress throughout is that the true type of Labrador should be preserved and that we should not sacrifice type, substance and character on the altar of speed.

L.H.

1957

## LORNA HOWE'S INTRODUCTION
## TO THE SECOND EDITION

It is gratifying to know that a new edition to my book has been called for, and I have done my best to comply with the publisher's request to add such information as will keep the book abreast with recent developments. There is, however, not a great deal that can be added other than to record modern conceptions of the qualities required in a Labrador, changes of personnel of the Labrador Club and some rather vital decisions affecting the Labrador taken by the Kennel Club. Most of this additional information has, to avoid repagination of the whole book, been embodied in an addendum, but here and there the text has been amended to amplify certain statements or to bring the records up to date.

The popularity of the Labrador as a gundog waxes rather than wanes; indeed in the number of registrations at the Kennel Club it is second only to the Cocker. The total for 1958 was 4672, which exceeds the 1957 total by 263. My earnest hope is that its popularity will continue to grow and that new owners of Labradors will find help and encouragement in this book to advance the interests of the breed.

I have no reason, so far as gundogs are concerned, to regret having 'gone to the dogs' so many years ago, and I hope I may have been of some help to those working with the breed I love so much.

L.H.

1959

## GEOFFREY WARING'S INTRODUCTION
## TO THE FIFTH EDITION

When I was asked to rewrite Lady Howe's book, *The Popular Labrador Retriever*, it was not without a great deal of careful thought that I eventually accepted on the basis of co-authorship. Perhaps it would interest readers to know why I decided to do it this way, when I would rather have written a completely new volume which would, of course, have been much easier.

To me the name of Lorna, Countess Howe, has always been synonymous with Labrador Retrievers. She it was who formed the first breed club, circa 1916. She formulated the breed standard – in fact practically every good thing about the organization of the Labrador Retriever world, which we now take so much for granted, was done on her initiative, wholly or in part.

Her kindness and consideration to anyone with a genuine interest in the breed were unparalleled. She was, and I am sure all who knew her will agree, willing and able to impart her knowledge and experience for the asking. As one who benefited from her wisdom in Labradors, I can say this with justification. Many years ago when I raised a query with her about the breed, not without some trepidation, a novice asking one who was at the peak in the breed and had been for many years, her reply, in great detail, was very enlightening. There was no suggestion of 'talking down' to a novice but instead a really shining example of dedication to the breed. Her attention to temperament in Labradors was extremely keen and I suspect that it was her lead and example to others in this respect that makes us so proud to boast of the breed's wonderful temperament today.

These were some of the points – there were obviously many more – which I turned over in my mind before I finally agreed to accept the publisher's invitation. To my mind the name of Lady Howe should always be known and remembered with affection and thanks in the Labrador world – and if by my small contribution I can help in that direction by keeping Lady Howe's name on this book I am delighted so to do.

In the early chapters of her work Lady Howe describes The Hon. Arthur Holland-Hibbert, later Third Viscount Knutsford, as the breed's greatest benefactor. This I would not deny but, without any doubt at all, I am sure that Lady Howe earned for herself the title of the breed's greatest benefactoress and we should all remember her as such.

In the ensuing chapters I have endeavoured to retain as much of the original work as possible, because I consider that it is the essence of many years' shrewd painstaking experience of breeding fieldwork and historical fact.

For example, Chapters 1 and 2, 'Origin' and 'The Breed's Greatest Benefactor', are as they were in the original edition; the text is unaltered.

Chapter 3 which dealt with Dual Ch. Banchory Bolo in the original work, I have retained but renamed the chapter 'Some Famous Labradors at Home and Abroad' (Chapter 4). Then Bolo takes pride of place and to lead the field. Here I considered it essential to include some of the famous strains from overseas, albeit some of these or their forebears were bred in the UK. It occurred to me that the world-wide interest which is now shown in Labradors warranted their inclusion. They have earned it by right – what is more I feel Lady Howe would agree.

I have attempted to lay greater emphasis and given more detail to the chapter on Breeding. In this I have not delved into the geneticist's world, there are many works devoted entirely to this complex subject by authors better equipped than I to give advice, I have contented myself with the simpler facts of genetics. Other chapters have been adapted or restyled for easier reference.

A section of this book is also devoted to sickness and ailments. The idea of this is not to try to turn every owner into a veterinary surgeon, but simply as a reference to which he can turn if he is in trouble with his dog. The symptoms given are in some cases the result of experinece, unfortunately, and in others assistance has been sought from the veterinary profession. In all cases owners are advised to seek veterinary advice except in the most minor troubles. Whenever possible treatment and remedies have been given but despite this my advice to the owner of a sick dog is to consult the veterinary surgeon as early as practicable if there is the slightest doubt. Delay is often dangerous and sometimes can be fatal; do not take any chances.

The sketches of kennels and suitable boxes for whelping, and the like, are based on ideas which we have found to be sound in principle. I give them to you as ideas which can be adapted to suit your particular problem and environment.

In order to give UK breeders some ideas about what goes on in other parts of the world in Labradors, I have attempted to explain some of the systems. So often UK breeders have been unable to find out how or why some exported dogs have become champions so quickly. An appreciation of the system concerned may bring in its wake a better understanding.

In this connection I would like to thank Lieutenant-Colonel Redvers Dunbar for a wealth of information from Australia. Although he is now trying to curtail some of his doggy activities, Redvers has been Vice-President of the Canberra Kennel Association (the ruling body in Australia Capital Territory), President of the ACT Companion Dog Club (all breeds obedience), Vice-President of the ACT Gundog Society, member of the committee of the Guide Dogs for the Blind, member of the committee of the Canberra All Breeds Kennel Club. His wife, Jean, is also a member of some of these committees. They own two Yellow dogs, Australian Ch. Ramah Royal Archer UD and  Australia Ch. Woodlark Wimmera CD.

Mrs Charlotte Todd, Whiskey Creek Kennels, Hart, Michigan, USA, gave me a good deal of information from the USA. Her aim in breeding is one Countess Howe would applaud, i.e. to rear sound, healthy, good-looking working Labradors. She is keenly interested in genetics and has spent some time on delving into hip dysplasia with the local veterinary college. She owns one of the rare chocolate Champions the bitch Whiskey Creek Brown Bruina.

I would also like to thank, most sincerely, Mr W. Brown Cole, for all his skilled veterinary help and above all my wife and daughter, Jean and Gillian, without whose help my part of this book could never have been written. Their detailed day-to-day knowledge and experience proved an unfailing source of information which they quite cheerfully imparted. This was, on occasion , accompanied by some quite warranted destructive criticism which proved quite salutary. It is to Jean that I would like to dedicate my part of this book.

G.W.

1975

# GEOFFREY WARING'S INTRODUCTION
## TO THE SIXTH EDITION

It seems only yesterday that the fifth edition was published and now the book is being updated for its sixth edition. In the intervening period there has been a relatively small decrease in the number of registrations. This is probably a good sign in that the Labradors numbers are stabilizing and we need not fear any dramatic 'explosion' in terms of numbers bred. The figure given for registrations in 1976 under the new Kennel Club system give in themselves no real comparison with earlier figures, except that the breed is only beaten in numbers bred and registered by German Shepherd Dogs (Alsatians) and Yorkshire Terriers. So at the top of the popularity league there has been no great change of late.

Ch. Cookridge Tango, the only chocolate Champion at the time of going to press with the fifth edition, has now been joined by the bitch, Sh.Ch. Follytower Merry Go Round of Brentville, and by the first chocolate dog champion, appropriately named Ch. Lawnwoods Hot Chocolate. This dog has now been exported to the U.S.A.

Enthusiasm for the breed has not waned either in U.K. or any other country I have visited. Indeed, to see for example the way the Labrador devotees at the other side of the world in New Zealand are zealously looking after the breed is most heartening. Here at home two more breed clubs with ambitious programmes for the future have been formed and the officials of the clubs are quite correctly taking their responsibilities very seriously.

There is one aspect which, in the opinion of many, does

deserve more consideration and that is Labrador rescue. A dog – all too often a Labrador – which is 'in the way' when the family want to go on holiday is turned out, some even at service areas on the motorways. To put it callously, those who survive and end up in the local dogs' home are probably under sentence of death within a very short time. Most other breed clubs have efficient rescue schemes, why cannot the Labrador clubs join forces and do likewise?

Perhaps for the seventh edition this situation will have been resolved because the breed deserves it.

G.W.

1978

## GEOFFREY WARING'S INTRODUCTION
## TO THE SEVENTH EDITION

At the time of printing this, the seventh edition, it is sad to report that the show world and the field trial world still appear to be as far apart as ever. Few show dogs appear in the field and even fewer working dogs appear in the show ring. There are far too many show champions whose owners do not attempt to have them qualified as full champions. The test for this qualification is relatively simple and it really is a pity that more owners do not take advantage of it. There are of course many material advantages to be obtained from gaining the full title – e.g. a more obedient dog, higher prices for stud and puppies, in addition to personal satisfaction. The last time there was a dual champion in Labradors was 1948 – this must be a sad reflection on the breed today.

There are many reasons which can be advanced for this, not least of which is lack of time. But in over thirty years one would have thought someone would have found the time to breed and train a dual champion. Could it be lack of incentive? Whatever the reason, let us hope that before the next edition of this book appears we can report a new dual champion and give readers all the details.

One serious setback experienced by many breeders and owners has been the dreaded disease known as canine parvovirus – it has been described as 'the disease of the century'. Sufficient for me to say that it has caused heartache for many and it has taken its toll of Labradors as well as many other breeds. In order to give some ideas of its cause and effect I have written about it at the end of Chapter 12 – The Labrador in Sickness. I am pleased to report that there is now an effort being made at Labrador rescue by several Labrador Clubs.

Registrations up to 15,002 for 1979 leave me with mixed feelings. The list given in Appendix A ends at an all-time high, and I am quite sure that the effects of this will not all be good.

G.W.

1981

# GEOFFREY WARING'S INTRODUCTION TO THE EIGHTH EDITION

The registration figures are fairly constant now at about 15,000 and Labradors remain very firmly near the top of the registration totals, second only to GSDs (Alsatians) in 1982 and 1983. Sadly, however, I am unable to report that we have a new dual champion in our midst so fame and fortune still await the breeder to achieve this after such a long period without one.

Happily two facets – rescue and parvovirus – have fared better. The former is now thriving in several areas and much good work is being done by the selfless individuals running the schemes. So far as parvo is concerned, the veterinary profession now seem to have this under much more control for which we are all thankful.

G.W.

1985

# 1
# Origin

In the latter part of the eighteenth century a certain Lieutenant
Cartwright, RN, travelled extensively in Newfoundland. In his
book on his travels, he writes: 'Providence has even denied
them [the aboriginal Indians] the pleasing services and companionship of the faithful dog.' From this statement, which is
reliable, I think we may suppose that there were no dogs in
North America. If we accept this statement, it seems reason-
able to assume that the Labrador Retriever was brought by
Europeans to those parts when they began to settle there.

Labrador is said to have been discovered in the year 1000,
but it was not until 1498 that Englishmen first went there in
search of fish. The English were followed one hundred and
fifty (approximately) years later by men from other nations –
Portugal, France and Spain. Reports are written of the inroads
made by wolves, but the author adds that these were kept from
camps by fires, dogs and other means. In the early days trade,
mainly in fish, was carried on with the West Country. In
England in those days the black hounds of St Hubert were
much prized and it is well within the bounds of possibility that
some of these dogs found their way back to Labrador and that
they were the ancestors of the modern Labrador. It is doubtful
if the real origin of the breed will ever be decisively settled, but
it is certain that as the fishing industry increased in Labrador a
breed of dog was founded there that has become world-
famous. It seems an established fact that there were two distinct types of this dog, a larger, stronger and long-haired dog
and a lighter smooth-coated variety. The larger, heavier dogs

were used as draught animals to pull sleighs and generally make themselves useful. The lighter, smoother coated variety were taken by wildfowlers and fishermen and were used to retrieve game from rough seas, and also to retrieve fish which would otherwise have escaped. Both these varieties found their way to these shores and attracted attention. They were known as Newfoundland dogs – which, of course, was confusing.

Finally, about 1812–1814 Colonel Peter Hawker sought to make the matter clearer and called the larger dog the Newfoundland and the smaller the lesser Newfoundland, or the Labrador or St John's dog.

Lord Malmesbury lived near Poole, in Dorset, in those days. He was greatly attracted by the smaller variety and he and Colonel Peter Hawker bought several dogs from the fishermen from Newfoundland, who doubtless found a brisk and remunerative trade to repay them for their enterprise. Colonel Hawker in his book *Instructions to young Sportsmen*, written in 1814, describes the Labrador 'as by far the best for every kind of shooting', and continues:

Oftener black than of another colour, and scarcely bigger than a pointer, he is made rather long in the head and nose, pretty deep in chest, very fine in the legs, has short or smooth hair, does not carry his tail so much curled as the other [presumably the Newfoundland] and is extremely quick in running, swimming and fighting . . . Poole was till of late years, the best place to buy Newfoundland dogs, but now they are become scarce owing [the sailors say] to the strictness of those . . . tax gatherers!

The Duke of Buccleuch, Lord Malmesbury and Lord Home were all favourably impressed by the Labrador as a worker on land and in water. In 1867 a picture was made of Lord Home's Nell, then about eleven years old. Apart from four white feet, she is a typical specimen of the breed so popular. The Border Country down to the present time has ever been a stronghold of the breed. The owners of these original kennels were proud of the breed and did their utmost to keep it pure. That the breed became so popular there is surely emphasized by the fact that Robert Burns describes the breed thus:

*His hair, his size, his mouth, his lugs*
*Shew'd he was nane o' Scotland's dogs*
*But whelpet some place far abroad,*
*Where sailors gang to fish for cod.*

These words seem to portray the Labrador and none other.

To encourage the breeding of sheep a law was introduced into Labrador in 1885 for the destruction of practically all Labradors. In a matter of ten years or so the quarantine laws came into force in England and these two laws virtually ended any extensive trade in dogs between Labrador and this country. At the time this must have seemed hard, but on the whole it probably did good, for once it became extensively known that to trade in Labrador dogs was a lucrative business no doubt there would have been an influx of inferior dogs: so possibly out of evil came good.

One amusing story is, I think, worth repeating, and as it was told to me by Lord Knutsford I can vouch for its truth. Lord Knutsford, then the Hon. Arthur Holland-Hibbert, was anxious to import a Labrador dog for breeding purposes as an outcross to his own famous Munden strain, so he asked a friend to try and get one. The friend tried in vain, receiving the reply: 'You will get a better one nearer home from a young fellow called Holland-Hibbert who lives at Munden, Hertfordshire.'

It is fortunate that the early breeders of the Labrador, such as the Dukes of Buccleuch, the Earls of Home and Malmesbury, the Hon. Douglas Cairns, Sir Richard Graham, and the Hon. Arthur Holland-Hibbert went to such infinite trouble to keep their strains pure and the pedigrees of their dogs intact, for now we are reaping the benefit.

As soon as the Labrador became known in England his praises were sung by those who came in contact with him.

This is an account of his early history as far as I can discover. From this beginning the breed has developed into the Labrador of today – a dog which excels in working ability, is a valued companion to man and a dog which has abundantly proved that he can hold his own with all breeds at shows. Surely if a motto is needed for the Labrador it could very aptly be 'I came, I saw, I conquered.'

In 1878 a dog called Malmesbury Tramp was born. He can be described as one of the tap roots of the modern Labrador. From him came Avon, a well-known dog which was in the Duke of Buccleuch's Kennel. Avon was born in 1885 and when mated to Buccleuch Gyp produced Buccleuch Nith. This dog did a great amount of good. He was mated with Munden Sarah, this union producing Munden Sixty, a dog which exercised great influence for good in Lord Knutsford's kennel and in other kennels of that time.

Another dog which also did much good in the 1880's was Kielder. It was really through the mating of this dog with a bitch named Susan that the real foundation of the famous Munden kennel was laid. In direct descent from them came Waterdale Gamester, which when mated with Birkhill Juliet produced the illustrious Peter of Faskally, a dog which proved himself to be one of the great field trial Labradors of all times.

Born in 1908, Peter was bred by Mr Watson of Birkhill and passed into the hands of Mr David Black, who has owned so many famous dogs. Later Peter was acquired by Captain A. E. Butter in whose name, and when handled by him, he was so brilliant at field trials. His wins included the Champion Stake. It is interesting to know that Peter was the sire of F.T. Ch. Patron of Faskally, which also won the Champion Stake, as did Patron's son F.T. Ch. Tag of Whitmore, thus making the record of three generations winning that distinction.

I believe Mr Twyford considered Tag one of the best, if not the best, field trial dog he ever owned, and he certainly owned a goodly company.

Returning to Peter, he can surely be accounted as a dog which did untold good to the breed. No fewer than thirty-two of his progeny actually won, or were placed in field trials. He sired a Bench Champion in Withington Dorando and two field trial Champions in Peter of Whitmore and Patron of Faskally. Peter of Faskally did a very great deal of popularize the Labrador Retriever.

Amongst other sons of Peter's was Sandal of Glynn, a dog which owing to the 1914–18 war, was prevented from competing at field trials. He sired only one litter. In that litter the only dog was Dual Ch. Banchory Bolo. From Bolo came many famous Labradors.

To return to the main tap roots of the breed, great prominence must be given to Netherby Boatswain – from Boatswain came Brayton Sir Richard and Warwick Collier, the latter being the sire of such famous dogs as Esk, Brocklehirst Bob and Kinmount Don. Brayton Sir Richard's progeny included Brayton Swift and Munden Sovereign, names which appear in so many pedigrees.

Boatswain when mated to Netherby Jill produced Kielder, a dog whose name is very famous in old pedigrees. Among other dogs he produced was Lord Verulam's Sweep, born in 1889. Among his sons was Netherby Tar, a dog famous in the Border country, from which came so many famous dogs.

Another dog which did an immense amount of good, and would have done more had it not been for the 1914–18 war, was Ch. Ilderton Ben, bred by Mr Thompson in 1913. He was by a dog called Bobby (Smiler – Athol Lass) ex Nell (Rover – Jet.) He passed into the hands of Mr Reay, of Northumberland, for whom he won third prize in the Gamekeepers' National Association's Trials in 1915 and qualified as a Bench Champion. I acquired Ben in 1916 and kept him until he died in 1924. He was one of the best-proportioned dogs I have seen, and a beautiful Labrador. He did much good at stud and would doubtless have done more but for the war. He sired one Dual Ch. namely Banchory Sunspeck, three champions, Grately Ben, Teazle of Whitmore and Baree of Faircote, and four winners field trials and others that gained recognition. Certainly outstanding was Banchory Don, a dog which, owing to an injury to his head, could never be shown but which did much good to the breed.

Tramp, Boatswain and Ben seem to have been the tap roots from which modern Labradors have descended; their names appear in nearly all pedigrees today.

It is also stated that in the period 1450–1458 a merchant, a native of Bristol named John Cabot, sailed from Bristol with a crew of Englishmen and later claimed to have discovered Labrador. He took with him on this voyage his son Sebastian, who went on to Hudson Bay and was much taken with the sleigh dogs and the dogs owned by fishermen there.

There can be no doubt that the Labrador owes a very great deal to the Dukes of Buccleuch and their family. They have from the very first given every support to the breed and have always kept a most representative kennel at Langholm, going to endless trouble to find suitable dogs and import them to benefit the breed.

A most informative book has been written on the breed by Lord George Scott, which gives a full and varied history of their breed.

In the book kept by the late Lord Knutsford which has very kindly been lent to me by his son, the present Lord Knutsford, I have found much of interest. In the cuttings from various newspapers, and in the pictures it contains, there is a great deal of information. A cutting dated May, 1896 taken from a paper called the *Country House* states:

Sixty or seventy years ago there was considerable trade between Poole in Dorset and Labrador, and it is a fact that by these trading vessels the breed (Labradors) was first brought to England and that excellent sportsman, the then Earl of Malmesbury, became possessed of them. So highly was he pleased with their work, especially in water, that he kept them until his death. About the same time, or perhaps a little later, the Duke of Buccleuch, the Earl of Home (who died in 1841) and Lord John Scott imported some from Labrador. They were kept pure for many years.

Lord Knutsford himself writes of the breed: 'I believe the Labrador Retriever to be unequalled for sporting purposes either on land or in water.'

The main early supporters of the breed in the North and in the Border Country at that time were, as far as I can discover, the Duke of Buccleuch, the Earl of Home, Lord John Scott and Sir Richard Graham of Netherby. Later Mr A. Nichol, the head keeper at Brayton, was also a very strong and ardent supporter of the breed. His dog Ch. Brayton Swift in later years was a big winner and was sire of Ch. Type of Whitmore, one of the great winners of his age.

A gentleman who refused to divulge his name and wrote over the name of 'Preserver' stated that the Labrador did not

come from Labrador at all, but was the result of a cross between a Pointer and a Newfoundland. In his argument against
this, Lord Knutsford wrote to *The Field* that:

. . . 'Preserver' having been proved wrong over this statement, produces further mystification by quoting various sayings from mys-
terious individuals whose names are not to be divulged.

Lord Knutsford goes on:

. . . that if the Labrador is indeed the production of a cross, it is
curious that like all cross breeds they do not throw back! That is one
of the remarkable things about them, how strong the Labrador blood
is.

On looking at the photographs in that book I am greatly
taken with the one of Avon (1896) which bears a great resemblance to Ch. Ilderton Ben and of Nero, about the same
period . . . to Ch. Withington Dorando. In that book also
appears a photo of a dog called Rufus, reproduced from the
*Sporting Magazine* of 1832. It does not state if the dog is black,
yellow or chocolate; one of the two latter colours seems suggested by the name. Rufus is not what one might call a typical
Labrador, his tail being rather feathered but not what is
usually described as really 'Flat Coaty'. He had apparently very
strong, well-shaped hindquarters, well-bent thigh and his
hocks are well set under him. He appears long in back and
slack of ribs. His ears are not well set and are inclined to be
sheep-doggy and semi-folded in head; he is distinctly snipy
and cut away in muzzle, which is too long and pointed. He has
white toes on all four feet but has good straight legs but lacks
bone. His coat appears rough and long. On going through
various newspaper cuttings in Lord Knutsford's book, which
contains different theories expounded by different people as
to the origin of the Labrador, I found in a letter to *The Field*
written in 1930 an answer to an article written on the Labrador, to which Lord Knutsford responded:

As far as I can ascertain – and I have been trying for many years – the
statement that the present Labrador results from a Pointer cross is
without foundation. Certainly some of the founders, Lord Malmesbury, Sir R. Graham, the Duke of Buccleuch, Lord John Scott or Lord

Verulam never tried such a cross, and I have bred Labradors ever since 1893 and have never used a Pointer. I believe that the attenuated look of many of the so-called Labradors today arises from breeding anything and everything so long as it has a smooth coat and a sort of look of a Labrador, but such curiosities cannot be called Labradors.

If Lord Knutsford wrote this in 1930 I wonder what he would have written of the dogs masquerading under the name of Labradors which appeared after the 1939 war and which still appear, alas, at field trials, and also at shows. Of course the modern craze for speed makes this light, racy and whippety dog popular. I believe in America there ia also a craze for speed, and lightly built leggy dogs with no bone or substance are winning. This is all wrong; these dogs may be racing machines but they are not Labradors. I am convinced that the old type of Labrador, which did not gallop too fast for its nose, collected more game in the aggregate than some of these what may be called speed merchants do today. Moreover, there was less game left uncollected, and left for an official picker-up to collect later.

In going through the pedigrees in Lord Knutsford's book one is struck by the recurrence of the names of dogs like Kielder from Sir Richard Graham's kennel at Netherby – Avon, Nith and many others from the Duke of Buccleuch's kennels, and Ned bred by Lord Malmesbury, also a dog from his kennels called Sweep (1877) apparently imported from Newfoundland: also the names of dogs from the kennels of Lord Ruthven and Lord Wimborne, Lord Home and others. There are two photos of Lord Home's Nell, one standing and one lying down. She appears to have been a typical Labrador, her main fault being white toes on three of her feet (two fore feet and the off hind foot), as was so frequently the case in early days. She appears to have a beautiful and very sagacious head with good width between well-placed and shaped ears, and has what the Scots call a 'wise-looking' head. She was whelped in 1855 and the photos I have before me were taken in 1867; beyond a white muzzle, she does not show signs of age and must have been a real 'laster'. On the opposite page appears a photo of Munden Solo (Dual Ch. Banchory Bolo ex Banchory

Betty) whelped 1923 and it is amazing how similar the two are in type, which is further proof of the purity of the breed. Stranger, as his name implies, was an imported dog, originally from Labrador, but as far as I can gather the late Mr W. Stuart Menzies of Arndilly, Craig Ellachie, found him in Norway. He wrote about Stranger to Lord Knutsford, in a letter dated May, 1911:

What I must have told you was that I found Stranger on the quay at Trondgerin, Norway, and his owner, an emigrant agent, said he had brought the dog over from Newfoundland via Canada, but I found out no details.

There is a photograph of Stranger which shows him to be a very good-looking dog, with good bone, beautiful neck and shoulders. Well set-on good tail with powerful quarters. I cannot trace any of his progeny, which is a pity because his appearance suggests that he ought to have done the breed much good.

Among the letters in Lord Knutsford's book there is one from Colonel Cotes of Pitchford Hall, Shrewsbury, dated, 16 July 1908, who wrote:

I enclose you a photograph from a picture of Jim, my father's Labrador, that was bought at Poole by Mr Portman, father of the present Lord Portman, 1832. He was an extraordinary good dog in the Field and is the ancestor of my present retrievers. The Captain of the ship who sold him to Mr Portman said he was one of the best bred dogs in the Island. He had a certain amount of coat more than the present Labradors have.

There is a letter from Sir Richard Graham, dated 21 October 1907, who wrote:

It is quite true, about 40 years ago there was a dog here which came from Edenhall very like a Labrador to look at which was half Mastiff and was called Tar; he was an excellent retriever and a very good night dog. He was never used as a stud dog except for breeding rabbit catchers' dogs of which he sired some very good ones. The first Labradors were brought here about 50 years ago by James Cran who came from the Hirsel (Lord Home's) and I think they came from Langholm originally.

On 3 November 1907, Sir Richard Graham wrote to
Lord Knutsford:

I have got 9 old Labradors and 7 puppies at the moment – 1887 I
think is as far back as any of my Labradors go. Lord Malmesbury may
have kept their pedigrees longer as a good many now go back to Lord
Malmesbury's Sweep 1877 and his Juno 1878.

In Lord Knutsford's book there are a number of groups of
Labradors and also many single ones. One cannot help being
struck by the type of Labrador he was so deeply attached to.
There is a study of four Labrador heads – Munden Saba,
Sandfly, Sorrow and Sovereign – which are so typical of the
breed and of the type he kept and bred. So many of the photos
of the dogs he had seem so similar to the best of those one sees
today. Judging from these photographs, and from various
conversations I had from time to time with him, he would not
tolerate anything in the shape of a lightly got up or leggy dog.
He always stressed the point that a Labrador is a dog which
should stand up to a really hard day's work and that the dog's
somewhat broad chest enabled him to do this. He was also
very particular about the right Labrador coat which, in some
cases, we appear to be losing. He also liked a dog with a broad
skull, not finely chiselled like the flat coat, with a pronounced
stop and large expressive eyes, not dark and piercing, but of
hazel or burnt sugar colour.

I feel that if we follow Lord Knutsford's ideal Labrador we
shall not go wrong; we certainly shall not be doing something
that might result in irreparable harm to the breed.

# 2

# The Breed's Greatest Benefactor

THE HON. ARTHUR HOLLAND-HIBBERT

later

THIRD VISCOUNT KNUTSFORD

No history of the Labrador could be complete without a chapter devoted to the breed's greatest benefactor, the Hon. A. Holland-Hibbert, later Third Viscount Knutsford. His knowledge of the breed was indeed profound and his devotion and support most loyal. He was amongst the first to recognize its great merits. From the outset he supported the breed in every way possible.

He owned his first Labrador, Munden Sybil, in 1884. Bred by Lord Grimston at Gorhambury, St. Albans, Sybil traced back to Kielder, which was by Boatswain belonging to Sir Richard Graham and which was imported from Newfoundland. Of Sybil Lord Knutsford said: 'A timid creature but a wonderfully good bitch for nose, pace, endurance and marking.'

A dog whose name appears in so many pedigrees was Munden Sixty, whelped July, 1897. He won a first prize at Carlisle Dog Show in August 1900. Carlisle, and in fact all the Border Country, was ever a stronghold of the breed.

Lord Knutsford wrote of Sixty (in the book in which he kept a record of his Labradors) that 'he was black with no white and a well-made dog'. That he was a great favourite with his master is made clear by the closing remark about him which reads: 'To the everlasting grief of all who knew him this splendid dog died August, 1901.' His daughter Munden Single, born March, 1899, must have been exceedingly good to look at. In an article in *Our Dogs*, 1904, she is referred to as the finest Labrador bitch ever seen on or off the bench. She was further

Dual Ch. Banchory Bolo. Born December 1915, died July 1927.
*From the painting by Ward Binks*

Ch. Judith Aikshaw. Born December 1951

Lord Home's Nan, born 1855. Photograph taken in 1867

Stranger. Imported about 1911 by Mr W. Stewart Menzies

Ch. Holton Baron (*Thomas Fall*)

Dual Ch. Staindrop Saighdear (*Thomas Fall*)

Dual Ch. Bramshaw Bob, Best Dog in Show at Cruft's 1932 and
1933 and at twelve other Championship Shows

Ch. Banchory Danilo, winner of 33 challenge certificates and Best in
Show Kennel Club 1925 (*Thomas Fall*)

referred to in this paper as having been described by a man
who had handled retrievers all his life as 'the best game finder
and steadiest retriever he had ever seen'.

Lord Knutsford wrote of her: 'Had to end her glorious life
Sept, 1909.' He continued: 'She now reposes in a glass case in
the Natural History Museum, Kensington, as an example, but
it is a bad representation.' Lord Knutsford's remarks were
always downright. Of one dog he wrote: 'A queer under-bred
head, dead and not mourned for.'

In 1902 came Munden Sovereign, a name which also
appears in so many pedigrees. He was by Sir Richard ex Munden Single. Sovereign must have been a beautiful dog. The
head study I have before me as I write is really perfection, with
beautifully set ears, wide forehead and very expressive eyes. In
the note regarding his end Lord Knutsford wrote that he had
to be destroyed in 1913, having been bitten by Shekel, the only
*dark-eyed* and the only *bad-tempered* Labrador ever born at Munden. Of one dog he owned later he wrote: 'Went all wrong
body and soul.' Lord Knutsford was certainly candid about his
own dogs, but he was ever kind about other people's.

During the years of the 1914–1918 war the Labrador kennel
at Munden became practically extinct. It was after this war that
I gave Lord Knutsford a puppy (which he registered as Munden Scarcity by Ch. Banchory Lucky ex Banchory Betty) on the
condition that he should eventually breed from her with dual
Champion Banchory Bolo. This mating produced Munden
Solo and Ch. Banchory Danilo; the latter won thirty-three
Challenge Certificates on the bench and was adjudged best
exhibit in the Kennel Club Show in 1925.

Later he owned Munden Squeezer with which, when he was
in his seventy-ninth year, he wond the Non-Winners' Stake at
the Herts, Beds, and Bucks Trials, handling the dog himself. I
think the last dog he ever bought was Rab of Cadrona, from A.
McCrindle in January, 1934, Rab having won the 5s. Members' or Gamekeepers' Stake held at Idsworth by the Labrador
Retriever Club in which there were seventeen runners.

This stake, which was held annually at Idsworth was always
attended by Lord Knutsford. He was a brilliant shot. I remember him so often telling me how he looked forward to these

particular trials. His annual speech made at the luncheon
there was always eagerly awaited by all who were privileged to
hear it. He was elected Chairman of the Labrador Club at the
formation of the club, an office he held to the end of his life.
He took the greatest interest in the club and it is certain that it
is largely due to his wise guidance that it was formed and
occupies the happy position it does today. From the formation
of the club up to the day of his death he took the deepest
interest in all connected with its welfare.

I acted as Hon. Secretary to the club throughout his time as
Chairman. No Secretary could wish to have a kinder or more
loyal and considerate Chairman than he was. It was at the
Gamekeepers' Trials in 1935 that he collapsed when speaking
at the luncheon, and died, to the great grief of all present –
gamekeepers from all parts of England and Scotland, men
who looked on him as their friend. All had the most profound
admiration for him. I shall always treasure what Lady
Knutsford wrote to me – that as he had not died at Munden she
was thankful that his death took place at Idsworth among
friends so deeply attached to him.

To him the Labrador breed and all those who love it owe a
debt of gratitude which can never be repaid. The most we can
do is to try to keep the breed as he would have wished it to be –
a dual purpose dog, not one in which the working and show
bench types are entirely different as in so many breeds
today.

There is at the present time some danger of this. Let us
beware – before it is too late. The great dogs of the past have so
ably upheld both beauty and brains that we should try to keep
this very high standard. What has been done can surely be
maintained. I remember so well Lord Knutsford saying to me,
not once but many times, that he was so proud that the Labrador had beauty and brains, and that surely people who wanted purely show dogs could seek another breed and not divide
the Labrador into what might virtually be classified as dogs
which were of practical use out shooting for collecting game
and dogs which were purely knights of the show bench. The
Labrador has proved so decisively that he can do both that is it
up to those who love the breed and have its interest deeply at

heart to see that this high reputation is maintained. There could be no more suitable memorial to Lord Knutsford than this, an objective he had so close to his heart.

During the year previous to his death Lord and Lady Knutsford celebrated their golden wedding. Naturally such an occasion could not pass unnoticed by the Labrador Club. All members were circularized and an appeal made for funds for a suitable presentation. Never was an appeal more generously supported. Subscriptions were limited to one guinea. Sufficient was quickly collected and a very beautiful golden inkstand was purchased. This was presented to Lord Knutsford at that final meeting which ended so tragically. It was a small tribute to one who had done so much to benefit and popularize the Labrador.

# 3

# The Breed to Date

With the formation of the Labrador Retriever Club in February 1916 under the chairmanship of the Hon. Arthur Holland-Hibbert and with Mrs Quinton Dick (later Lorna, Countess Howe) as Hon. Secretary arrangements for the necessary encouragement and protection for the breed began to be made. At a meeting held on the second day of Cruft's Show at which Flatcoated retriever breeders were present the wins of a dog called Horton Max exhibited by Mr A. Shuter were discussed. Mr Reginald Cooke of Flatcoats asserted that whilst Horton Max won in Labradors he won with a Flatcoat closely related to Max. It was after this meeting and the discussions that the Labrador Retriever Club was born. One of their first duties was to draw up a standard of rules and a standard of points.

Lorna, Countess Howe writes:

The main object of the club was to encourage and protect the breed which had proved so eminently successful for work and which was rapidly coming to the fore as a force to be reckoned with in the judging for Best in Show at Championship Shows. Naturally much time had to be spent before a suitable set of rules was drawn up and in this as in the drawing up the standard of points, the help given by the late Mr Burdett-Coutts was invaluable. It may give an idea of the care and trouble expended in drawing up the standard of points when it is pointed out that this standard drawn up in 1916 remains in force today and has been accepted by the Kennel Club. From the very first it was known that a dog suitable for work was essential, and right well has the Labrador fulfilled the expectations of those who placed such great faith in the working ability of this breed. The committee also realized that everything possible should be done to encourage gamekeepers, for it was rightly appreciated that in the hands of the gamekeeper rested much of the future of the breed. This policy has certainly paid great dividends.

Naturally, at the time of the formation of the club, all field trials were at a standstill, as we were struggling for our very existence. When field trials were resumed the Labrador club was invited by the Earl of Lonsdale (a member of the Committee) to hold the first Field Trial Meeting at Lowther. A good entry was obtained but unfortunately the meeting had to be abandoned owing to heavy snow. The following year the first Field Trial Meeting was held by permission of Sir Francis Boughey at Aqualate in Shropshire. Two stakes were held, an Open won by Mr Twyford's Tag of Whitmore and a Junior won by my Banchory Dancer.

It was then decided to hold two separate Field Trial Meetings comprising an Open Stake and a Puppy and Non-winners' Stake. In 1925, to help the numbers of members paying a 5s. members' subscription, a Stake was also provided, this being called the 5s. Members' Stake. This has been held regularly in the month of January and has always been extremely popular. In the years preceding the Second World War the dogs competing in this Stake were well able to hold their own, either at trials or at shows with the best dogs in the country. I am glad to say that this Stake is still continued and in this last season the work was of a particularly high standard. The winner is qualified to run in the Champion Stake the following season. It has twice been won by a dog belonging to Mr R. MacDonald named Rockstead Footspark, a dual Champion, and undoubtedly he has fully demonstrated his dual ability. He won the Stake in the 1954 season at the age of nine and half years, which proves that the Labrador is indeed a breed which lasts. In the 1955 season the Stake was won by Mr J. Cady, of Whitmore fame.

In 1938 the first Championship Show was held at Nantwich. These shows were resumed after the war, the first being held at Reading in 1947.

In 1952, owing to the death of Captain Eccles, the Assistant Secretary, it was held in conjunction with Cruft's. In 1953 the Club again held its own show at Ascot by the kind permission of Mr Terry Clare. In 1954 and 1955 the show moved to Phyllis Court, Henley, by permission of Sir Geoffrey Betham who hospitality is so deeply appreciated by all who have experienced his kindness.

In 1938 the Labrador Club had a great honour paid to it: His late Majesty King George VI became Patron of the Club. Upon His Majesty's lamented death Her Majesty the Queen graciously consented to become Patron, an honour deeply appreciated by all members. His Majesty King George VI took great interest in the breed and kept some fine specimens at Sandringham. His Labradors – Wolferton Jet – Wolferton Dan and Ben – soon became well known at many shows, where they were winners of Challenge Certificates and other awards. King George VI was particularly fond and proud of his Labradors. His Majesty preferred yellow Labradors. Her Majesty the Queen has run dogs in her name at trials and to everyone's great pleasure won a Stake in 1956.

Countess Howe writes on the various colours in the breed in the post 1914–18 war period as follows:

### THE BLACK LABRADOR

The kennel of the late Mr T. W. Twyford of Whitmore will never be forgotten either at field trials or on the show bench. Under the able management of Mr J. Cady, it held a marvellous record. F.T. Ch. Tag of Whitmore won the Champion Stake in 1920 and Dual Ch. Titus of Whitmore won it in 1923. Another celebrated inmate of this famous kennel was Ch. Peter of Whitmore, a Labrador of great character and type. Ch. Type of Whitmore (born 1909) was almost invincible in the show ring in the 1912 to 1916 period (he also ran with distinction at field trials), and among many other famous inmates were Champions Thelma and Twilight.

Mr Twyford did much to help in the formation of the Labrador Retriever Club and was one of the original members of the Committee, remaining on it up to the time of his death. He was always willing to help with wise advice and sat on the small committee set up to draw up rules for the club's administration. Upon the death of Mr Twyford, Mr Cady carried on the kennel, though considerably reduced, for his son, Mr H. Twyford, and remained with him until Mr Twyford's death. Mr Cady evidently cannot forsake the Labrador for he still keeps some and runs them with success at trials. He is a member of the Committee of the Labrador Club and his services as a judge at trials and shows have been much sought after.

A gamekeeper member who ran and exhibited Labradors at shows with great success was the late Mr McCall, who lived at St Mary's Isle, Kirkcudbright. He was also a member of the Committee of the Club and was a renowned judge of the breed.

Other gamekeeper members, now dead, were Mr J. Dinwoodie, who bred many good dogs, Mr Carruthers, who prefix Orchardton was so well known, and Mr Campbell, a member of the Committee, who was head keeper at Arundel. A man who did untold good to the breed – in fact to all breeds of gundogs – was the late Mr C. Mackay Sanderson, who compiled the *Labrador Retriever Stud Book*. This book is a complete record and history of the breed and is a book all lovers of Retrievers should possess as it deals with all breeds though compiled specially for the Labrador Club.

The late Mr T. Parmley will always be remembered by Ch. Manor House Belle, perhaps generally accepted as the best bitch of all time. I should like to see her and Judith Aikshaw together for comparison. Belle was not only beautiful herself but she produced some beautiful sons and daughters, such as Ch. Withington Dorando, Ch. Coats Lu, Manor Wyn, Bradfield Lancer, and Banchory Bute. Mr Allbones always seemed to have a good Labrador. Perhaps his two most famous were Ch. Alby Twink (a yellow) and Ch. Alby Mother's Ruin (a black). A judge always sought after, either for field trials or shows, was the late Mr. J. H. Hulme. His Ch. Withington Ben and Withington Dinah were two of the best Labradors I have ever seen. I owe much to Mr Hulme's kindness. In 1914 I went to see him at his home near Manchester when I was just beginning to get my kennel of Labradors together. He gave me much wise advice and I could always depend on this until his much regretted death. From him I purchased on that day in 1914 Ch. Withington Dorando.

A man who has done much for the breed is Mr David Black who, I am happy to say, is still with us. He had much to do with the training of F.T. Ch. Peter of Faskally and F.T. Ch. Patron of Faskally. I shall ever be grateful to him as he sold F.T. Ch. Balmuto Jock to me. Jock (or John as he was always called), owing to his age of course lacked experience, but the education he had received at Mr Black's hands stood him in good stead for the rest of his life. He will ever go down in the history of working gundogs as a really great dog with super intelligence and nose.

The name of Mr J. Alexander will always be famous. He was for years the trainer of the late Duke and Duchess of Hamilton's dogs – both Labradors and Spaniels. He was a wonderful trainer. His dogs loved him and he had a mutual understanding with each one of them. I think his name will always be remembered as one of the really great trainers in gundog history. Mr T. Gaunt, my kennel manager, was at one time with Mr Alexander at the Duke and Duchess of Hamilton's places at Dungavel, Balcombe in Sussex and Ferne in Wiltshire. Both Gaunt and Alexander had great success with the dogs in their care. Gaunt has the same quiet way with his dogs and they respond by giving of their best to him.

Another of the earliest and staunchest supporters was Mr Owen Mansel who owned Belle Chienne and many other good Labradors.

## THE YELLOW LABRADOR

There can be no doubt that the black and yellow Labrador Retrievers can claim a common ancestor. Both trace back to a dog called Neptune. It was in 1925 that the Yellow Labrador Retriever Club was founded – although as early as 1908 a yellow, Mrs Straker's Sandy, won an award at field trials. At that period the yellows were more throaty in neck than the blacks. They usually, and do at the present time, excel in density of coat and much-to-be-desired otter tail. At that time, namely the period 1925–1926, there was an attempt made to try to induce the Kennel Club to make a distinct register for black and for yellow Labradors, thus separating and making two distinct varieties of a breed that was fundamentally the same, had practically the same standard of points and could claim a common ancestor.

The absurdity of this idea can perhaps be more easily understood when I point out that at that time a dog, Ch. Beningbrough Tangle, winner of eighteen Challenge Certificates, was black in colour. Also winning at this time was his own son (from a black mother) Banchory Tawny, which was, as his name denotes, a yellow, and was, at one show, reserve to his father for the Challenge Certificate. He was later exported to India by H.H. the Maharajah of Patiala, where he became a champion. Tangle was a son of Dual Champion Banchory Bolo who was, as far as I can trace, entirely black bred, as was, I believe, Tawny's mother. The Kennel Club, having these facts before them, in its wisdom refused to grant a separate registration for blacks and yellows, for which decision we who have the interest of the breed at heart cannot feel sufficiently grateful.

The yellows have had from the start very loyal supporters. His late Majesty, King George VI, was a great admirer of the breed and had some exceedingly good specimens in his kennels, amongst them being the yellow St Mary's Charm, owned and bred by that great supporter of the breed, the late Mr W. McCall whose prefix St Mary's was so well known. Charm was bought, after winning the Gamekeeper's Stake (or 5s. Members' Stake as it is called) held by the Labrador Retriever Club in 1938, to present to his Majesty by members of the Club. Major Radclyffe, of Hyde Wareham, did much to bring the breed into prominence, his Neptune being the ancestor of the majority of the yellows of today. Neptune was by Mr M. Guest's Sweep ex Nell, bred by Major Radclyffe. Neptune produced many well-known dogs, his sons including Hyde Ben Mannie and other famous dogs. I think I am correct in writing that Mannie was the foundation on which the late Major Arthur and Mrs Wormald's Kennel was built. Mrs Wormald has at the present time the most representative kennel of yellow Labradors extant.

Other staunch supporters of this colour were the late Lord Wimborne and of course the aforementioned Major Radclyffe (in the South of England), whilst in the North, the Border Country, Dumfries and up to Inverness, this colour received most loyal support from Mr and Mrs F. Straker, the Earl of Feversham, Lord Middleton and many others. This was in the earlier years. After the 1920 period, and up to the 1939 war, many more breeders became attracted by this colour, amongst them Major Doyne Ditmas, whose Boghurst prefix became extensively known, and Mr Allbones with his beautiful dog Ch. Alby Twink who, with Mr Williamson's Reyen Lass, accounted for the Challenge Certificates at Cruft's Show, Reyen Lass gaining the award of Best of Breed in an entry which numbered 906. Many other breeders also patronized the colour and in 1938 the Champion Stake was divided between Mr R. G. Heaton's Cheverells Amber, a yellow, and Major Peacock's black, Greatford Shy.

Two of the three Dual Champions now existing are yellow – the late Mr Edgar Winter's Dual Champion Staindrop Saighdear, a dog teeming with Labrador character and most handsome, having everything that goes to make up a true Labrador, and Mrs Wormald's Dual Ch. Knaith Banjo, also a typical Labrador. The latter claims yellow ancestors, Saighdear being a great-grandson on both sides of his pedigree of Dual Ch. Banchory Bolo, who (except in colour) he much resembles. Saighdear is 75 per cent black bred – and was the first yellow Dual Champion.

The name of Ch. Banchory Danilo, a son of Bolo's, is found in many of the pedigrees of yellows today, Danilo's son, Ch. Badgery Richard, appearing frequently in pedigrees. Richard had a daughter Ch. Badgery Ivory, which, as her name denotes, was a pale yellow in colour and a typical and beautiful Labrador. At present time a bitch of this colour, Ch. Judith Aikshaw, is being exhibited. She is so similar in type and appearance to Ivory that I asked her owner the first time I ever saw Judith if she was descended from Ivory. Her owner later sent me her pedigree; she traces back on both sides of her pedigree to Ivory, Richard, Danilo and Bolo. This bears out the statement made by Lord Knutsford years ago when he answered correspondence appearing in various newspapers which claimed that the Labrador is a chance-bred dog. In this he stated that the Labrador is no 'come-by-chance' breed but one firmly established with a fixed type. The Yellow Labrador Retriever Club was formed in 1925 to protect and care for the welfare of dogs of this colour. Lord Middleton of Birdsall, Yorkshire, has a well-established kennel of yellows with which he has done remarkably well at field trials. The black and yellows are now equally well established.

The Yellow Labrador Club is most capably run by the Hon. Sec., Mrs Arthur Wormald, who took over the duties on the death of her husband, Major Arthur Wormald. The breed owes much to their unfailing interest in this attractive colour. This colour is fortunate in having among its admirers and breeders such experts as Mrs Radclyffe, whose dogs have run so well at trials, Mr J. Hart, whose prefix Landyke is so well known, Mr Outhwaite, owner of the Poppleton prefix, Mr Wrigley and many others who support the colour. A colour recognized by the Kennel Club and the Labrador Retriever Club, but which is not so numerically strong as the blacks and yellows, is the chocolate colour. One of the chief supporters of this colour is the Hon. Lady Ward of Chiltonfoliat, near Hungerford, the dogs from her kennel being very typical with particularly good tails and coats. The Earl of Feversham also had some typical specimens of this colour, his Nawton Pruna doing well at field trials in the years before the 1914 war. The late Earl of Lonsdale had a kennel of yellow Labradors at Lowther and his dog Ben was almost as well-known a figure in London as was his master.

Mrs Wormald's Dual Ch. Knaith Banjo is a dog which has done remarkably well at field trials and at shows in the post-war period. The Yellow Labrador Retriever Club holds an annual show for Labradors of this colour. Some shows have classes confined to this colour, but now all dogs, blacks and yellows are quite capable of holding their own without separate colour classes. The Yellow Labrador Club holds annual field trials confined to dogs of this colour. At one time some people thought that the yellows had not the same drive and determination as the blacks, but I think it is more a question of a dog's courage than of its colour. Two yellows who did remarkably well in this country were Jaffa and Ming. The former went to India, where he became a field trial Champion, whilst Ming qualified for this honour in America. The late Major Lucas had a very strong kennel of yellows before the last war, his Hawkesbury Joy being a particularly beautiful type.

During 1956 the blacks and yellows divided the Challenge Certificates awarded at championship shows very equally but it is not at all uncommon for the yellows to gain both Certificates. I think one can certainly find as many good specimens of the yellows as one can of the blacks – perhaps more. I was particularly struck with the yellows when I judged at the Labrador Club of Scotland recently, where both Certificates and the Reserves for that honour went to yellows.

The yellow Labradors owned by Mrs Radclyffe have always to be reckoned with at shows and field trials, but I do not think a dog which is not a genuine worker finds much welcome in her kennel.

Many of the best Labradors of today trace back to Badgery Richard, a son of Ch. Banchory Danilo. Sir Ian Walker, Bart., also has a kennel of chocolates, and so does Mr J. G. Severn, who has kindly given me much information about his dogs. He writes as follows:

My first experience of the chocolate Labradors was in February, 1938, when I visited Dr Montgomery of Sutton Ashfield, about three miles from Tibshelf. We had mated his black bitch Shelagh of Brasidonia to my black dog Danilo of Tibshelf. Danilo was by Marksman out of Fearless of Tibshelf. Shelagh was also 50 per cent yellow bred. Result: 4 blacks, 2 chocolate dogs, 1 cream bitch. I later bought Shelagh and mated her again to Danilo. Result just the same – 4 blacks, 2 chocolate dogs, 1 cream bitch. One of this litter I sold to a lady in Scotland and other I used for stud for a long time, mating to several blacks and yellows. The only chocolate bitch mated produced 6 chocolates, 1 cream. This was to a gamekeepers' bitch from

Wakefield. I did not have any of these, as the type did not suit me.

My present stud dog Chocolate Bronze was sired by Swank of Tibshelf ex Good Charm ex Dannyboy of Tibshelf, a black by Ch. Banchory ex Danilo, and was out of a black bitch Charming Wendy by Danpru ex Sunshine Betty (black). He has produced three litters, all chocolates, five to Sir Ian Walker's Kynock and two litters to Mrs Tibbitts's Chocolate Lady, litter sister to Kynock, but unfortunately the last litter of nine were all dogs – five bitches were booked. She has now been mated again to Bronze and we are hoping for better luck. Chocolate Soldier, a nice specimen owned by Col. Sir Ian Walker, Bart., of Osmaston Manor, Ashbourne, was sired by Midas of Metesford (yellow) out of Sea Otter of Metesford (chocolate). Formerly Miss Wills, of Metesford Prefix, has been able to breed several chocolates. I have now only four myself – Tibshelf Trustful, Joyful, James, Queen. I have given several to my friends and take a delight in showing them. I know we have all made mistakes in introducing outside blood which we have regretted afterwards. A vicious and a nervous strain, and when we read of the working strain and the Show bench strain, it is then when we realized that the writers know very little of what they are talking about. One does occasionally get one that won't work, and I have known quite a few that have failed after having distemper.

Mr Severn has for many years had a formidable kennel of blacks and has always had the welfare of the breed at heart.

Another powerful kennel which has both yellows and blacks is Whatstandwell Kennel of Mr and Mrs Taylor. Their dogs have got to be workers also, which is all to the good and as it should be. The late Mr Edgar Winter also kept Labradors of both colours; his most famous dog was Dual Ch. Staindrop Saighdear, a yellow of which I have written elsewhere and which is a model all breeders should strive to copy. The Hon. Lady Hill-Wood, whose name will ever be connected with the wonderful little black F.T. Ch. Hiwood Chance, also is a supporter of both colours.

There is little for me to add to these words of Lady Howe except to draw attention to Appendix A which shows the explosion in the Labrador population in the last twenty years. As I have said elsewhere, despite this tremendous increase the standards laid down so long ago have been maintained to a degree. Whilst there has been some bad temperament it has been minimal when compared with the total number of Labradors.

Perhaps the two things which have caused the largest ripples on the pool of tranquillity in the post 1939–45 war era are the discovery of hip dysplasia and progressive retinal atrophy in the breed. Let me hasten to say Labradors are not the only breed to be affected. After the first dramatic and sometimes impetuous actions following these discoveries it is pleasing to be able to record that breeders are now for the most part tackling both problems calmly and philosophically. They take care to breed only from clear and healthy stock and obviously this is the only way to eradicate this fault.

To give some idea of the size of one of the problems: hip dysplasia has been under continuous research in Germany since about 1920 in the German Shepherd Dog. Despite the half century of work there are still a large number of questions that apparently remain unanswered. We are told that a complex recessive gene is at the root of the trouble. This may well be, but from other quarters there is talk of 'induced' hip dysplasia. The veterinary profession are doing all they can to diagnose and help all breeders and there is no doubt in my mind that they will produce the answer.

In the meantime, with the cooperation of breeders and the guidance of the veterinary profession, we must continue to work for the wellbeing of the breed, thus carrying on the heritage which has been bequeathed to us by those early breeders.

# 4

# Some Famous Labradors at Home and Abroad*

*Dual Champion Banchory Bolo*

A history of the Labrador must certainly include mention of this remarkable dog. His sire was Scandal of Glynn and he was a most intelligent dog, a charming and beloved companion and a great game-finder. Unfortunately he died of canine typhus at the early age of five. He was the first Labrador I ever owned.

Owing to the 1914–1918 war breeding of all dogs was rightly severely curtailed, but Scandal had one litter bred by the late Sir John Harwood Banner, Bart. This litter consisted of thirteen puppies, of which only one was a dog. This dog later became Dual Champion Banchory Bolo, but he passed through many vicissitudes before he attained that dignity.

Born on 29 December 1915, he lived until 10 July 1927. I first saw him as a mere infant three days old and did not again see him until February, 1918. His father, Scandal, died in 1917. I was devoted to this dog and could not find one to replace him. I had several very good dogs, all most charming in their various ways, but I could not discover one among them that would fill the gap left by my beloved Scandal.

Eventually my husband thought of Bolo (or Bully as he was then called) and finally traced him. He had been through various hands, and various trainers had tried to train him. He was offered to me with the proviso that if I could not make anything of him I was to have him destroyed. In fact he had what

*The sections on Banchory Bolo, Dungavel Jet, Banchory Corbie, Balmuto Jock, Hiwood Chance, Banchory Donald, Bramshaw Bob, British Justice, and Ingleston Ben are by Lady Howe.

human beings would describe as a really bad police record. However, I accepted him gratefully.

It was arranged that I should meet him at Liverpool Street Station, so one February morning in 1918 I went there to greet him and found a disconsolate, surly dog, heavily muzzled. I took him to the house we had in Grosvenor Crescent and left him off his chain in my bedroom. It took me nearly an hour to catch him, so terrified was he. He must have got a chill on the journey – it was bitterly cold. He was ill for nearly three weeks. During those weeks he gained confidence in me and could hardly bear me out of his sight. When he got well I took him with me to Scotland and started to train him to be steady to the gun. This I did by at first shooting rabbits with a rifle out of a pony cart. He gradually learnt not to run-in and eventually became one of the steadiest dogs I have every known.

We then moved down to the place we had in Shropshire and I got Bolo ready to run in field trials. Unfortunately he went with me one evening to the stable yard where he heard one of the stable boys cracking a whip. The old terror came back to him and he bolted. Finally at midnight I gave up searching for him and went to my room, leaving the front door open. At 5 a.m. Bolo came into my room and got into his basket. When I was about to go to my bath an hour later I was horrified to see big splashes of blood on the floor. On examining Bolo I found he had two very deep wounds on his chest, a tear three inches long in his groin and his hind leg and hock torn so badly that the bone was visible. I was urged to have him destroyed but this I would not do. The nearest veterinary surgeon lived eight miles away; there was no telephone and I knew he would be away at a market town another eight miles away; so with the kennel man I had then I put twenty-three stitches into Bolo. He was so good and lay perfectly still until it was all finished. Of course there could be no question of competing at field trials that season.

The following season he became a F.T. Ch., winning the Open Stake at the Western Counties Field Trial Meeting and the Scotish Open Stakes in quick succession. He soon qualified as a Bench Ch., thus becoming the first Dual Champion Labrador.

It was as a sire that Bolo proved of such enormous value. As he was always with me he was not heavily used as a stud dog, but I think every litter sired by him contained a winner at trials and on the show bench. Most of the Labradors winning at trials and at shows today are descended from him. It was not because of his brilliance in these spheres that I valued him but because he was the most intelligent, the most human, dog I have ever seen. He was remarkably quick to learn and once he had learnt anything he never forgot. He was invaluable as a tutor when I was training young dogs – one could always rely on him to do what was wanted. He loved children and would dress up for them and play the buffoon with obvious pleasure.

If I was out on the high road and he saw anyone he thought looked at all doubtful in character he would walk just in front of me until whoever it was came level with me; then he would get between the suspect and me and then keep close to my heel.

He was always gentle with little puppies and never sought a fight with other dogs.

He had quite the best nose I have ever seen in a dog and with apparently the greatest ease he would collect runner after runner after several other dogs had failed. I have never had a dog with such great natural ability or one so anxious to please me in every possible way. I loved him dealy and it was a real and great grief when I had to have him put to sleep to save him from suffering. It was ten years before I had another personal dog, and that was a smooth Champion Griffon known to her friends as Binkie the Beloved. I am sure Bolo's mantle fell on her little shoulders as did that of Elijah on Elisha in days of old.

Bolo's name was known practically throughout the world. Many were the offers I had for him but I could not part with a dog which loved me so dearly and which I loved equally well. He had a beautiful head; when looking through the book in which Lord Knutsford kept a record of his Labradors and their parents I found a photograph of him with the inscription: 'A perfect Labrador's head.' He had the most intelligent and kindly expression. In hindquarters he excelled and he transmitted this feature to his progeny.

Of him *The Field* wrote:

*A Prince Among Dogs*

If ever evidence were needed of the character of a great dog, and of
his influence on the generations following him, it was to be found at
the Retriever Championship Trial held at Idsworth last week.
[December, 1932.]

After two withdrawals, there were twenty runners in the Stake. Out
of the fourteen who gained prizes or diplomas eight were descended
from the same Field Trial Champion.

They were: First, Main, grandson; Second, Banchory Becky, great
grand-daughter; Equal Third, Bryngarw Flute, grandson, and Pee
Wit of the Rhins, great grandson; Reserve, Rotchell Jock, grandson;
and three others who were awarded diplomas of merit – Beningbrough Taffy, great grandson; Tutsham Brenda, great grand-
daughter and Banchory Tern, grand-daughter.

All these look back to the same ancestor, Lorna, Countess Howe's
famous Bolo, who in his time was among dogs as Agamemnon was
prince among men.

Quotation from the *Labrador Retriever Stud Book*, by the late C.
Mackay Sanderson:

In order to assess the imprint from Lord Malmesbury's Tramp in its
wholeness and right proportion a separate feature has to be accorded
the line from F.T. Ch. Peter of Faskally through Scandal of Glynn,
which joined its fullest expression with the emergence of Dual Ch.
Banchory Bolo. Between the period which had given birth to Tramp
and the advent of Bolo some forty years later, no single figure had
arisen which had exercised such a great and moulding influence on
progress. Bolo's coming may be said to have breathed a spirit of new
life into the breed, the prestige enjoyed by this dog as a competitive
and stud force giving lasting impetus to Labradors' fortunes and sub-
sequently his name runs like a golden thread through all the vital
streams of progress. Bolo was undoubtedly triumphant and pre-
dominant during his period, his dominance being referable to
qualities other than are actually wrapt up in his prestige as a stud
force. He came at a time when prestige both in a competitive and
breeding sense was being put to rigorous tests. Behind the full story
of remarkable expansion during the last period lies the priceless contribution made by Bolo and his descendants. In the interval since
Bolo caught the imagination of the public, we can discern certain
events of change and significance and the feats of this remarkable dog
and his progeny give joy to the memory as one contemplates the
advance which followed. The name and fame of Bolo will always be

indissolubly bound up with the Banchory Kennel of Lorna, Countess
Howe of which he was such a distinguished inmate.

### Dungavel Jet

Famous kennels of Labradors were kept by the late Duke and
Duchess of Hamilton both at Dungavel in Scotland and Ferne
in Wiltshire and Balcombe in Sussex. The Duchess ran
Dungavel Jet herself to win the Kennel Club Open Stake in
1908. Their dogs were also handled and trained by the late Mr
J. Alexander and by Mr T. Gaunt, who later took entire charge
of the Duke's Spaniels which he ran with such outstanding success at field trials until the kennel was disbanded in 1925, when
I was fortunate enough to secure his services.

### Banchory Corbie

In the post 1914–1918 war period Banchory Corbie was one of
the most attractive dogs I have ever met. He was known to his
many friends as Corbie the Criminal. Why? I know not, for a
better behaved dog would be hard to find. He was a son of
Bolo's and was always with him in the house with me. In 1923
he won the International Gundog League Nomination Stake
and had every prospect of brilliant field trial achievement, but
unfortunately he broke his shoulder by galloping into a guard
post. That ended his field trial career, much to my regret as he
was a delightful dog to handle.

It also curtailed his career on the show bench, where he had
won one Challenge Certificate. I was once showing him at
Cruft's and when speaking to someone I heard people laughing. I looked round to see what they were laughing about and
saw Master Corbie sitting up in front of the Judges begging!
Where he had learnt this accomplishment mystifies me: I certainly did not teach him. He must have found it an exceedingly
lucrative trick as far as food was concerned, for if allowed to he
would go round the luncheon tables at the field trial meetings
at Idsworth begging and I think reaping a rich reward for
his enterprise.

Corbie was in character and temperament all that a Labrador should be. He was highly intelligent, very faithful, a wonderful watch-dog and guard, yet very gentle with children. He had the great game-finding ability which goes with good nose and the brains to use it. In rough he was fearless and would face the most punishing covert. He was a wonderful sire and when mated to Beningbrough Tansy (owned by the late Lord Chesterfield) they produced the famed field trial dogs, F.T. Ch. Beningbrough Tanco, Truant and Tan, also F.T. Ch. Banchory Ben, Tealer, Theine and Tar. These all had the same merry, attractive style of hunting. Corbie can justifiably be classed as one of the dogs which did great good to the breed.

### F.T. Ch. Balmuto Jock

Field Trial Ch. Balmuto Jock or John, as he was always called, holds a record in Retrievers which will be very difficult to surpass.

He was a wonderful dog and a joy to handle, for one could literally put one's hands in one's pockets and leave matters to John. If ever in difficulties he would spin round and look to see what was wanted and would take the least sign of direction, yet he never for one moment became dependent on his handler.

After my Bolo's death he always went about with me and when I went to London he came too. I think he must have walked in some acid in London in 1928, for the outer skin on all four feet came off, leaving the paws terribly sore and raw. This happened at the end of July. I made him a set of boots with thick leather soles and padded inside and laced over the joints of his legs, but of course he could do no work. By mid-September I left his boots off but still had to exercise him on very soft ground, except when I put his boots on again, when of course he could do no galloping. His hind feet healed first and we gradually got his front feet healed and hardened by soaking them in salt and water. He would sit solemnly, like an old gentleman, with his paws in a bowl of salt water for half an hour without attempting to move. To get him fit and hard I used to send him up and down the stairs on the soft carpet to retrieve a tennis ball, and so was able to run him in a trial in October. He won this and thereby qualified to run in the Champion Stake, which he won for the third time. This was the last time I ever entered him for a trial as I felt he had done enough.

He was an extraordinarily brainy dog and always willing to learn. He was a great character and I think every one who knew him loved him. I bought him from Mr David Black, who told me he was the most intelligent puppy he had ever trained. He ran him in trials as a puppy.

Mr Black also told me that he used to send him round to collect eggs from hens which were laying out and that John was invaluable for this purpose. He had one curious habit. When I had him he always used to go to some grass under a certain cedar tree, scrape the grass off and eat some of the earth. He did this every morning when at home but I never saw him do it anywhere else. I suppose there was some mineral in the earth.

I give his full record of wins at field trials.

When owned by Mr Black he won Certificates of Merit in the Gamekeepers' Association National Stake 1923 and 1924, after which I bought him.

He won 2nd in the North Western Societies Trials; 2nd South Western Counties and equal 3rd in the Champion Stake, 1924. In 1925 he won 2nd in the North Western Counties Trials; 1st all ages Western Counties C. of M. Gamekeepers' National Association C. of M. Labrador Club Open Stake; equal 3rd Champion Stake. In 1926 1st all ages Western Counties; 2nd Kennel Club all ages Stake; 3rd North Western Association; 1st Open Labrador Club all ages; 1st Champion Stake. In 1927 2nd Gamekeepers' National Stake; 2nd Labrador all ages Stake 1st Labrador all ages Stake; 1st Western Counties all ages Stake; 3rd Champion Stake. In 1928 Cert. of Merit Labrador Club; 2nd International Gundog League Trials; 1st Open Scottish Field Trial Association; 1st Gamekeepers' National Association; 1st Kennel Club all ages; 1st Champion Stake. In 1929, the last year he ran, he won 1st Southern Counties Association and 1st Champion Stake – the only Trials he ran in. He is the only dog to the present time that has won the Champion Stake three times. Truly a great record for a great dog.

### F.T. Ch. Hiwood Chance

I do not think anyone who ever saw her compete at field trials will ever forget little F.T. Ch. Hiwood Chance, owned by the Hon. Mrs Hill-Wood (later the Hon. Lady Hill-Wood). When I write 'little' I mean in stature, for she was very great in heart – always ready and alert to take any instructions from her mistress, yet by no means an automaton as are so many of the field trial winners of today. Chance had great courage and would always face any punishing covert. Invariably gay and happy in her work, she seemed to have the greatest understanding and love for her mistress. That she won the Champion Stake twice goes to show how reliable she was in her work.

### F.T. Ch. Muntham Raven

Owned by Colonel Thynne, was a most consistent worker at trials.

### F.T. Ch. Tracey Parma

Owned by the late Mr A. B. Simpson, was also a consistent worker and worked brilliantly in the 1932 Champion Stake.

The last three named were all daughters of Banchory Corbie.

### F.T. Ch. Banchory Donald

Was second in the 1932 Champion Stake. Donald in his work much resembled his grandfather, Bolo, as he had the same style and way of working. I acquired him from Mr R. Kelland (of Spaniel fame) as I had taken a great fancy to him. Shortly after he became my property I was asked by a former owner of Don's how I got on with him. I replied: 'Very well; he lives in the house and sleeps in my room. Why should I not get on with him?' I was told that he was supposed to be a woman-hater! He certainly never hated me. Neither did he Miss Lang, who lives with me, and was as devoted to Don as he was to her, and as he was to the two little Griffons, Ch. Binkie the Beloved and Bonnie the Brave.

*Dual Ch. Bramshaw Bob*

Bought from Sir George Thursby in December 1931, he had already won a field trial when in February, 1932, I took him to Cruft's Show, where a gamekeeper, Mr W. McCall, was judging the Labradors. Bob won all the Classes in which I had entered him (six, I think). On the second day of the show he won the Cup for best of all breeds. Cruft's Show was, and still is, a great meeting place for gamekeepers. I shall never forget the overwhelming reception they gave Bob when the award was announced; it was so kind of them. They were pleased that a working gundog should receive this much-coveted award. I took Bob to the Scottish Gundog and Terrier Show at Edinburgh shortly afterwards, where he was again Best in Show, and soon afterwards to Manchester, where he again won Best in Show and so became a show bench Champion and a little later became a field trial Champion and so entitled to the much sought after title of Dual Champion. At Cruft's Show in 1933 he was again awarded Best in Show, an honour he won at Championship Shows thirteen times, a good record for a genuine working gundog. He was always used for his legitimate work and he worked equally well for either Gaunt or myself. His sire, Ch. Ingleston Ben, was runner-up in Labradors to Bob at Cruft's in 1932. Ben's other sons, Ch. Cheverells Ben of Banchory and Ch. Banchory Trueman, won many Challenge Certificates, Ben winning Best in Show all breeds at Cruft's in 1938 and at the Ladies' Kennel Association in 1939.

Dual Ch. Staindrop Saighdear, Dual Ch. Knaith Banjo, Ch. Landyke Sheba, Ch. Judith Aikshaw, Ch. Ballyduff Whatstandwell Rowena and Ch. British Justice are six Labradors which in the opinion of Countess Howe 'stood out' as typical

Labradors, full of character and worthy representatives of the breed. Countess Howe says that in striving to imitate their type, with their substance and quality, breeders cannot go far astray and will benefit the breed.

### Ch. British Justice

Takes a very exhalted position among black Labradors in the post-war period. He was the true type of Labrador. He had a charming disposition and character; he was good in his work and ran well at trials. A well-known all-round judge with a high reputation once said after judging him and giving him the Challenge Certificate Best of Breed that he was a dog one had to handle and go over carefully to realize how good he really was. He had won twenty-one Challenge Certificates when he died at the early age of five years, a very great loss to the breed.

### Ch. Ingleston Ben

No one interested in the welfare of Labradors can overlook the great good done to the breed by Ch. Ingleston Ben in the 1928–1936 period. Bred by the late Mr Dobie of Dumfries, he later passed into my hands. He had a brilliant bench career and distinguished himself at field trials. As a sire he was of great value to the breed, being the sire of one Dual Champion, eight Champions, two field trial Champions, and of ten winners of Field Trial Stakes.

It is quite impossible to mention all the dogs and breeders by name in the post-war era. Some have been outstanding, e.g. Mr and Mrs H. A. Saunders – Liddly; Mrs A. Radclyffe – Zelstone; Mrs G. Broadley – Sandylands; Mr and Mrs Grant Cairns – Blaircourt; Mr and Mrs Horace Taylor – Whatstandwell; Mr F. Wrigley – Kinley; Mr K. Hart – Landyke; Mrs Docking – Ballyduff; Mrs Purbrick – Strattonley; Mrs Roslin Williams – Mansergh; Mrs Wormald – Knaith.

There are obviously many others. Those, as I have said, are far too numerous to put in print here but their names appear with their champion dogs in Appendix B.

On the subject of famous Labradors Lady Howe writes:

From the earliest days of the Labrador's appearance in this country Scotland and the Border Country have been strong-holds of the breed. One can safely state that the breed owes an immense amount to the Dukes of Buccleuch, the Earls of Home, Sir Richard Graham and others for their support of the breed. I well remember in 1920 going to the field trials held by the Gamekeepers' National Association at which two Stakes were run, one for gamekeepers and one for ordinary mem-bers. The Gamekeepers' Stake, or Castle Milk Stake as it was called, had a wonderful entry of dogs which would have graced any show and which were equally good at their legitimate job of finding and collecting game. At that time Mr C. Mackay Sanderson was Secretary of the Association, and very ably he filled this position which he held until his death, an irrepar-able loss not only to the Labrador breed but to all gundog owners and to field trials.

The Scottish Field Trial Association flourished at that time with the able assistance of the Secretary, the late Mr Formby.

The Open Stake held by this Association ranked in those days as one of the three best in the country, the others being the Kennel Club and the International Gundog League – the latter being the first big Society to be founded.

Many famous kennels were situated in Scotland. Most not-able were those of the Dukes of Buccleuch, the earliest suppor-ters of the breed. Later came the Hon. W. J. Hewitt, the Labradors of Mr McCall of the famous St. Mary's Isle prefix, Mr Dinwoodie with the beautiful Brocklehirst dogs (now for-tunately carried on by his son Mr T. Dinwoodie with the prefix Lochar), Mr Carruthers with the Orchardtons, Mr C. A. Phillips, who did so much for Spaniels, of Dildawn, Mr Dobie of Ingleston fame, Mr D. Black with his Balmutos, Mr Annand and many others. South of the Border – the Birdsall dogs of Lord Middleton, and Lord Joicey's 'of Flodden' dogs.

The names of Mrs Wormald, of Annan, and the late Major Wormald will ever be famous in yellow Labradors, their Knaith prefix being a household name word in the breed. The name of the late Captain A. E. Butter will ever be remembered in field trial history, as will that of the late Mr Charles Alington. In the South of England there are no stauncher supporters of the breed than Mr and Mrs H. A. Saunders who, under the prefix Liddly, have won high honours at shows and field trials.

Mr Owen Mansel will be remembered as a keen enthusiast.

In America there ia a great demand for Labradors, the pioneers there being the late Mr J. Carlisle, Mr Lord, Mr and Mrs Ferguson, Dr and Mrs Milbank. The breed there quickly became popular. The Labrador Retriever Club of America was formed, the President being Dr Samuel Milbank, one of the original admirers of the breed on that side of the Atlantic. This Club holds a show for the breed and field trials. The field trials seem to have enormous support. Most interesting is the Record of field trials and shows I was kindly sent by the Labrador Club of America. Taking 1952, the latest record I have, there are records of fifty-eight meetings beginning on 2 March 1952, and ending on 22 November 1952. Some Stakes were confined to Labradors but the majority were open to all – with one Stake confined to Golden Retrievers and one for Chesapeake Bay Retrievers. One held on 24, 25 and 26 October 1952, numbered fifty starters, which strikes one as a large entry for only two judges to deal with.

Between 1934 to 1952 the entries for retrieving dogs placed at trials were:

|  | 1st | 2nd | 3rd | 4th | Total |
|---|---|---|---|---|---|
| Labradors | 354 | 322 | 301 | 302 | 1279 |
| Goldens | 67 | 70 | 82 | 65 | 284 |
| Chesapeakes | 20 | 33 | 40 | 46 | 139 |
| Curly Coats | 0 | 2 | 1 | 2 | 5 |
| Irish Water Spaniels | 0 | 0 | 3 | 0 | 3 |

This shows the preponderance and popularity of the breed.

I understand the water test in America is particularly severe. At some trials a whole day is devoted to work in water, sometimes in difficult and testing conditions. It is perhaps the Labrador's adaptability for this form of work which contributes to his popularity.

A large number of dogs were also exported to India, where at one time field trials were immensely popular. His Highness the Maharajah of Patiala and His Highness the Maharajah of Jind both organized field trial meetings. Several people who judged at those trials have told me of the work there and of the necessity for dogs of high courage and working ability to pass some of the exacting tests encountered in a day's work.

I had several invitations to judge both in India and America at field trials and at shows, and it has always been a source of regret that I was not able to accept these invitations. I have exported dogs to both these countries, and many others, including China. I have often wondered if any of the descendants of the dogs I exported to China still remain. I doubt it! One thing can be safely stated, wherever the Labrador has gone he has become popular. He has a high reputation in France, Belgium and Holland; he has made a name for himself in Africa (Kenya particularly), Australia and New Zealand.

Since writing this I have received, through the kindness of the Labrador Retriever Club Inc., of America, a schedule of their trials held on Friday, Saturday and Sunday, 22, 23 and 24 April 1955.

Messrs J. A. Stockwell and Mahlon B. Wallace were the judges. Three Stakes were scheduled: the Derby, which corresponds, I conclude, to our Puppy Stakes, a Limited All-Aged Stake and an Amateur All-Aged Stake. In the Derby there were 24 entries; in the Limited All-Aged 52 and in the Amateur All-Aged 34. This amounts to a total of 110 entries to be assessed in three days by two judges. One does not know the conditions, but it certainly seems an enormous task for two judges. Personally, I should be very sorry to have to do it. In fact, nothing would induce me to do so! I have been told by people who have been to these trials, and have seen the work, that it is much more artificial than the work we have over here. I gathered, too, that the dogs are subject to much more of what I would call artificial handling and obedience to signals.

I have also heard that a more leggy, racey type of dog is preferred and that speed is greatly valued. It would be indeed a great pity if in breeding for speed the true type of Labrador should be lost.

Before the last war the late Maharajahs of Patiala and Jind took an enormous interest in field trials and shows. Their trials were always well run and provided very severe tests both in water and on land.

They imported into India many of the best gundogs of that period and held trials for Retrievers and Spaniels. Both Maharajahs handled dogs themselves and also engaged professional handlers from this country. These trials were exceedingly well supported – many dogs who had competed against each other in Great Britain fought their battles again in India. From accounts I have received from people who had judged at these events dogs of high courage were needed as some of the covert was exceedingly punishing. I exported several dogs to India; one I had bred, F.T. Ch. Bryngarw Flute, meeting with a tragic end. He was literally stung to death by bees, a horrible end for any dog.

I do not know if field trials are still held but shows most certainly are. They seem to be extremely popular and many of our famous judges officiate there and in Ceylon.

The Maharajah of Patiala was one of the quickest and best shots I have ever seen. He adored his dogs and so did the Maharajah of Jind, though severely handicapped in training work by deafness.

Shows also take place in Ceylon where from all accounts they are exceedingly popular.

# 5

# Type, Colour, Character and Standards

The Kennel Club publishes the standard for each breed in groups. This standard is in effect the specification or blueprint for the breed.

The breed clubs are used to make recommendations for this standard based on a particular format. Each breed club does this and submits it to the Breed Council who in turn submit one composite and agreed version to the Kennel Club. After approval by the Kennel Club Committee it is printed and is available for anyone to purchase for a modest sum. It is also reproduced in a number of breed clubs' year books.

Most countries in the world follow closely the standards issued in the UK with only minor variations. There are some notable exceptions to this, one example of this being in the height when the English standard is compared with the American standard.

## KENNEL CLUB STANDARD 1950 (AMENDED 1968)

### (Reproduced by permission of the Kennel Club)

GENERAL APPEARANCE: The general appearance of the Labrador should be that of a strongly-built, short-coupled, very active dog, broad in the skull, broad and deep through the chest and ribs, broad and strong over the loins and hindquarters. The coat close, short with dense undercoat and free from feather. The dog must move neither too wide nor too close in front or behind, he must stand and move true all round on legs and feet.

HEAD AND SKULL: The skull should be broad with pronounced stop, so that the skull is not in a straight line with the nose. The head should be clean cut without fleshy cheeks. The jaws should be of medium length and powerful, and free from snipiness. The nose wide and the nostrils well developed.

EYES: The eyes of medium size, expressing intelligence and good temper, should be brown or hazel.

EARS: Should not be large and heavy and should hang close to the head and set rather far back.

MOUTH: Teeth should be sound and strong. The lower teeth just behind but touching the upper.

NECK: Should be clean, strong and powerful and set into well-placed shoulders.

FOREQUARTERS: The shoulders should be long and sloping. The forelegs well boned and straight from the shoulder to the ground when viewed from either front or side. The dog must neither move too wide nor too close in front.

BODY: The chest must be of good width and depth with well-sprung ribs. The back should be short coupled.

HINDQUARTERS: The loins must be wide and strong with well-turned stifles; hindquarters well developed and not sloping to the tail. The hocks should be slightly bent and the dog must neither be cow-hocked nor move too wide or too close behind.

FEET: Should be round and compact with well-arched toes and well-developed pads.

TAIL: The tail is a distinctive feature of the breed; it should be very thick towards the base, gradually tapering towards the tip, of medium length and practically free from feathering, but clothed thickly all round with Labrador's short, thick, dense coat, thus giving that peculiar 'rounded' appearance which has been described as the 'otter' tail. The tail may be carried gaily, but should not curl over the back.

COAT: The coat is another distinctive feature of the breed, it should be short and dense and without wave with a weather resisting undercoat, and should give a fairly hard feeling to the hand.

COLOUR: The colour is generally black or yellow but other whole colours are permitted. The coat should be free from white markings but a small white spot on the chest is allowable. The coat should be of whole colour and not of a flecked appearance.

SIZE: Desired height for dogs 22–22½ inches, bitches 21½–22 inches.

FAULTS: Under or overshot mouth, no undercoat, bad action, feathering, snipiness on the head, large or heavy ears, cowhocked, tail curved over back.

*Note:* Male animals should have two apparently normal testicles fully descended into the scrotum.

## AMERICAN STANDARD

(Reproduced by permission of the American Kennel Club)

GENERAL APPEARANCE: The general appearance of the Labrador should be that of a strongly-built, short-coupled, very active dog. He should be fairly wide over the loins, and strong and muscular in the hindquartes. The coat should be close, short, dense and free from feather.

HEAD: The skull should be wide, giving brain room; there

should be a slight stop, *i.e.* the brow should be slightly pronounced, so that the skull is not absolutely in a straight line
with the nose. The head should be clean-cut and free from
fleshy cheeks. The jaws should be long and powerful and free
from snipiness; the nose should be wide and the nostrils well
developed. Teeth should be strong and regular, with a level
mouth. The ears should hang moderately close to the head,
rather far back, should be set somewhat low and not be large
and heavy. The eyes should be of a medium size, expressing
great intelligence and good temper, and can be brown, yellow
or black, but brown or black is preferred.

NECK AND CHEST: The neck should be medium length, powerful and not throaty. The shoulders should be long and sloping.
The chest must be of good width and depth, the ribs well
sprung and the loins wide and strong, stifles well turned, and
the hindquarters well developed and of great power.

LEGS AND FEET: The legs must be straight from the shoulder to
ground, and the feet compact with toes well arched, and pads
well developed; the hocks should be well bent, and the dog
must neither be cow-hocked nor be too wide behind; in fact,
he must stand and move true all round on legs and feet. Legs
should be of medium length, showing good bone and muscle,
but no so short as to be out of balance with rest of body. In fact,
a dog well balanced in all points is preferable to one with
outstanding good qualities and defects.

TAIL: The tail is a distinctive feature of the breed; it should be
very thick towards the base, gradually tapering towards the tip,
of medium length, should be free from any feathering, and
should be clothed thickly all round with the Labrador's short,
thick, dense coat, thus giving that peculiar 'rounded' appearance which has been described as the 'otter' tail. The tail may
be carried gaily but should not curl over the back.

COAT: The coat is another very distinctive feature; it should be
short, very dense and without wave, and should give a fairly
hard feeling to the hand.

Ch. British Justice, winner of 21 challenge certificates
(*Thomas Fall*)

Dual Ch. Knaith Banjo (*Thomas Fall*)

Ch. Whatstandwell Coronet (*Thomas Fall*)

Ch. June of Sandylands. Born 1938
(*Thomas Fall*)

Ch. Sandylands Truth. Born 1960
(*Anne Roslin-Williams*)
These two Sandylands champions exemplify breeding
to type by Mrs. Gwen Broadley

Ch. Cookridge Tango, the first Chocolate
Labrador to become a champion in the
UK to date (*Anne Roslin-Williams*)

Ch. Cornlands My Fair Lady
(*Timothy Hills*

Ch. Ruler of Blaircourt (*C. M. Cooke*)

F.T. Ch. Zelstone Moss
(*C. M. Cooke*)

Ch. Braeduke Joyful (*Sally Anne Thompson*)

Ch. Kinley Skipper

COLOR: The colors are black, yellow or chocolate and are evaluated as follows:

(a) Blacks: All black, with a small white spot on chest permissible. Eyes to be of medium size, expressing intelligence and good temper, preferably brown or hazel, although black or yellow is permissible.

(b) Yellows: Yellows may vary in color from fox-red to light-cream with variations in the shading of the coat on ears, the underparts of the dog, or beneath the tail. A small white spot on chest is permissible. Eye coloring and expression should be the same as that of the blacks, with black or dark brown eye rims. The nose should also be black or dark brown, although 'fading' to pink in winter weather is not serious. A 'Dudley' nose, (pink without pigmentation) should be penalized.

(c) Chocolates: Shades ranging from light sedge to chocolate. A small white spot on chest is permissible. Eyes to be light brown to clear yellow. Nose and eye-rim pigmentation dark brown or liver colored. 'Fading' to pink in winter weather not serious. 'Dudley' nose should be penalized.

MOVEMENT: Movement should be free and effortless. The forelegs should be strong straight and true, and correctly placed. Watching a dog move towards one, there should be no signs of elbows being out in front, but neatly held to the body with legs not too close together, but moving straight forward without pacing or weaving. Upon viewing the dog from the rear, one should get the impression that the hind legs, which should be well muscled and not cow-hocked, move as nearly parallel as possible, with hocks doing their full share of work and flexing well thus giving the appearance of power and strength.

APPROXIMATE WEIGHTS OF DOGS AND BITCHES IN WORKING CONDITON: Dogs – 60 to 75 pounds; bitches – 55 to 70 pounds.

HEIGHT AT SHOULDERS: Dogs – 22½ inches to 24½ inches; bitches – 21½ inches to 23½ inches.

*Approved 9 April 1957*

The slightly bigger dog which appears to be preferred by our friends in the USA is also the preference of a number of breeders on the continent. I have heard several explanations of this but the main one is that the larger and therefore stronger dog is much better able to cover the local terrain than the smaller dog. This is a view I do not share, but it is an opinion I must respect.

In general appearance the Labrador is a well built, even heavily built dog. Perhaps 'stocky' is the best word to describe him. He has an air of quiet confidence about him. This together with an obvious power and agility gives him distinction.

Unlike many breeds the Labrador has changed little in general appearance over the years. Reference to some of the photographs in this volume will confirm this. Their backs are more level, dogs are shorter in the coupling, and colours are whole nowadays, but this could also be said of some of the earlier dogs. What has happened is that now the proportion of dogs carrying these attributes is probably much greater.

There have been views expressed over the years and these I have heard many times that there are two types of Labrador, the gundog and the show dog. In my experience nothing could be further from the truth. All Labradors are potentially working dogs. True some are better than others either in the field or on the bench, but this does not alter the basic fact. In addition a large percentage of show dogs attend training classes and go 'picking up' whenever time and opportunity permit. I am quite sure that it is only the lack of time and/or opportunity which prevents some Labradors from attending.

There is no doubt that these sessions are great fun enjoyed equally by dog and owner.

Figure 1 shows the points of the Labrador. Perhaps now it would be as well if we went into some detail about the standard of points recommended by the breed clubs and approved by the Kennel Club.

GENERAL APPEARANCE: As I have said, in outline he will be stocky, of good strong bone and substance, 60–70 lbs weight in a height of not more than 22½ inches which means fairly con-

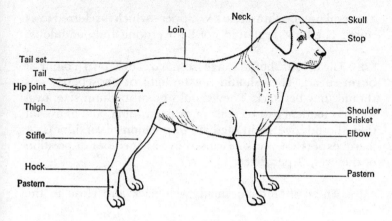

*Figure 1* Points of the Labrador

centrated power in bone and sinew in a not very large animal. He must look active and strong enough to be out all day in the field covering the worst of ground, able to carry heavy birds safely to hand under the most difficult conditions even swimming against strong currents. He should present a square 'picture' rather than a rectangular one.

HEAD AND SKULL: The skull must be broad but not coarse, and there must be a definite 'stop' (see Figure 2). When viewed from above the shaping should be apparent and any tendency to thickness of the cheekbones e.g. like a Bull Terrier should be penalized. The muzzle should be square, not too long and

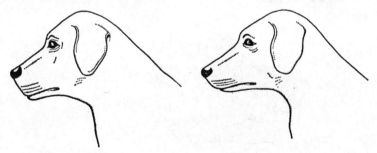

*Figure 2* Heads: (left) correct (right) bad, narrow 'snipy'

above all not too thin – like a Whippet – which is referred to as snipy. The muzzle should not be overdone and pendulous.

EYES: The colour should range from hazel to brown (colour of burnt sugar). They should not be light or gooseberry, nor should they be black. They should be of medium size, oval with no tendency to be sunken or protruding, and above all they should give an immediate impression of kindliness. A 'hard' expression, i.e. one caused by either colour or position of the eyes, is penalized.

EARS: These should be small, well back and close to the head.

MOUTH: This is a very important point: obviously the teeth themselves must be strong and sound. The standard calls for the lower teeth to be just behind but touching the upper teeth. This is called a scissor bite (see Figure 3).
If the lower teeth protrude beyond the upper teeth, the dog

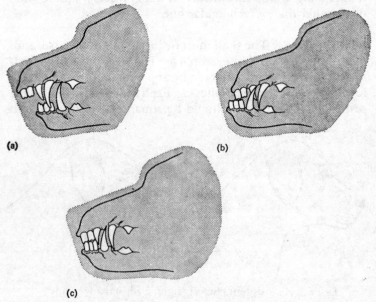

*Figure 3* The bite (a) overshot (b) undershot (c) correct

is said to be 'undershot'. If the upper teeth protrude beyond the lower teeth he is said to be 'overshot'.

NECK: This must be longish with no appearance of throatiness, strong and set into well placed shoulders. Short necked or thickness spoils the balance and refined overall picture.

FOREQUARTERS: Shoulders long and sloping which together with a strong well placed neck gives the dog the balance so very necessary in a working dog.

The forelegs must be straight from the shoulder to the ground viewed from any angle. They must be well boned.

When viewed from the side pasterns should be straight not slack (see Figure 5)

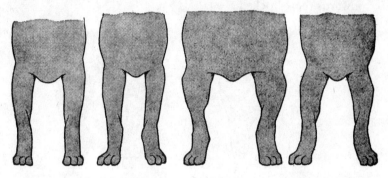

*Figure 4* Fronts (left to right) correct; too narrow; wide and out at elbow (Queen Anne legs); tied in at elbow

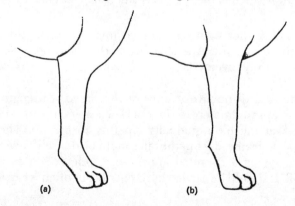

*Figure 5* Side view of front legs (a) weak pastern (b) correct pastern

BODY: While a dog is wanted with plenty of lung and heart room in other words a good depth of chest and spring of rib is required a barrel chest which is inclined to produce faulty fronts is to be avoided. So also is a slab-sided animal which will produce other faults, notably narrow fronts.

The standard demands a short coupled dog i.e. the loin is short – the distance between the last rib and the pelvis. If the back is long the dog is said to be 'long cast' and therefore should be penalized because the aim is a short coupled or 'cobby' dog.

HINDQUARTERS: The stifles must be well turned, never straight (see Figure 6) and when viewed from the rear the back legs must not be too close (close behind) nor with the hocks turning inwards (cow-hocked).

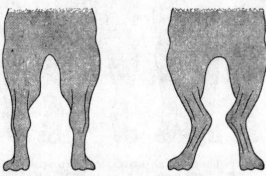

*Figure 6* Hindquarters (a) correct (b) bad, 'cow-hocked'

FEET: Small, rather tight well arched toes. They should resemble those of a cat. Any splaying of the toes and general slackness is to be avoided.

TAIL: This is a distinctive feature of the breed. In length it should be approximately to the hocks. In shape it should be very thick at the base gradually tapering to the tip. There should be no feathering but the tail should be densely covered with coat giving a rounded appearance, referred to as the 'otter' tail. It should be carried horizontally but often is carried higher (referred to as 'Gay') but must never be carried curling over the back (see Figure 7).

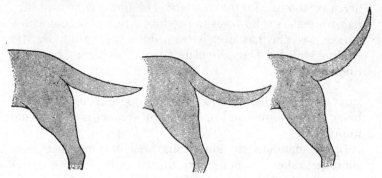

*Figure 7* Tails (left to right) correct; too low; high-placed, tending to curl over back

COAT: This is another distinctive feature of the breed. It is two-fold, a longer outer harder coat (slightly harsh to the touch) and a very dense short undercoat. Far too often single coated dogs are seen and this is not correct. The coat should not show any wave.

COLOUR: The Labrador Retriever can be either black, chocolate (liver if you prefer) or yellow. The colour must be whole and not of a flecked appearance. A small white spot on the chest is permissible. The yellow can range from a fox red to a pale cream.

Original Labrador colour was black and all dogs of the present day could trace their ancestry back to the black Labrador. There is little doubt however that the most popular colour today is yellow so far as the general public is concerned, although very recently the black is receiving a little more favour. Chocolates (or liver) are a very small minority; this colour either appeals or it does not. Those to whom it appeals are enthusiastic, others appear completely uninterested. With blacks or yellows the owner of one colour will discuss with interest the other colour, but they rarely want to discuss chocolates.

This may be due to the palish eye of the chocolate which in fairnes is complementary to the coat and pigmentation, but is of course too pale for the standard. The aim of chocolate Labrador breeders is however to produce a rich dark coat with a darker eye. This has already been done successfully by Mrs Pauling with her first chocolate Champion bitch Ch. Cookridge Tango.

MOVEMENT: The Labrador is a working dog and therefore must be generally sound and of course movement is of supreme importance.

In the standard straight fronts, well balanced neck and shoulders, short coupling, well turned stifles, good quarters and well balanced tail are all demanded. When these are put together you should have a dog which when moving is four square, i.e. his fronts are straight and true and his back legs are moving in the same plane, so much so that when viewed coming towards you, you can only see his front legs. Likewise when moving away from you, you can only see his back legs.

If the ground had a light covering of snow and your perfect moving Labrador was moved his back feet would go almost exactly into the imprint made in the snow by his front feet.

Far too many dogs nowadays move badly in front: either they are pin-toed (toes turning in) or they plait with their front legs. In addition of course there are the faults behind when sometimes the back legs or feet actually cross. Dogs with such faults in movement are doubtful stayers.

CHARACTER

So far we have discussed the looks of the Labrador in general and in detail but we have only touched on what is possibly his finest attribute\– his temperament. On this I can say with the utmost conviction it is unbeatable. For this we have to thank all those early breeders who took such care to see that it remained unspoiled. Today that tradition is carried on religiously, and very rarely do you hear any displays of bad temper among a collection of Labradors.

In the show ring it is dealt with quite ruthlessly, normally by the judge asking the exhibitor to remove the dog from the ring immediately. No matter how good looking such a dog may be one such display will create a long-lasting impression in the minds of the onlookers.

All Labrador breeders guard this temperament zealously, and this is one of the reasons why I think seasoned breeders are so willing to assist and advise the newcomer about stock and matings.

The Labrador is wonderful with children, a good guard, and a loyal companion. In the field he is intelligent and fearless possessing a good 'nose' and never giving up a scent easily.

These characteristics have been recognized by the discerning and this recognition has caused a meteoric rise in registrations in the breed in recent years. In 1912 there were 281 registrations at the Kennel Club. In 1972, just sixty years and two World Wars later, there were no less thatn 13,880 registrations. It doesn't take a mathematician to see that a continuation of this trend would lead to 20,000 in 1982.

The grave danger inherent in such a rise in numbers is indiscriminate breeding by ill informed people. Such people are jumping on the bandwagon in the hope of quick profits. Fortunately this is a forlorn hope, and they soon jump off. It only needs one such litter, where perhaps little or no thought and less experience has gone into selecting the right mate, to cause endless trouble later on. It is gratifying to be able to say that so far such happenings have been few and there have been no disastrous consequences. Those which have occurred have been relatively insignificant, and the genuine enthusiast has been extremely successful in keeping the breed true in most respects.

It is well known that Labradors have been used as guard dogs by the Services in both peace and war, and even today they can be found engaged on these duties in many parts of the world. From the handler's point of view they are easier to train and handle than most dogs. No doubt this quality is hereditary, a result of the fact that their forebears were 'handled' in the field for very many years, both taking directions and obeying them. It is, therefore, almost second nature for the Labradors of the present day to take to such work. They have guarded airfields and other defence installations, they have been used as mine-detectors, and they have worked as message-carriers. All this is surely evidence of their intelligence and courage.

It these two qualities need further proof it can be found in many of our police forces, where Labradors are rapidly becoming ever more popular as police-dogs. One of the latest uses to which they have been put is in the detection of dangerous drugs; again the breed has proved that it is quite capable of such work, and it is understood that more dogs are to be trained in this field of crime detection and prevention.

On the subject of police work Lady Howe writes:

What Mr H. S. Lloyd (of Ware Cocker fame) who was in charge of the large establishment set up for the training of dogs in the critical times of the last war, showed me in tracking work, stale scent and scent discrimination and methods of arresting criminals left me with the definite opinion that the Labrador is as good at police work as he is at his legitimate business. It hink he has more tenacity of purpose than many much-vaunted dogs possess; no one will ever get the better of him by rough treatment. If he receives punishment he will take it like the great-hearted dog he is but he will not give in to bullying or threatening, and where many of the much-advertised breeds would retire on receipt of such punishment from an evildoer the Labrador will defend with his life what he has been left to guard. Left to his own devices, he likes to go through life peacefully, but once he is on his mettle it is well to beware of him. I suppose a Labrador is quite one of the easiest tempered dogs in existence, thinking no harm, expecting none, but once his temper is aroused he is more than capable of holding his own.

He was, and still is, much sought after by the police as a dog which will guard, track, and protect his master. After trying many breeds for these purposes it was found that the Labrador was undoubtedly the best. There is an authentic story of a break in a long stretch of gas piping. This meant that the whole line might have to be pulled up, at great expense. Instead, a happy idea was born – to call in the services of a dog to detect

the exact spot. A Labrador was called in and he soon discovered the break, thus saving a great deal of money and trouble.
The Labrador is in use in our police force of today and I
believe many a criminal has been brought to book by the
sagacity of one of these specially trained dogs. They are as
unflinching in their attack upon a dangerous criminal as they
are pertinacious in their determination to do their master's
bidding at all costs.

As a guide dog for the blind I think the Labrador has proved
himself to be supreme. He was chosen for this work for his
steady temperamemt and dependability in all circumstances,
although I would not advocate breeding solely for this or any
other single purpose as I think it would tend to rob the breed
of the indefinable measure of greatness it possesses. I would
like to quote from a guide-dog owner:

Lassie, my first Labrador, had only one fault and that was the most
adorable because she would not be left without me. Otherwise as I
have often written and said during the nine years of her working life,
she worked, played, looked and kept well. As a guide dog she was in
fact ideal – both temperamentally and physically. Her response to
everything whether as part of her work or her life in general was
absolutely right and there were very few days when Lassie was not a
happy, healthy, useful and beautiful dog.

I found she was always ready to take the initiative when required
and she showed herself able to rectify those errors of judgment which
any blind person inevitably makes from time to time due to lack of
knowledge of their surroundings. Besides being a wonderful guide
she was, moreover, just right as a dog. Her clean tidy coat and beautiful manners made her a joy to take anywhere. She accompanied me
to various places where dogs are normally barred which gave me
cause for pride in her behaviour.

A wonderful tribute for a wonderful breed of dog.

We are not however, dealing with a guide dog or a police
dog in particular, but with the Labrador breed as a whole. Of
the Labrador one can say that he will want to be the everyday
companion and friend to you and your family young and old.
He will want to be a working dog which is his natural calling.
Whatever you call upon him to do you can be confident that,

given ordinary simple training, he will master it quickly. One thing is certain, the house is enriched by his presence. Very few who have lost such a friend, for one reason or another, can bear the house without him. We have had many owners visit us, obviously very distressed at their loss, looking for another puppy – not, they assure us, to take their dog's place because no dog could ever do that. After a short time, however, whether the owners agree or not, it is a fact that their new puppy has filled the gap.

Lady Howe continues:

Once a Labrador gets hold of your heart it will not let you escape.

Labradors are certainly most adaptable; they seem content to do whatever comes to hand. They never seem out of place. People may think that their size makes them difficult to keep in a small house but this is not so. He must have his own special place to lie in. If he comes into the dining-room he should be made to sit or lie quietly on some spot where he will be out of the way and not liable to trip people up. Above all, he must not be allowed to beg from all and sundry. They are so adaptable, so intelligent, that the rules of the house are soon learnt.

One of the nicest dogs I ever had in the house was F.T. Ch. Banchory Donald. His two companions in the house were two Griffons. They had a big basket to lie in at meal-times in the dining-room. It was amusing to watch them file into the dining-room, always in the same order, all three get into the basket and lie quietly there until called out.

Dual Ch. Banchory Bolo always lived in the house and (let it be only whispered among those who say that living in the house ruins a gundog) he always slept on my bed. Banchory Corbie, F.T. Ch. Balmuto Jock and Dual Ch. Bramshaw Bob had the free run of the house. They never abused their privileges. I am convinced, as I have stated elsewhere, that the more a dog is with one the more intelligent and astute he becomes but of course he must be treated consistently and understand that he must do as he is told.

I think it is wrong to bring any dog into the house during the day, perhaps allowing him to be by the fire, and then at night put him out into a draughty, cold kennel. This is surely asking for trouble. It usually ends either in pneumonia or rheumatism and invariably in great discomfort for the dog. I could not sleep in comfort if I thought a dog which had worked hard, perhaps in water, was outside in an uncomfortable kennel with insufficient bedding. Most of a Retriever's work is done in winter, some of it in bitterly cold water. It is only fair and right that such dogs should receive, on returning to their kennels, a look-over, thoroughly dried if wet, given a warm meal (not hot but with the chill off), given a final run out, then put into a draught-proof kennel with plenty of bedding so that a really restful night is ensured.

Some people may think this undue fussing but if looked at only from a commercial point of view it is commonsense. A dog that is a good worker is of value both at home and abroad. Considered from a sentimental point of view, it is only kindness and a small payment for work faithfully carried out for an owner's pleasure and possibly profit.

Forty years have now passed since I first owned a Labrador. Many waters have passed under the bridges since those days. Times have changed and we have changed with them, but I can honestly say that if I had that time over again I would still choose Labradors as ideal in every way both for work and as companions. I can also say with all sincerity that I do not think anyone could have had more genuine happiness than I have had given to me by my dogs.

# 6

# Choice, Care and Training of the Puppy

CHOICE

Before even considering the choice of a puppy some self-searching questions must be asked and answered truthfully.

1 Am I prepared to spend a few minutes every day on grooming and feeding?

2 Am I prepared to spend a few minutes a day on training?

3 Am I prepared to exercise a dog, in all weathers, for approximately one hour each day when it is fully grown?

If each answer is an unqualified 'yes', then it is fair for you to proceed. However, you must remember that at all times the happiness of your pet will depend entirely upon you, and that you are contemplating a companionship which, normally, will endure for a period in excess of ten years. Once you have made up your mind, the next step is to consider how to go about your purchase.

This can be an exciting event, even for hardened breeders. There is something about choosing a puppy which we hope will be the best out of a litter – either in looks for show, brains for fieldwork, or character as a pet – which appeals to most of us. It may well be that this appeal is to the gambling instinct in all of us, because there is little doubt that it is a gamble to try to pick the puppy which eventually will excel in any particular aspect. How often the poorest-looking little mite in the litter has turned out, in the end, to be the best. No matter how experienced you may be, it is a fact that the only sure way of keeping the best of the litter is to keep the whole litter. This is the reason why some well-known breeders do not sell their stock until it is at least six months old.

Would-be purchasers of today are fortunate in that they have many bodies to whom they can turn for advice. There are Labrador Retriever Clubs in most countries who will be pleased to supply the names and addresses of member breeders in any particular area. The main aim of all these clubs is to preserve and strengthen the good name of the Labrador Retriever, and most of the members are dedicated in this respect. Should you not wish to go to the trouble of writing to one of these breed clubs, a telephone call to the secretary of your local canine society, or to a veterinary surgeon, will produce the names of local breeders.

Buying a puppy from a well-known breeder – and we stress well-known – is in itself an insurance policy for satisfaction. They guard their reputations zealously, and insist upon giving satisfaction with any stock they sell. They will help and advise you with most of your problems, even after you have had your dog for some considerable time.

When you go to buy your puppy it is best to be frank with the breeder, particularly if it is your first dog. If you are asked questions, such as 'do you want the dog for showing, or as a pet-companion, or for work with the gun?', it is not for any sinister reason. These questions are asked with the object of choosing a puppy from a mating, or from a litter, which is most likely to give the qualities you seek. And please do not say you are looking for a pet, and then blame the breeder if your puppy does not go on to win all the prizes at the local shows.

You will already have decided which of the three colours you prefer – black, yellow or chocolate (sometimes described as liver) – but have you decided upon the sex? While a bitch requires a little more care when she is in season (normally twice a year), she is so much softer and sweeter by nature, and so loyal, that she more than compensates for the little extra trouble you have to take with her. The male is rather more headstrong in character and, therefore, requires a little more firmness in handling. He also has a greater inclination to wander than a bitch, and this tendency has to be curbed whenever possible if his owner wants to avoid the troubles it can cause; the earlier the better.

Obviously, therefore, there are arguments for and against each sex. For example, if you want a dog for work with the gun you could be let down if you choose a bitch, who might come on heat during the shooting season. If this is not acceptable, then a male must be your choice. That is not to say, or imply, that a bitch is not as good in the field as a male; nothing could be further from the truth. There are many owners who put up with the loss of their gundog for the times she is in season because they contend that she more than makes up for this at other times. If, however, you want a family pet where this eventuality is not quite so important, the female of the breed would be our recommendation. How to cope with her season is dealt with on page 126.

The breeder will be very pleased to discuss all these points with you. He will also show you the dam of your puppy, perhaps not looking her best after coping with a litter of demanding puppies, but you will get a fairly clear image of what your puppy will grow to look like, and what its temperament is likely to be. Often the breeder will be able to show you the sire and dam and many relatives of the litter you are viewing, and this is excellent from the purchaser's point of view.

Despite all that has been said about breeders of repute, it seems obvious that anyone about to purchase a puppy would like to know the main breed points which they should look for. They are as follows:

1  A bold puppy, not one which slinks into the corner.

2  A kind expression with a dark eye.

3  A well-developed but short body, with good strong bones and a deep rib cage.

4  A nice action when moving, i.e. the puppy moves smoothly with no signs of lameness in either front or rear legs.

5  A good tail – at the root, short, tapering to the end – described as an 'otter' tail.

6  A good coat, which means a harsh topcoat and a dense, soft undercoat. This is very difficult to forecast in a puppy, but

if you have seen the parents they will have given you a good indication of how the puppy will be clad when he is older.

Avoid puppies showing any or all of the following signs:
1 Watery eyes.
2 Running nose.
3 Signs of rash – look at the stomach and under arms.
4 Patchy coats, i.e. where the coat obviously has been 'got at' by lice or other parasites.

Having seen all the puppies which are for sale, it may well be that you do not want the best in the litter. This puppy could be too expensive, especially if it is a potential show or field trial winner. Here again it pays to be honest with the breeder in explaining your requirements. He may well be able to help by offering a puppy which, for some reason quite unimportant from your point of view, is what is called a 'throw-out'. This means that it is less expensive because it has no potential as a prize-winner, but it might be just right as a family pet.

The usual age to buy a puppy is at about eight weeks; but it can be, and often is, bought later than this without detriment to the dog and owner relationship. When a breeder is selling a grown dog, it normally is done on a 'trial period' basis; but this 'trial' usually does not apply to puppy sales. However, most reputable breeders would take stock back should something quite unforeseen go wrong.

When you have chosen your puppy with the points mentioned in mind, and with the help of the breeder – and remembered the purpose for which your pet has been purchased – there remains one last important chore – documentation. The breeder should supply you with:
1 A properly completed and signed pedigree.
2 A Kennel Club Registration Card if the puppy is registered at the Kennel Club.
3 A transfer form, duly signed, if your puppy is registered at the Kennel Club.
4 A signed registration form if the puppy is not registered at the Kennel Club.
5 A diet sheet; or a list of items, giving quantities showing your puppy's daily needs. This is absolutely essential in order

to avoid any dietary upsets which might result from your feeding vastly different foods. (Our own diet sheets, for puppies from eight weeks to one year old, are given in Chapter 9.)

If you have paid a good price for your puppy, you may wish to take the precaution of insuring him against any loss. Reference to the dog press (*Our Dogs* and *Dog World* both published weekly) will give you the names and addresses of companies who specialize in this type of insurance. Should you decide to take out a policy of this type, do be sure to read the small print so that you are in no doubt at all as to the cover your premiums will give you. Check with the breeder whether the pup has had any inoculations.

Before ending this section on choosing your puppy, there is one other point which should be emphasized.

Please, before you make your purchase, do remember that you are not buying an inanimate toy for yourself or for your children. A puppy is a living creature which feels pain, and reacts to cruelty as a human being does, but without the same deep reasoning. Equally, it responds without reserve to kindness, and this should be the cornerstone of the relationship between you and your puppy.

Children, of course, can be very kind to animals; equally they can be very cruel, often without meaning to be. We would urge parents to supervise most carefully the behaviour of children for whom pets are bought, to guide them in the right way to care for their animals, and to emphasize the importance of kindness and consideration. Results in the character of both child and puppy will prove the wisdom of this advice. Above all, do not let a small child pick up a heavy puppy – he may drop and seriously hurt the pup, and this may leave an indelible mark on the child's mind in addition, possibly, to doing irreparable damage to the dog.

CARE

When you have made up your mind to buy the puppy you will have decided where he is going to have his kennel or 'spot' indoors (see Chapter 9). If he is to live indoors for a time, at least until he has finished teething, it would probably be wise to provide him with a strong cardboard box of suitable size. This is easily replaced should he play havoc with it, and you won't be so exasperated watching him tear this up as you would if you had bought him an expensive basket. Nevertheless if he does tear his bed he must not be allowed to get off scot free – he must be scolded.

Whilst feeding and housing the puppy are obviously matters of great importance, his health and well-being cannot be allowed to go without mention.

You have selected your puppy, collected his papers and diet sheet, and you have asked the breeder about inoculations.

Normally a puppy will not have been inoculated against any diseases at the age of eight weeks when you pick him up. Because he is carrying a gradually reducing number of antibodies from the bitch which may render an injection useless, most veterinary surgeons will not inoculate him until he is three months old. You have therefore a gap of one month during which you must take care that your puppy is not allowed to roam and sniff where other dogs have been, thus exposing him to any disease which they could have been carrying. His activities must therefore be seriously curtailed until he has been inoculated.

*Inoculations*

Veterinary science has provided us with benefits which dog-owners and breeders would be foolish to ignore. Perhaps the most important of these are the inoculations against hardpad, distemper, hepatitis and leptospirosis. There are two main forms of inoculation, one covering the first three named diseases, and the other the last. All of these are serious diseases for dogs, and even if they did not actually kill, you would be very fortunate if your dog remained unaffected in later life. For this reason I would like to deal with these first, before discussing the general care and the health of your dog.

HARDPAD: A strain of distemper, highly contagious, so called because it does in fact, cause the skin on the dog's pads to harden to such an extent that as he walks he sounds as if he has wooden shoes on.

DISTEMPER: A highly contagious virus disease which normally affects the nerves of the spinal cord, or the brain. There are many known strains of distemper and, while it attacks dogs of all ages, those under twelve months are particularly susceptible.

HEPATITIS: Another highly contagious virus infection which affects the liver, also known as Rubarth's disease.

LEPTOSPIROSIS: (1) Canicola. Sometimes called Stuttgart distemper; an infection of the kidneys. (2) Jaundice. A disease of the liver.

Puppies under twelve months are particularly prone to hardpad and distemper, and if they do pick up one of these dreaded diseases they seldom survive. Veterinary research workers have provided the answer with inoculations at the age of three months which normally give complete immunity. These inoculations should be boosted periodically, as recommended by your veterinary surgeon. You will see that this leaves an apparent danger period up to three months. Very briefly, during the larger part of this period the puppy carries immunity in the form of antibodies which it received from its mother, but, as the puppy is weaned, the effect of these antibodies weakens until they are virtually useless against the onset of the virus. It is at this point that inoculation is essential. To be doubly sure, up to the age of three months your veterinary surgeon can inject your puppy with a serum which will protect him until he can have the full inoculation. Although the complete inoculation against all these diseases costs a few pounds it is well worth the expense – as anyone who has seen dogs suffering from any of these diseases will agree.

When you have bought your puppy, do make the appointment with your veterinary surgeon for this treatment immediately. Until this has been done you should be very careful where you allow your puppy to go.

Every puppy should be taught to be clean in the [
properly on the lead, to obey at least simple comm[
come when he is called. Such training should start [
simple form from the moment of acquisition.

You must remember, however, that you have ta[
animal from his mother and the rest of the litter where h[   ]s
warm and cared for, and where he knew every sound and
smell. You have transported him to a strange place, amid
strange people, there are no familiar sounds or smells, and of
course he now has no brothers or sisters. He must feel lost and
it is up to you to gain his confidence and show him that he has
come to a far better home.

This is not easy because whilst you are doing this you have at
the same time to be firm and make sure that he knows you are
the master. There will therefore be times when you are in a
dilemma knowing that if you scold him for something when
you are beginning to gain his confidence you may have to start
from scratch again. Should this be your problem settle for
gaining his confidence at first because there is no doubt in my
mind this is by far the more important. Everything else can
follow.

A Labrador is a naturally clean dog and normally gives
warning of wanting to go out from a very early age. It would be
unusual if a puppy never made a mistake; when he does you
must scold him, but do this gently. *Never hit a puppy.* Show him
that he must go outside. The main object is to avoid a mess
indoors. Here there are two simple rules to follow: whenever
the puppy wakes take him outside; when he has done what you
have taken him out for praise him, and take him back
indoors.

The same rules apply after each meal. The important thing
to remember is that praise is as essential as scolding.

As I have said, Labradors are naturally very clean dogs and
they always head for the door whimpering when they want to
go out. If their cries go unheeded, they start 'circling' near the
door. Both of these actions are your cue to take the dog
out.

If you have to leave a puppy soon after you have acquired

him, place some newspaper near to the door, and you will find that he will use this if he needs to. This is not something normally advocated, but it is far better for him to wet a newspaper than anything else. To be quite fair, a new puppy should not be left for any length of time. He is like a baby and hasn't the power to retain. All he knows is that he is uncomfortable and must relieve his discomfort.

So far I have used the term 'scold' and I would like to explain what I mean.

I have said *never hit a puppy*, and I would qualify that slightly by saying never hit a Labrador. You are dealing with an intelligent and sensitive creature whose one wish, once you have gained his confidence, will be to please you. Normally your tone of voice is quite sufficient for him to know whether he is in or out of favour. If you 'growl' your command at him he will know that this is no time for play. If the worst comes to the worst, then take him quite firmly under the chin and make him look at you, at the same time saying 'No'. You will find that this is usually the most serious punishment you will have to mete out.

For the baby puppy even a quick movement towards him may, and certainly a dive to grab him will, scare him. So, although both of these mean little or nothing to you, do remember the effect they may have on the puppy. This will depend on the temperament of the puppy, and therefore the owner has to apply a little elementary doggy psychology. Whatever happens, however, you do not want to be the unwitting cause of your dog being hand shy.

While on this subject of cleanliness, never never rub his nose in his droppings. This is absolutely stupid and inexcusable.

One question often asked goes something like this, 'We want to call him "X". How can we make him understand this?'

The first thing that the new owner must learn quickly is that a dog has a very limited understanding of what you are saying. He knows by your tone of voice whether you are pleased or otherwise and he will react accordingly, but a long conversation means nothing to him. Eventually he will learn simple commands but words must be kept to an absolute minimum – for example: 'Go', 'come', 'sit', 'stay', 'down'. As far as possible use one word, but make each quite different in sound.

When you take your puppy to give him his meal let him see the bowl of food and call 'X'. When he comes stroke him, say 'Good boy' and let him have the food. After this has happened a few times he will associate 'X' with something pleasant, either food or being fondled, and you will have no further trouble with the name problem.

Real training should not start in earnest until the dog is about four months old, but there is a lot of preparatory work which can be done before then, and it can and does start almost from the day you take your puppy home. You start with the name and the cleanliness. Then you have to spend a few minutes each day brushing him and here again you have the opportunity to make him, for example, stand still whilst you groom him. Always remember to praise him when he has done just what you wanted. I cannot emphasize too much that during this preparatory period you must take great care that you are not building up any malpractice, but are trying to establish an association of ideas for the future. For example, when you call your dog you want him to come to you, so don't call your dog and then when he comes, scold him. As far as he is concerned you called him and he came, and now you are telling him off and he just doesn't understand. He thinks that as he came when you called he therefore warrants praise, so he does, for he has obeyed the command.

Scolding should only be done while the dog is actually doing something wrong – when he has as it were been 'caught in the act'. There is no point in scolding some time after the event, when the dog has probably forgotten all about it. Do be particularly careful about this point.

*Lead Training*

The law asks ever dog owner to make sure that his dog wears a good collar with a name and address on it. The new owner should therefore equip himself with one each of these – certainly from the time the puppy is inoculated. The best collar I have found is made of leather and is rolled rather than being just a plain strap. This type does not appear to be quite so hard on the coat around the dog's neck as the flatter variety.

For a lead I always choose a leather one about four feet long and with a good strong clasp. The lead may well be too much for the puppy, if you feel this to be so, try a nylon one which is a collar as well. This is only for the lead training.

The great thing with lead training – as with most dog training – is to do it little and often. Don't get up one morning and in a burst of enthusiasm say that today you are going to train your dog to the lead. It doesn't work like this. Some Labradors, even puppies. take to the lead the moment it is put on, and apart from being taught not to pull or make a figure eight in front of their owner, thus endangering life and limb, they never look back, and are therefore quite easily trained.

Others, I am afraid, are quite the reverse and these are not always the timid ones; therefore the owner has to proceed slowly and carefully, just a few minutes at a time until the dog is fully adjusted and quite happy with the lead. Your patience will always be rewarded, so do not give up with the most difficult dog.

It is always better to start your training somewhere where there are few distractions, and again remember to praise him when the dog does well.


## Obedience Training

Let me hasten to say that by obedience training I am not referring to Test C obedience training as performed by some of our top obedience dogs at the big shows, but simply rudimentary obedience.

This can become the foundation of all your future work with the dog, whether as a companion or as a shooting dog. It must therefore be done with care.

Let me say first of all that there are many dog training classes up and down the country which do a very excellent job up to a very high standard. Dog and owner could do worse than attend such classes where the many problems associated with dog training are highlighted.

Incidentally, one of the first comments which the new owner attending will hear from the old-stagers goes something like this: 'Of course it is not difficult to train the dogs. The biggest trouble is training the owners.' The wisdom of this remark becomes apparent very quickly. Such classes do, however, provide a very useful service to the community, and one which is enjoyed by owners and dogs alike.

The only equipment required for this training, other than your leather lead, is a choke chain about 22 to 24 inches long.

This is a chain with a loop at each end and therefore the chain has to be fed through one of the loops before being placed over the dog's head. An important point here is that the chain should 'run' freely i.e. tighten and slacken. In order to do this the straight part of the chain is on the top.

Never leave a choke chain around the dog's neck as a collar. Only a short time ago while driving down a country lane I saw a dog lying in the gutter. I thought he had been hit by a passing car, but when I approached I saw that he had his right front paw threaded through the chain and couldn't extricate it. It

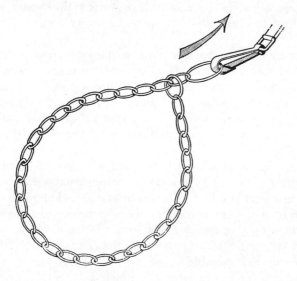

*Figure 8* Correct position for check chain

took a local farmer and myself several minutes to free him.

All exercises should be carried out on the lead until you are certain that the dog knows exactly what you want him to do and, what is more, that he will do it.

The first exercise is to consolidate what you taught him as a puppy: how to walk properly at your side on the lead. You want him to be level with you, not in front and not lagging the full length of his lead behind you. You must use the choke chain to 'position' him, giving the command 'heel'. Don't forget to praise him every time he does a good exercise.

The next exercise is to stop, so while moving on the lead you call 'halt' at the same time stopping yourself. If you want your dog to sit every time you stop, you will give the command 'halt, sit' and for the first few times you will have to put pressure on his rump at the same time saying 'sit'. He will soon get the idea and when you stop he will automatically halt and sit even without the spoken command.

This exercise is followed by the 'down', that is the dog lying down. Again the procedure is similar to the sit except the command becomes one of 'halt, sit, down' or just 'halt, down'. Again you will at first have to apply pressure at the shoulders to make him go down until he grasps what you want him to do.

You then come to the 'stay' either in the sitting position or in the down position or both. Having sat or downed your dog, go to the farthest extent of the lead in front of him, at the same time holding up a 'stop' hand saying 'stay'. Again he will soon understand what you want. This exercise is finished by calling the dog to you 'come' and of course lavish praise for an exercise well done.

When you are absolutely certain that the dog fully understands these exercises, then you can try them without the lead. If you fail, back on the lead again until you feel you can confidently try again. It is far better not to overdo the exercise, particularly with a young dog. Fifteen minutes a day is quite enough. If you do decide to go to training classes you will find these extremely valuable.

Once you have successfully completed these you have an excellent companion, one ready to be taught to be a good shooting dog. He is steady, he will on command walk to heel, sit, go down, stay and come. What is even more important to you as his owner is the satisfaction and pride you will have in your dog. It is a pleasure to have a dog like this with you.

In the world of obedience training one of the exercises in which difficulty is encountered is the retrieve. This is the very *raison d'être* of the Labrador and should cause little or no trouble. Many breeders start teaching, if such is necessary, the dog to retrieve from the early days of puppyhood.

It is all a 'game' to the puppy and it is surprising how quickly and eagerly a puppy of eight weeks will retrieve an object thrown for him. Gentle encouragement to return it to hand soon meets with success as will a hand placed on his rump restrain him from rushing to pick the object up the moment it is thrown.

A word of warning here: do take care that your puppy does not pick up sharp sticks. I had the misfortune to see a puppy knock such a stick so that it went down his throat and pierced him right through to the shoulder. It was only with great difficulty that it was extricated, and only careful nursing managed to save the dog.

A useful 'dummy' for the retrieve is a piece of wood wrapped in an old sock or encased in some sacking. You can later add feathers to the sacking to get your dog used to picking up feathered objects.

# 7

# Starting a Kennel

To establish a strain in any breed of animal takes a great deal of time, endless patience, careful culling and often considerable expense. It has been done in Labradors by careful breeding over a very long time by Gwen Broadley with the famous Sandylands strain, the late Grant and Mrs Marjy Cairns with the Blaircourt, and the late Mr Severn with the chocolate (liver if you prefer) Tibshelfs.

It would be difficult if not impossible to tell you in detail how this is achieved. In the broad sense we have all in our mind's eye the picture of our perfect Labrador. Each picture will differ to a greater or lesser degree, although all pictures will come within the standard of the breed. To quote one or two extreme examples, it may well be that one breeder likes a bigger type of Labrador and that therefore his picture will be based on dogs at the top end of the breed standard. Another may have as his ideal one at the middle or lower end of the height scale. This in itself may not sound very much but, as the standard gives heights for dogs 23½ inches and bitches 22½ inches, a difference in height of something in excess of one inch is involved, this can make a tremendous difference in the appearance of the finished products when viewed together. A particular colour may be the preference; e.g. the late Mr Severn spent many years breeding chocolates. The diffuclties here were in pigmentation and colour of eyes. These have still to be completely overcome. Other breeders go for minor differences in shapes of head and other features. When all these features are welded together to form the complete entity in the breeder's mind's eye, it is the constant reproduction of dogs of similar type which is known as a strain.

If the reader glances at the two photographs of Gwen Broadley's Sandylands dogs, he will see that the two dogs span thirty years of breeding. He will also notice the remarkable similarity which has been maintained over such a long period and it is hoped it will last for a very long time to come.

Earlier I mentioned the late Grant Cairns and his wife Marjy; in their case I feel sure they would agree that Ch. Ruler of Blaircourt fulfilled their idea of the ideal in a strain. This view was shared by many, not only in this country but all over the world. Ruler certainly left his mark on his progeny in many ways but perhaps the most gratifying was the temperament he endowed.

It is quite impossible to mention all the types but Ch. Whatstandwell Coronet, bred by Mr and Mrs Horace Taylor, whose Whatstandwell prefix has been so famous for so long, must be mentioned. The Whatstandwell strain called for mainly yellows, the dogs being masculine in build and appearance without being 'overdone' and the bitches decidedly feminine. In effect at a glance the onlooker can tell the dog from the bitch; how I wish other breeders would copy this one, to me, essential attribute in any strain. Nowadays more than a glance is required to separate the males from the females. Some of the dogs have smaller heads and some of the bitches more doggy heads; this, together with a general narrowing of the height gap between the sexes, I consider to be quite wrong.

Famous for show and working, were the Liddly blacks and yellows belonging to Mr and Mrs H. A. Saunders. It is interesting that all blacks are called after trees and flowers, and all yellows after food. Mrs Audrey Radclyffe's excellent working kennel carries the Zelstone prefix.

In some quarters of the field trial world great stress is placed on speed or intelligence, appearance mattering little in comparison as long as the dog is presentable. Here, therefore, is an intangibility in the strain, difficult to define but nevertheless an intent which is often met.

## Selection of Brood Bitch

There must, of course, be a starting point and it is here where the brood bitch to start the breeding programme must be selected with great care. It is possible to start with a puppy – and selection of a young puppy is dealt with in Chapter 6 – but in a case such as this it is better to buy an older bitch, say eight to twelve months. This is normally more costly, but you can see fairly clearly what the finished product will look like on maturity. Obviously one must be chosen which seems to possess as many of the attributes you would wish for as possible but there may well be a considerable shortfall.

There is of course no violent objection to choosing a puppy, particularly if the parents are known, and if a previous mating of the same parents has produced the type of bitch you are seeking. Should this be the case, obviously there is a good chance of your being lucky.

If you choose an older bitch, exercise patience before you embark on your breeding programme. There are one or two 'musts' to observe first; for example the confidence of the bitch must be won, and although this may take a little time it will pay dividends in the long run.

Housing or kennels for your bitch must also be considered, details of some you may find suitable are contained in Chapter 9.

You may consider a veterinary examination is necessary, particularly in respect of hip dysplasia and progressive retinal atrophy (see end of Chapter 3).

A discussion with the breeder of your bitch regarding your plans and hopes may result in some worthwhile suggestions. After all, the breeder may well have a wealth of experience from which you can benefit, and this should not be spurned.

There is then the all important question of a sire. After the choice of brood bitch this is the next most difficult decision. Remember that there are two parents to every puppy and each will have faults as well as good points. These faults are passed on to their progeny as certainly (sometimes I think more certainly) than the good points which no doubt you will wish to enhance.

It may take two or three litters from the bitch to show that you are even on the right lines. A word of warning: please do not become so absorbed in your plans as to forget any consideration for her – she must *not* be treated like a puppy producing machine.

Again I would stress that unless you are extremely fortunate time and patience are essential before you embark on this process of establishing a strain.

Obviously your choice of sire must fit in with the bitch you have chosen and possess as many of the attributes you require for your ideal as possible. It is not essential for the sire of your choice to be a champion. You need a dog conforming closely to the standard but complementary to the bitch. It may well be that you will choose a complete 'outcross' as the sire. That is a dog which is no relation to your bitch at all. Such a mating may well give good results at first but to continue this procedure with subsequent litters, while possibly producing first-class puppies, is likely to give a considerable variation in type, and will not give the constant feature you are seeking.

Therefore having produced a first-class litter from an outcross mating, the method to adopt in order to establish these qualities in future litters is to mate the progeny in their turn with not too close relatives who themselves carry these qualities either in their blood or in fact. This is termed 'line breeding'.

Normally the idea of line breeding is to choose a particularly outstanding dog and mate related bitches to that dog in the hope that his particular good qualities and/or characteristics will be handed down to his progeny. The best chance of success in this is where the dog and bitch are top quality. The further the pair are from the 'outstanding dog' the less the chances of success.

Most breeders hold the view that cousins who themselves possess the necessary characteristic qualities poroduce the best results. Another view is similar, that of uncle mated to niece.

The most certain way of establishing a type or strain is of course 'in-breeding'. By this we mean the mating of very close realtives (father to daughter, brother to sister). Although this is practised widely in some breeds it is not to be embarked upon by the novice, or for that matter by the experienced breeder without a very careful study of the risks he is running.

Bearing in mind the basic idea of in-breeding, i.e. the carrying in duplicate, as it were, of the genes of the best points of the outstanding dog, it must be remembered equally that you are duplicating and therefore accentuating the faults. Ideally then in-breeding is only for the perfect dog and the perfect bitch.

This is partly true of line breeding also but to a very much slighter degree and this method of establishing a type, although the results are produced more slowly, is infinitely safer.

In a preceding paragraph Ch. Ruler of Blaircourt was mentioned and also how he left his 'mark' on his progeny. Many good stud dogs have this capacity and they are termed prepotent sires. No matter which bitch they are mated to they stamp the puppies with some degree of resemblance to themselves. A knowledge of this capacity in the sire is invaluable if, for example, he has a particularly good point, say, a typical otter tail which he invariably passes, and this happens to be the very point which needs strengthening in your litter. The same applies to typical heads, compactness, etc.

One mistake often made by the novice is to look for a stud dog which is over-exaggerated in one respect, for example having a very big coarse head, to mate to a bitch inclined to be narrow in head. The resultant progeny will most likely be a mixed bag, some resembling father, some mother. The required result was of course a proportion if not all, correct: the only way to achieve this is to choose a dog with a correct head.

This then is the general principle which must be emphasized: breed to the correct point and do not expect nature to produce a compromise. Above all follow the excellent concept that you should only breed from sound and healthy as well as good-looking stock.

When you have been presented with the first litter you are then faced with the problem of which members to keep in order to carry on your breeding programme. This is probably

Aust. Ch. Ramah Royal Archer UDX, CDX (Yellow) and Danish Int.
Ch. Ramah Raisin (Chocolate). Litter brother and sister at four months
Forsaken by mother and hand-reared

Aust. Dual Ch. Ellenarta Garnet CM, CD, his dam Aust. Dual Ch.
Baldorra Jewel CM, and his litter sister Aust. Ret. Trial Ch. Ellenarta
Tahitian Pearl

Aust. Ch. Karnmore Ruler (*Barkleigh Shute*)

Aust. Ch. Ramah Royal Archer (imported)

Aust. Ch. Duffton Glen Angus had a wonderful record, including three BIS and sixteen Group wins

Aust. Dual Ch. Baldorra Belle (*The Australian*)

AFC, FC and Nat. Amateur Ret.
FC Super Chief

NFC, AFC, CFC Cork of
Oakwood Lane

Am. Ch. Whygin Gold Bullion at ten years old (*Jansken*)

the most difficult and expensive task of all. Puppies are ready for sale at eight weeks, and Labrador puppies at this age cost a good deal in good food (and there is no such thing as a cheap food). Unfortunately it is quite impossible for even the most experienced breeder to pick out the best puppy at this age, and there is little alternative to keeping the puppies until they are nearly six months old before you can confidently make your selection. One compromise here is to make a preliminary selection (which could be wrong) at eight weeks to reduce the numbers (see Chapter 6) and hence the expense, and repeat this process every four weeks or so until you are left with approximately the number you want.

The next step, that of mating the puppies of the litter, which is your first real step in starting your strain, is now all important. It is at this point that you must decide which programme of breeding you are going to follow, and which stud dogs you will use. Such a programme should be forward looking, not only to the next litter but the one after, and the one after that.

Eventually when you are breeding puppies to a type, litter after litter, then you can say that you have established your strain or kennel. Do remember, however, that this cannot be done overnight, and that often a fair amount of expense is entailed before you achieve the results you are seeking. Although there is a lot of heartache in the process there is a credit side to breeding Labradors in that they are really wonderful dogs to be with any age. Their company and the enjoyment and pleasure they give is something to be treasured. This enjoyment is doubled and trebled when you have achieved your objective, and the puppies you are breeding conform to a type both in looks and in temperament in keeping within the standard of the breed.

I have heard it said many times that the most successful breeders are the breeders who can cull ruthlessly. This means disposing of unwanted animals either by having them destroyed, selling them cheaply, or finding 'good' homes. Without being sickly or sentimental I find the idea of putting down healthy stock abhorrent. Selling cheaply can be inviting future trouble for the dog on the basis of 'easy come, easy go'.

If a 'good' home can be found this is fine, but I must confess to dismal failure in this when I have looked for one although I appreciate some breeders have been very fortunate in this direction.

# 8

# Breeding and Whelping

Breeding must not be undertaken lightly. Before embarking on this extremely interesting aspect very careful consideration must be given to the pros and cons. In addition there are, I feel, one or two fallacies which should be exploded.

First of all, if the reason for breeding a litter is to make a quick profit, my earnest advice would be 'do not'. Far too many puppies end up either in the Dogs' Home, or having to be put to sleep because of this.

A Labrador bitch will usually produce a litter of six to eight puppies, sometimes fewer, often more. From the age of two to three weeks, the bitch's milk is not enough to ensure really good quality stock, and therefore in addition to giving her all the good and nutritious food she needs, the puppies' food must be supplemented. The quality of the supplement must be good. All this adds up to a fair amount of expense as can be seen from the diet sheets given in the next chapter.

When the puppies are ready to be sold at eight weeks, it is most unlikely that they will all go at once, or even within a week or two. Often one or two puppies cannot be sold for some time, perhaps months. If the breeder lacks facilities for keeping such puppies, life will become very difficult indeed, to say nothing of the financial loss incurred while the puppies grow.

These points must be considered most carefully by the would-be breeder before a decision to breed is taken.

Let us turn now to some of the myths about breeding which must be dispelled. For example, how often one hears 'I decided that my bitch must have a litter for the good of her health' or 'I must find a bitch for my dog to mate'. Admittedly procreation is the natural order but there is absolutely no evidence to prove that a bitch which does not have a litter lives a shorter or a more unhealthy life than a bitch which has had one or more litters. The same applies to the dog and in fact here I would strongly advise that unless the dog is going to be rgularly used at stud it is far better not to use him at all, though much must depend on his temperament.

Finally there is the time factor. Breeding is a twenty-four-hour-day occupation for the breeder, with no holidays or time off until the litter is completely off his hands. The work is pleasant but demanding. Time schedules are important and must be followed closely. There is little time left for many other chores if the litter and mother are to be properly looked after.

If, however, after carefully considering all these points the would-be breeder decided to go ahead, then I can offer him the consolation that it is a fascinating hobby and one which the devotee never ceases to enjoy.

In Chapter 7 (Starting a Kennel) I touched briefly on hereditary diseases such as hip dysplasia, progressive retinal atrophy and entropia. Before the mating it is essential to ensure as far as possible that sire and dam are free from these defects. It is quite irresponsible to breed without checking these points. If you breed from unhealthy stock you are only storing up trouble for yourself and – more important – the breed, and this must be avoided at all costs. A visit to your veterinary surgeon will settle these points.

Perhaps before going into the question of the actual mating some consideration should be given to the stud fee and similar arrangements.

It is essential that these formalities are clearly understood by both sides from the outset. Perhaps a brief résumé of the normal arrangements would be helpful.

First of all, it is normal for the bitch to visit the dog, and if any other arrangement is made (e.g. the dog visiting the bitch) then it is customary for a fee in respect of any additional expense incurred by the owner of the stud dog to be added to the stud fee. In any event transport for the bitch including return transport are the responsibility of her owner. Here I must emphasize that if you have to send your bitch by rail there are certain important things to remember. Some are listed below:

1 Do make sure that your transit box is adequate in size and strength to withstand rail travel and has a pointed roof so that nothing will be stacked on top.

2 Label it clearly with feeding and watering instructions when necessary.

3 The comfort of your bitch at this time is essential.

4 Choose only through trains and do not risk changes en route. Rather than this take you bitch by car to a station from which she can be put on a through train.

5 Advise the consignee as soon as you are ready to despatch and make sure that there is someone at the other end to meet her.

6 Do *not* be satisfied until you are certain that your bitch is safe at her destination.

7 Follow a similar procedure for her return.

8 Remember that the telephone is far better and quicker than a letter in these cases so don't for economy's sake, resort to post to tie up all the loose ends.

9 K.C. regulations now require that both the stud dog and the brood bitch should be registered in the active register if their progeny is to be registered at the Kennel Club (see pages 115).

The normal procedure for payment is to pay a fee for the service, and here it must be stressed that the fee is paid normally for the service, *not for the result*. In other words if no puppies result the fee is not returnable. Most stud dog owners agree, however, that if there is no result from a first mating, they will allow a second mating free at the next season, subject to the dog being available. There may be variations of this arrangement but this is the basic position. Stud dog owners should make any such arrangement clear in writing on the stud receipt and then both sides know exactly where they stand.

If it has been agreed to give a puppy in lieu of a stud fee, exactly which puppy must be clearly agreed, preferably in writing. If it is to be the pick of litter regardless of sex, the best bitch or the best dog, both parties must fully understand this.

It may be more than one puppy e.g. first choice and third choice. There are many variations, but with goodwill and the arrangement put in writing there is no reason why there should be any trouble. In cases where a stud fee is not paid immediately the stud dog owner will not normally hand over a copy of the dog's pedigree until the transaction is finally completed.

One final point: do tell the owner of the stud dog the moment the bitch comes in season even if you have booked his service months ago. The stud dog owner can then ensure that the dog will be available at the right time.

Remember to tell the owner of the stud dog whether your bitch is a maiden bitch, with whom there may well be a little difficulty, and do take a copy of your bitch's pedigree with you to be seen and considered by the stud dog owner. If he sees that the pedigrees will not 'nick-in' for any reason then he will tell you, and perhaps make some suggestions about other dogs who would be more suitable.

There is now the question of when to mate the bitch. A bitch normally comes in season, or on heat (oestrum) twice a year, in the spring and the autumn. The approach is recognizable in that there is a swelling of the vagina, and she becomes quite friendly and excitable. This is soon followed by a show of colour i.e. slight bleeding from the vagina. The bitch will usually be ready for mating when this colour has stopped on or about the eleventh or twelfth day from the commencement. At this time she will be extremely friendly and will begin to make overtures to any dog she sees. She will probably bark, push them with her nose and finally present her rear with her tail switched well to one side.

There is a more scientific method of telling readiness and this is by use of Test Tape.

The only real test of course, and the one in which you are interested is the acceptance of the dog. So as soon as any of the foregoing conditions have been reached i.e. colour stopped, eleventh/twelfth day, then it is time to take her to the stud dog. Take her on a good strong collar and lead and if you want to be popular, do not in any circumstances let her run all over the stud dog owner's property. Make sure you have left off such things as Amplex for at least forty-eight hours beforehand.

Unless you have been to a mating before please also forget all preconceived ideas about it.

The owner of the stud dog will want you to hold your bitch securely until he sees how she reacts in the presence of the dog which he will also bring in on a strong lead. The first reaction is normally one of slight suspicion followed quickly by some friendly pushing and jostling. At this point the bitch often becomes a little frightened when the dog starts to mount her, and she needs the help and support of her owner, and this is really one of the main reasons why we always prefer the owners to be present. It does help to give the bitch confidence.

It is highly desirable to secure a 'tie' at the mating which can last ten minutes or longer. Once a 'tie' has been made infinite care must be taken to se that the dog in getting down and turning does not hurt the bitch. Frequently at this point the mating can fail because the bitch in her already highly excitable condition suddenly lunges and the tie is broken – do therefore take great care to see that the bitch, especially a maiden, is held firmly.

Obviously the less assistance and the less force used the better, but at the same time you will find that it is often well nigh impossible to allow them to mate naturally, as such an attempt usually ends with a tired dog and bitch through constant playing but no satisfactory tie.

Some bitches are so difficult that they have to be muzzled or sometimes even tranquillized (although I have never known a really successful mating with a tranquillized bitch). Muzzling is necessary because often a bitch who is obviously ready for mating (which she shows by such means as turning her tail) will fly at the dog every time he goes near her. If this is allowed to continue for long the dog will refuse to have anything to do with her. When she is muzzled, apart from the threats which the dog can ignore, trouble is usually eliminated, and the mating can proceed fairly easily. An effective muzzle in most cases is a nylon stocking pulled over the bitch's head. This is usually quite sufficient a deterrent.

The gestation period is usually sixty-three days from mating (see table). Some breeders like two matings and if you are one

# GESTATION TABLE

| Served January | Due to Whelp March | Served February | Due to Whelp April | Served March | Due to Whelp May | Served April | Due to Whelp June | Served May | Due to Whelp July | Served June | Due to Whelp August | Served July | Due to Whelp September | Served August | Due to Whelp October | Served September | Due to Whelp November | Served October | Due to Whelp December | Served November | Due to Whelp January | Served December | Due to Whelp February |
|---|---|---|---|---|---|---|---|---|---|---|---|---|---|---|---|---|---|---|---|---|---|---|---|
| 1 | 5 | 1 | 5 | 1 | 3 | 1 | 3 | 1 | 3 | 1 | 3 | 1 | 2 | 1 | 3 | 1 | 3 | 1 | 3 | 1 | 3 | 1 | 2 |
| 2 | 6 | 2 | 6 | 2 | 4 | 2 | 4 | 2 | 4 | 2 | 4 | 2 | 3 | 2 | 4 | 2 | 4 | 2 | 4 | 2 | 4 | 2 | 3 |
| 3 | 7 | 3 | 7 | 3 | 5 | 3 | 5 | 3 | 5 | 3 | 5 | 3 | 4 | 3 | 5 | 3 | 5 | 3 | 5 | 3 | 5 | 3 | 4 |
| 4 | 8 | 4 | 8 | 4 | 6 | 4 | 6 | 4 | 6 | 4 | 6 | 4 | 5 | 4 | 6 | 4 | 6 | 4 | 6 | 4 | 6 | 4 | 5 |
| 5 | 9 | 5 | 9 | 5 | 7 | 5 | 7 | 5 | 7 | 5 | 7 | 5 | 6 | 5 | 7 | 5 | 7 | 5 | 7 | 5 | 7 | 5 | 6 |
| 6 | 10 | 6 | 10 | 6 | 8 | 6 | 8 | 6 | 8 | 6 | 8 | 6 | 7 | 6 | 8 | 6 | 8 | 6 | 8 | 6 | 8 | 6 | 7 |
| 7 | 11 | 7 | 11 | 7 | 9 | 7 | 9 | 7 | 9 | 7 | 9 | 7 | 8 | 7 | 9 | 7 | 9 | 7 | 9 | 7 | 9 | 7 | 8 |
| 8 | 12 | 8 | 12 | 8 | 10 | 8 | 10 | 8 | 10 | 8 | 10 | 8 | 9 | 8 | 10 | 8 | 10 | 8 | 10 | 8 | 10 | 8 | 9 |
| 9 | 13 | 9 | 13 | 9 | 11 | 9 | 11 | 9 | 11 | 9 | 11 | 9 | 10 | 9 | 11 | 9 | 11 | 9 | 11 | 9 | 11 | 9 | 10 |
| 10 | 14 | 10 | 14 | 10 | 12 | 10 | 12 | 10 | 12 | 10 | 12 | 10 | 11 | 10 | 12 | 10 | 12 | 10 | 12 | 10 | 12 | 10 | 11 |
| 11 | 15 | 11 | 15 | 11 | 13 | 11 | 13 | 11 | 13 | 11 | 13 | 11 | 12 | 11 | 13 | 11 | 13 | 11 | 13 | 11 | 13 | 11 | 12 |
| 12 | 16 | 12 | 16 | 12 | 14 | 12 | 14 | 12 | 14 | 12 | 14 | 12 | 13 | 12 | 14 | 12 | 14 | 12 | 14 | 12 | 14 | 12 | 13 |
| 13 | 17 | 13 | 17 | 13 | 15 | 13 | 15 | 13 | 15 | 13 | 15 | 13 | 14 | 13 | 15 | 13 | 15 | 13 | 15 | 13 | 15 | 13 | 14 |
| 14 | 18 | 14 | 18 | 14 | 16 | 14 | 16 | 14 | 16 | 14 | 16 | 14 | 15 | 14 | 16 | 14 | 16 | 14 | 16 | 14 | 16 | 14 | 15 |
| 15 | 19 | 15 | 19 | 15 | 17 | 15 | 17 | 15 | 17 | 15 | 17 | 15 | 16 | 15 | 17 | 15 | 17 | 15 | 17 | 15 | 17 | 15 | 16 |
| 16 | 20 | 16 | 20 | 16 | 18 | 16 | 18 | 16 | 18 | 16 | 18 | 16 | 17 | 16 | 18 | 16 | 18 | 16 | 18 | 16 | 18 | 16 | 17 |
| 17 | 21 | 17 | 21 | 17 | 19 | 17 | 19 | 17 | 19 | 17 | 19 | 17 | 18 | 17 | 19 | 17 | 19 | 17 | 19 | 17 | 19 | 17 | 18 |
| 18 | 22 | 18 | 22 | 18 | 20 | 18 | 20 | 18 | 20 | 18 | 20 | 18 | 19 | 18 | 20 | 18 | 20 | 18 | 20 | 18 | 20 | 18 | 19 |
| 19 | 23 | 19 | 23 | 19 | 21 | 19 | 21 | 19 | 21 | 19 | 21 | 19 | 20 | 19 | 21 | 19 | 21 | 19 | 21 | 19 | 21 | 19 | 20 |
| 20 | 24 | 20 | 24 | 20 | 22 | 20 | 22 | 20 | 22 | 20 | 22 | 20 | 21 | 20 | 22 | 20 | 22 | 20 | 22 | 20 | 22 | 20 | 21 |
| 21 | 25 | 21 | 25 | 21 | 23 | 21 | 23 | 21 | 23 | 21 | 23 | 21 | 22 | 21 | 23 | 21 | 23 | 21 | 23 | 21 | 23 | 21 | 22 |
| 22 | 26 | 22 | 26 | 22 | 24 | 22 | 24 | 22 | 24 | 22 | 24 | 22 | 23 | 22 | 24 | 22 | 24 | 22 | 24 | 22 | 24 | 22 | 23 |
| 23 | 27 | 23 | 27 | 23 | 25 | 23 | 25 | 23 | 25 | 23 | 25 | 23 | 24 | 23 | 25 | 23 | 25 | 23 | 25 | 23 | 25 | 23 | 24 |
| 24 | 28 | 24 | 28 | 24 | 26 | 24 | 26 | 24 | 26 | 24 | 26 | 24 | 25 | 24 | 26 | 24 | 26 | 24 | 26 | 24 | 26 | 24 | 25 |
| 25 | 29 | 25 | 29 | 25 | 27 | 25 | 27 | 25 | 27 | 25 | 27 | 25 | 26 | 25 | 27 | 25 | 27 | 25 | 27 | 25 | 27 | 25 | 26 |
| 26 | 30 | 26 | 30 | 26 | 28 | 26 | 28 | 26 | 28 | 26 | 28 | 26 | 27 | 26 | 28 | 26 | 28 | 26 | 28 | 26 | 28 | 26 | 27 |
| 27 | 31 | 27 | MAY 1 | 27 | 29 | 27 | 29 | 27 | 29 | 27 | 29 | 27 | 28 | 27 | 29 | 27 | 29 | 27 | 29 | 27 | 29 | 27 | 28 |
| 28 | APR. 1 | 28 | 2 | 28 | 30 | 28 | 30 | 28 | 30 | 28 | 30 | 28 | 29 | 28 | 30 | 28 | 30 | 28 | 30 | 28 | 30 | 28 | MAR. 1 |
| 29 | 2 | 29 | 3 | 29 | 31 | 29 | JULY 1 | 29 | 31 | 29 | 31 | 29 | 30 | 29 | 31 | 29 | DEC. 1 | 29 | 31 | 29 | 31 | 29 | 2 |
| 30 | 3 |  |  | 30 | JUNE 1 | 30 | 2 | 30 | AUG. 1 | 30 | SEP. 1 | 30 | OCT. 1 | 30 | NOV. 1 | 30 | 2 | 30 | JAN. 1 | 30 | FEB. 1 | 30 | 3 |
| 31 | 4 |  |  | 31 | 2 |  |  | 31 | 2 |  |  | 31 | 2 | 31 | 2 |  |  | 31 | 2 |  |  | 31 | 4 |

of these then the matings *must not* be more than thirty-six hours apart. Personally, if the mating results in a good tie I would not have a second mating.

Once your bitch has been mated she needs a little extra care so that she won't stray during the remainder of the period of her season.

The time to worm her before she has her litter is not earlier than three weeks after the mating, or not later than four weeks after mating. Do make sure that you are using only the safe worm tablets supplied by a veterinary surgeon.

Exercise for a healthy bitch in the first six weeks should be quite normal. Obviously as she becomes more cumbersome she will slow down and virtually decide for herself when she has done enough.

You will probably find she likes more short walks than long rambles. Be careful about her jumping or being bumped by other dogs.

Feeding the 'in whelp' bitch follows a similar pattern. During the first three weeks her diet should be her normal one to which has been added necessary vitamins. The amount she will need of these will depend almost entirely on the quality and varieties of food she is receiving normally. The better her normal diet and the more complete, the fewer additions she will need. Some of the additions which can be used with advantage are: Raspberry leaf tablets, wheat germ capsules, wheat germ oil, Canovel tablets, Vetzyme tablets, Vionate vitamin powder, Stress, Vivomin, calcium tablets, halibut liver oil. Choose from this list with care – most items can be obtained from the Boots' veterinary counter. Calcium tablets need not be given until about halfway through the gestation period.

Before the bitch is given this additional diet one must be reasonably certain that she is in whelp, and this can be the most difficult assessment to make even for the highly skilled professional at four to five weeks a slight swelling around the flanks is a good sign.

Before the third and sixth week increase her number of meals to two per day, but do *not* double the total intake immediately, although this should increase by about 25 per cent at the fourth week to nearly double by the time she whelps. At this time start with the Raspberry leaf tablets.

*Proposed diet sheet for the 'in whelp' bitch from four weeks to whelping*

| | |
|---|---|
| *Breakfast:* | Approx ¼ lb biscuits and ⅓-pint of milk with glucose or brown sugar. To this add your necessary additons. |
| *Lunch:* | 1 cup of biscuit meal (terrier size) soaked in gravy to which has been added ½ lb of meat or tripe or fish. Don't forget many nutritious leftovers in the 'green' line are often thrown away. These are invaluable for the bitch. Again your additions can be included. |
| *Evening Meal:* | Approx ¾ lb of meat varying from lunch. Any further additions required for the daily intake. |

Be careful on several important counts:

1 In searching for variety in your bitch's diet you may be tempted to buy meat or offal from pet shops. Don't forget these be boiled thoroughly.

2 Make sure she is not constipated.

3 Make sure she is kept warm and comfortable, throughout the whole period.

4 Rub a little olive oil into her undercarriage during the last two weeks before the puppies are due. This will make the skin soft and pliable.

5 At least two weeks before your bitch is due to whelp you must make your mind up where you will want her to have her puppies. Once you have made a suitable quiet place ready you can introduce her to it gradually. This will help give her a feeling security, knowing that she has somewhere to whelp when her time comes. A description of a suitable whelping box if indoors and equipment for outdoors is contained in Chapter 9.

6 Do not increase your bitch's intake to the extent that you are making her fat as this will only cause trouble when her time comes to whelp. What you want is a fit bitch who will have her puppies naturally and quickly. If you feel that the diet she is on may be fattening then reduce the carbohydrate content.

## Whelping

There are one or two things which should be done during the

waiting period between mating and whelping. It has already been mentioned that some quiet quarters for the bitch and/or whelping box should be arranged. There are other things on which perhaps a brief dissertation might be useful

1 Collect as many clean newspapers for bedding for the bitch and the puppies as you can. It is surprising how many you need and if you have a good supply the bitch and her brood will always have a clean bed.

2 Do check with a useful book of reference (e.g. Olwyn Gwynne-Jones' *The Popular Guide to Puppy-Rearing*) on points to be watched and remembered.

3 Have ready a sterilized bowl, scissors, cotton, cotton wool, T.C.P., towels, hot water bottle (rubber), a little brandy, feeder and emergency puppy box (clean box about 18 by 12 by 12 inches).

The first signs of your bitch whelping is one or more of the following symptoms:

1 She will lose her appetite.

2 She will want to be left alone.

3 She will probably keep looking behind.

4 She will pant and shiver a great deal.

5 She will dig furiously at the newspaper you have so carefully laid on her bed until they are like pieces of confetti. Don't scold her for this as it is all part of her labour, and if you have done your conservation job properly you will have plenty more papers anyway.

6 Her temperature will become subnormal approximately eight hours before the puppies present themselves.

7 She will be enlarged and will show a watery discharge. None of the above symptoms should cause any alarm providing that they occur anywhere between two and three days of the sixty-third day. If they are occurring say a week before consult your veterinary surgeon with whom you should have made some preliminary arrangements earlier in case you needed his assistance.

Likewise once your bitch commences to strain in earnest she must not be allowed to do so in vain for longer than two hours without you consulting your veterinary surgeon. This may be caused either by a dead puppy in the passage, or by one lying the wrong way (resulting in a breech birth), and professional skill is required. A dead puppy is usually heralded by a heavy green discharge and a caesarean section may be called for – this is quite straightforward nowadays. Any amateurish effort at pulling or assisting without full knowledge can do more harm than good and should not be attempted.

There is one way help can be given to a bitch if, as often happens a pet bitch or a maiden bitch is a little overwhelmed by the first puppy she may sit looking at it instead of tending it. You will have read that the puppy is born within a protective membrane, similar to a polythene bag, to which is attached the afterbirth. If your bitch is disinclined to touch it simply tear away the membrane around the puppy's face letting the bitch see what you are doing. Usually she will then take over and finish the chore, but she may not until you have done two or three puppies.

The procedure is quite simple:

1 Remove membrane with your fingernails.

2 Tie off the umbilical cord using a piece of thread dipped in diluted T.C.P. Make the knot about ½ to 1 inch from the puppy's tummy.

3 With sterile scissors cut the umbilical cord about 1 inch below the tie (the opposite side to the puppy of course).

4 Dab the cord with a little T.C.P.

5 Encourage the bitch to lick the puppy. If she won't, do not force the issue, simply dry the puppy off on a towel, and either put to suckle or if not possible put it on the hot (not too hot) water bottle.

6 It is important that the puppies suckle fairly soon because this makes them and the dam contented. In addition of course the food is exactly right to start the puppies off.

During the course of her whelping it does help if you exercise her, but always keep her under strict supervision. A bowl of cold milk too is acceptable. When the bitch has finished her labours she will be pretty exhausted especially if she has produced a large litter. Just clean her and her bed of newspapers, settle her puppies around her and leave her quiet and warm.

It is unusual once the bitch has settled with her litter that further trouble should develop, but you should always be prepared for an emergency. Any untoward happening is usually heralded by the dam showing indifference, and in extreme cases antagonism, to her puppies. The breeder should always be on the look out for any signs of this, and must track down the cause.

It can be any one of a number of things but the most common are:

1 A feeling of insecurity especially if many people are being allowed just to have a peep at the puppies – this is to be avoided particularly during the first two weeks. It can cause more trouble even with a bitch who is normally very placid, than it is worth. For the sake of the dam and her litter it is far safer to risk incurring the displeasure of the curious.

2 As regards nutrition, the dam is normally a very good mother and will give the puppies all she is able even to the detriment of herself. This may even cause her to drain herself of calcium and become paralysed. The first symptoms of this are a general restlessness and a slight rise in temperature. She does not want to be bothered by the puppies. Should this happen the remedy is simple, to call your veterinary surgeon at once. He will simply give her a fairly large injection of calcium and the results are miraculous. Obviously the earlier you spot this, the better. If you do not catch it early then you will most likely find the bitch in a state of paralysis in which case the remedy is similar to that already described.

There is sometimes a rare (I am glad to say) case where the bitch is lost during the whelping. It is most unusual but unfortunately it does happen and one is left with orphan puppies to rear. This is about the most time-consuming task of them all unless your veterinary surgeon can find a foster mother. The puppies must be tended and fed every two hours night and day for the first ten days to two weeks. Then the time between the night feeds can be gradually increased to four, and later six, hours. The daytime feeds should be every three hours.

For this you need a bottle with a very small teat. These are

not easy to find and in view of the low cost it it probably as well
to have one in stock just in case of any trouble with any one of
the puppies. Again you will find that one of the reputable pet
shops or Boots can procure one for you. A suitable one is
advertised in the *Kennel Gazette*.

The food for the puppies can be one of the specially prepared milks although we have found that Ideal or Carnation
evaporated milk are just right. What must be borne in mind is
that a bitch's milk is extremely rich and therefore any substitute must be made equally rich. Experience has taught that
evaporated milk diluted one part milk to two and a half parts
water is about right, and to this add a little sugar or
glucose.

The milk should always be fed at approximately body temperature; take care it is not too hot.

After each feed if you take a piece of cotton wool and gently
rub the lower part of the tummy the puppy will urinate. All
that needs to be done then is to wipe away any surplus food
and put it back in its heated box. The two essentials with
orphan puppies are food and warmth. You must provide both
if you want to rear them successfully. After the first two weeks
you can then encourage them to take other food (see Weaning,
page 113).

Do remember to clean all feeding utensils scrupulously; this
is essential.

*After Whelping*

For the first forty-eight hours after she has whelped the bitch
should *not* be given heavy or solid food. She has consumed the
afterbirth and in the wild state this would be sufficient to keep
her going for some time. She may, however, be given a light
but nutritious diet. This should be given in small quantities
four or five times a day and should consist of milk, eggs, and
invalid foods e.g. Complan, Bengers, etc., to which can be
added vitamins. Again I would stress the importance of
calcium and if a deficiency is suspected Collocal 'D' can be
given. Do *not* overdo the quantity thinking you are being kind

because you can do more harm than good; adhere strictly to the dosage recommended.

After the first two days you can feed a little raw minced beef or some boiled fish. Gradually increase the quantities until the bitch's diet at the end of ten days is approximately as follows:

*Morning:*   ¾ to 1 pint of milk with biscuits, Farex or similar foods. Add 1 teaspoonsful of Neo Ferrum and 2 halibut liver oil capsules.

*Midday:*    1 lb of meat, tripe or fish.

*Evening:*   ¾ to 1 pint of milk and biscuits or similar to which has been added 1 small teaspoonsful of Collocal 'D'. Alternatively tinned rice pudding.

*Bedtime:*   Biscuits and gravy.

It is imperative that whilst the bitch is feeding the puppies water is available to her at all times.

If the puppies show any signs of soreness then it will most likely be because the bitch's milk is tending to be acid. If you see this, add some antacid to one of her meals, and the trouble should soon clear.

Diarrhoea often attacks the bitch a few days after she has whelped. This must be remedied quickly. Usually a gruel made of arrowroot with glucose will do the trick, or you can sprinkle a little arrowroot or cornflour on her morning meal. Should the diarrhoea persist consult your veterinary surgeon and he will probably prescribe an antibiotic. The main point here is to correct the situation as early as possible.

Most bitches have a heavy discharge during the first few days following whelping which will gradually disappear in the next six weeks. Normally apart from cleaning no further attention is necessary. If however it persists and is objectionable consult your veterinary surgeon.

During the first two weeks after whelping it is essential that the bitch and puppies are disturbed as little as possible. Do not over-handle and above all do not agitate the bitch by taking strangers to see the litter. There have been many cases where this has resulted in an otherwise gentle bitch and good mother turning on her puppies. Patience is vital and well rewarded. If they are left alone and kept quiet the bitch will tend her puppies calmly, and the end product is far better than it would have been had the mother been nervy and worried during the first vital weeks.

When the bitch decides that she wants to leave the puppies for a time (usually about the end of the second week), she will make her intention quite clear, and you will know she wants to go out. When she has left her puppies for the first few times it is very interesting to watch her on her return to the 'nest'. She will 'count' and check over each one meticulously.

During the first day or so examine the puppies carefully to check that the mother has cleaned them properly when they were born. Pay particular attention to behind the ears, under the chin and tail, and in the fatty folds of their legs. If they are not clean, a warm solution of T.C.P. dabbed on the area with cotton wool will soon put it right. It is advisable to repeat this process every few days to ensure that they remain clean.

Likewise with the bitch a similar solution will clear up any nastiness from her discharge. In addtion of course it makes the whole whelping box smell sweet and wholesome.

Check the puppies' nails within a few days of birth and weekly thereafter to see whether they need cutting. If they are allowed to become too long they scratch the bitch and make her very sore. So much so that if it is bad she will not let them feed. The nails are quite easy to trim with a pair of sharp scissors, but take care not to leave any jagged or sharp edges.

There is no necessity to have dew claws removed, this is a matter of personal preference.

Keep the bitch's nipples clean and make sure they don't become sore. A little lanolin rubbed over them every so often will help to prevent this.

Remember to keep a watchful eye of the progress of the puppies and watch for fading or ailing puppies. The former is one which has a form of streptococcyl infection, and in this case you should consult your veterinary surgeon immediately. This is also true in the case of the ailing pup unless the cause is obvious and the remedy available.

*Weaning*

This will commence usually when the puppies are about three weeks old. There are exceptions to this: if, for example the litter is a large one or for some reason the bitch is unable to cope, then obviously the sooner you supplement what the bitch is giving them the better. A sure sign that the puppies are not getting enough to eat is discontent after the bitch has fed them.

As we have already said when discussing the feeding of orphan pup's a bitch's milk is particularly rich. It is much stronger than cow's milk. We have therefore to find something as near as possible to the bitch's milk if we are to avoid dietary upset, and if we want the puppies to accept the substitute easily.

There are proprietary brands of such substitutes available, and many breeders use them with great success. Mostly these are in powder form and when reconstituted with water in the correct proportions provide a very palatable and successful substitute.

We have used evaporated milk (Ideal or Carnation) very successfully for many years. A dilution of one part milk to two parts warm water with a little glucose added seems to be very acceptable; it must be sweet.

Start by giving each pup a tablespoonful to lap. It is a very messy business to begin with and if you don't hold the pup's front feet you will find that he soaks most of it up in his feet. Fortunately the little ones soon get the idea and in a day or so are little or no trouble, apart from the amount they somehow manage to get on their coats. Normally the bitch will clean them off well, and if she does not you *must*. If you don't the coats will be a sticky mass within a few days and you will have great difficulty in cleaning them. This applies no matter which type of milk you have chosen to feed.

Providing the bitch is in good condition after her whelping and her natural chores for the last few weeks, she can now be taken off Neo Ferrum or halibut oil and Collocal 'D'. These vitamins should be mixed with the puppies' milk but the quantities *must be small*. For example two halibut oil capsules should be sufficient for about eight puppies or one drop for each pup or one *very small* spoonful of Collocal 'D'.

As they become used to lapping, the quantity of milk should be increased so also should the frequency of the feeds so that at five or six weeks they are having three such milk feeds per day. To one of these three meals can be added Farex or similar. An acceptable change is one of the creamed rice puddings.

The puppies can be introduced to meat about a fortnight after they have started to lap, say about four or five weeks old. Again this is a messy business to start with. Scrape lean raw meat (beef) until you have pulpy juicy mass and try each pup with a teaspoonful gradually increasing this. Later, introduce minced beef, fish etc. until when they are completely weaned they are having four or five meals per day gradually building up to the menu for the eight week-old puppy (see page 120–21).

When the puppies reach the age of six weeks they should be treated for roundworms. Here again I would strongly recommend that you obtain the tablets from the veterinary surgeon. This worming nowadays is a relatively simple affair and requires no fasting, and no ill effects result providing the dosage given is correct. The improvement in the puppies after this treatment is quite remarkable. If worms were present in largish quantities the puppies go from pot-bellied and poorly coated ones to fairly sleek good-looking youngsters. Obviously the difference depends on the amount of worms present.

It is sometimes the case that the puppies have to be wormed before they are six weeks old. For this there are some special preparations on the market, but again caution is advised and you should consult your veterinary surgeon before you administer the medicine. Remember you are dealing with a highly sensitive and delicate young mechanism which the giving of an ill-considered chemical compound can upset very seriously; caution is essential.

Perhaps the most important item to remember before, during and after the whelping is cleanliness. Cleanliness of the kennel and surroundings, cleanliness of all utensils used in feeding, and above all cleanliness of the bitch and puppies.

This way such unpleasant things as lice and the like are avoided.

### Registering the puppies at the Kennel Club

To register or not to register always give rise to a dilemma for the new breeder. Because it is extra expense, usually at the time when the litter are proving expensive in food, many new breeders steer clear of it. Despite the cost, however, it is well worthwhile to register the puppies with the Kennel Club, and indeed this sometimes can be a good selling point.

It is quite a simple procedure providing the brood bitch and stud dogs themselves have been registered in the Kennel Club active register. Within a month of whelping, forward K.C. Form 1 (application for recording of a litter) duly completed to the Kennel Club. The litter will be recorded (no names given) and a litter pack will be sent to you. This pack holds the partially completed forms for registering each puppy. These you complete or give to the purchasers of the puppies. When named, the puppy is entered into the basic register. To show, breed or export, application must be made to the Kennel Club for entering in the active register.

### Breeding of Dogs Act 1973

Before closing this chapter on breeding I feel sure that many readers would like to know that legislation was introduced by Parliament in 1973 to control this activity. The Act became law, and with effect from April 1974 anyone who has more than two bitches maintained for the purposes of breeding and later selling puppies has to register with his local authority.

The intention of the Act was good but, like many such Acts, it was pushed through with unseemly haste – and those who should have been consulted to help make it more realistic were not even approached. We have therefore ended up with an Act which will have to be amended at an early day if it is to be truly effective. For example, the owner of two bitches, from which four litters each are possible, does not have to register, whereas a more responsible breeder with more than two bitches who might not have anything like this number of litters, does have to register. There are similar anomalies, but perhaps the most serious anomaly occurs in the application of the Act by Local Environmental Health Officers and their Assistants. Some are extremely good and tackle the subject from a commonsense point of view. Others, perhaps lacking experience or knowledge, try to enforce a form of legislation which was never intended by aligning this new Act with the earlier one on the Boarding of Dogs. Thus the breeder/owner of say three or four bitches is placed in a quite impossible position and has to spend quite unwarranted sums of money before a licence is granted.

The Act was introduced at a time when local area boundaries were being reorganised and when there was a shortage of Environmental Health Officers. As a result veterinary surgeons and others have been called upon to assist with the inspections. The net result is a widely differing standard of rules and regulations throughout the country. To those who are affected by this Act and want to start breeding I can only advise patience in the hope that amendments to the legislation will remove most, if not all, of the problems.

### Selling the Puppies

If you have used a well-known sire as the stud dog the owner of the sire will want to know the results of the mating, and will in all probability assist in the sale of the litter. It would be quite unfair and unrealistic to expect the sire's owner to sell all the puppies, which is clearly the responsibility of the breeder.

Advertisements in the press are the usual method of sale. It is better to make the advertisement clear and concise giving the purchase price of the puppy. Once you have stated the price don't allow yourself to be beaten down, for if the prospective purchaser is keen on having the pup he will pay a reasonable price without haggling.

When selling a litter over which you have spent many long hours of care, to say nothing of money for food etc., it is always advisable to make a few judicious enquiries to satisfy yourself that it is going to a good home. If the purchasers don't appear very keen, or if for example they are buying a dog when they really wanted a bitch, take great care because as likely as not they will be back to return the puppy sooner than you think.

A period to avoid in puppy sales is Christmas. Many well-meaning people buy puppies as Christmas presents and after the first excitement has died down the puppy is unwanted. After Christmas the homes for unwanted and lost pets are full of such unwanted presents. This is not the fate you wanted for any of your litter.

Curiously enough, in our experience immediately after Christmas is normally a good time for selling puppies.

# 9

# Diet, Care and Accommodation

This is a subject that could fill a book in itself. Its importance to both dog and owner alike cannot be emphasized too strongly. A good and balanced diet will usually mean a healthy and happy dog, all other things being equal, and for the owner few of the worries involved in caring for an animal which is almost constantly sick and ailing, to say nothing of freedom from veterinary surgeons' bills which in these days of V.A.T. can be high.

It is false economy to feed poorly or injudiciously, likewise it is equally fatal to kill with kindness. The aim must then be as in most things in life the happy medium.

During the first weeks of the Labrador's life he received from the dam milk considerably richer than ordinary cow's or goat's milk. It is richer in fat and casein, and contains correspondingly less water. This richness is necessary to assist the rapid growth of the new-born puppy. In order to grow properly he must have the correct intake. Because the bitch instinctively realizes this, the good mothers, giving literally all they have to a litter, often put their own lives in jeopardy by not retaining enough for themselves. This is one of the reasons for eclampsia or 'calcium lack'.

Therefore, when a puppy is weaned this must be taken into account, and the milk given should be enriched (see Chapter 8, weaning, page 113).

It is also important to see that trace elements are included, for example, calcium, phosphorus, magnesium, sodium chloride and others. These are only required in small quantities, and if your dog is being fed good food will already be present in sufficient quantity to satisfy his needs.

He must have proteins to keep all the normal processes of the body going. He needs them particularly when is growing. These are found in meat, eggs, and fish, and to a lesser extent in vegetables. Some of the better commercial dog foods will give the proportion of protein contained in their food.

Carbohydrates are another 'must'; he requires these for energy. They are also necessary because with their usual bulky and fibrous nature they help to 'clean' the digestive tract as well as keep it working. These can be obtained in many forms, although the usual one is dog biscuits. It is also the part of the diet which must be reduced if the dog is putting on too much weight.

A proportion of fat is also necessary as it is a source of energy helping to provide body heat. It is also a vitamin agent.

Much is said nowadays about vitamins and the like, and many proprietary products, not only pet foods, make extravagant claims that their products contain such and such a vitamin which will not only allow people to feel twenty years old at eighty, but to retain their youthful looks, etc. etc. Most of this is quickly debunked by the responsible press and/or the medical profession. Similarly in the canine world such claims are sometimes made, but they meet with little success because of the vigilance of the veterinary profession, and the experienced breeders.

At the same time it can be truthfully said that the veterinary profession and many pet food manufacturers go to a great deal of trouble, and spend enormous sums of money on research, to establish what should be included in the dog's diet. It is now accepted that vitamins A,B,C,D, and E form part of the dog's nutritional requirements. These vitamins are made by chemical interaction on certain foods in the dog's normal body processes, or they are fed.

Vitamin A, essential for growth and body tissue maintenance, is present in liver, milk, eggs, carrots and liver oils.

Vitamin B is found in yeast, meal, milk and eggs. $B_{12}$ is essential in red blood cell formation, and vital for the development of healthy dogs, especially young ones.

Vitamin C is most necessary for healthy skin. In the case of a severe deficiency the dog will experience a form of painful cramp when he has been in one position for some time. This vitamin is found in green vegetables, grass and fruit. The outer leaves normally discarded when preparing meals in the kitchen can be used very effectively for your dog, and help prevent any lack of this vitamin.

Vitamin D promotes growth, particularly of bone. The sun's rays reacting on the fat in the skin produces it. It allows the absorption of calcium, and if it is not present then the bones will not calcify properly, the result being rickets and similar bone defects.

Vitamin E is concerned with sterility. A lack in a bitch will mean that a properly fertilized egg will not become embedded in the uterus, and she will therefore not produce. A lack is alleged to be caused by feeding rancid fatty substances which tend to destroy the vitamin present in the body.

Ignoring the proprietary pet foods perhaps we can now summarize briefly what a dog should have. He needs proteins, carbohydrates, minerals and vitamins A,B,C and D. The amounts and the variety must be left to the individual owner, but it must be emphasized that a pet dog lying around in the warmth is not expending energy, and therefore does not require the amount of food of a dog working hard in cold or wet conditions. It is very necessary to watch your dog carefully to make sure he is not too fat or too lean, and to adjust his diet accordingly.

Some suggestions as to feeding are:

*Puppy 8–12 weeks*

*Breakfast:* ⅓ to ½ pint of milk with either Farex, Brown bread, Porridge, Weetabix, Shredded Wheat, or fine puppy meal. Add a little glucose, halibut or cod liver oil (the oils should not be given between April–October as they tend to overheat), and a sprinkling of bone meal powder from your veterinary surgeon.

*Lunch:* ⅓ to ½ lb of meat, fish or tripe with a tablespoonful of grated carrot and green vegetable, and a pinch of salt.

| | |
|---|---|
| *Tea:* | ⅓ to ½ pint of milk or gravy on puppy meal. Allow it to soak in before serving. A good alternative here is rice pudding or egg and milk with biscuits. |
| *Supper:* | ⅓ to ½ lb of meat, fish or tripe. Try to vary from lunchtime. Again add grated carrot and green vegetable. |

Always have a hard biscuit for the puppy to chew, and of course water to drink even though he does think it is a fine paddling pool.

### Puppy 3–6 months old

| | |
|---|---|
| *Breakfast:* | ½ pint of milk, etc., as for puppy. |
| *Lunch:* | ½ lb of meat, etc., as for puppy. |
| *Tea:* | As for puppy, but increase slightly. This can be another meat meal, or as for puppy. |
| *Supper:* | A handful of dog biscuits or baked brown bread. |

### Puppy 6–12 months

| | |
|---|---|
| *Breakfast:* | As for puppy. |
| *Lunch and Tea:* | These meals can now become the main meal of the day at roughly midway between the times you previously gave him his meals. For example if you fed lunch at 1 p.m. and tea at 6 p.m. then this meal can be about 3 to 4 p.m. It should gradually become approximately 1 lb of meat, fish or tripe with vegetables, and approximately ¼–⅓ lb of wholemeat dog biscuits (terrier size) (soaked but not sloppy). |
| *Supper:* | A handful of biscuits. |

### Adult Dog from 12 months

| | |
|---|---|
| *Breakfast:* | A handful of biscuits and a drink of milk (optional). |
| *Main Meal* | ¾ lb to 1 lb of meat, fish or tripe with vegetables, and approximately ¼ lb of whole meal biscuits. |
| *Supper:* | A few biscuits. |

All changes in quantities should be done gradually. If you find that your puppy shows no inclination for one of the meals don't become alarmed, but reduce that meal, and see how he fares with other meals during the day.

All puppies vary, some will eat all you put before them, others are quite choosy, and will only eat what they want. The important thing to remember is that they receive a quota of proteins, carbohydrates, etc., during each day.

There are one or two rules which most, but not all, breeders observe. Most of us like to see a puppy, certainly up to five months and even a little beyond that, carrying a little fat. He can do this quite safely, and it is always a great advantage if suddenly he picks up something he shouldn't, as puppies will, and goes off his food. In no time puppies seem to go to skin and bone, hence the, if you like, insurance policy of carrying a little excess.

Once your Labrador has reached maturity then it is wise to try ot keep him just right. Adjust the intake as necessary to do this.

There are also other points which really should need no emphasis. Do make sure all his utensils are clean, and that he always has a supply of clean fresh water.

The best meat to feed is of course beef, but this is expensive unless you shop around for the cheaper cuts such as ox cheek. This minced, although tough, is good. If you use tripe make sure it is thoroughly clean before you feed it. It is, if unprepared, very smelly, and in summer the Mecca for all flies from miles around. Never feed fly-blown meat for that is only asking for trouble. Do not feed pork or mutton.

Fish is good and seems to be very well like by the dogs. Again be careful to remove all bones. We use coley or rock salmon.

Unless the meat is fit for human consumption, it should be cooked. Actually it is now against the law, I believe, to sell condemned meat except through certain licensed traders, and then it has to be par cooked.

A dog and a bone go together, or so we are told. Let the bone be a large marrow bone which he can chew to his heart's content without breakding off small sharp splinters which will give nothing but trouble when swallowed. These swallowed splinters frequently are the cause of an operation having to be performed on the dog to remove them. In extreme cases they can kill, so do beware of poultry bones, chop bones, pork, lamb and similar.

So far I have only mentioned the more conventional foods, but of course recently there has been a tremendous influx of all types of dog foods on to the market.

Stockfish from Scandinavia was one of the first, and this the dogs seem to enjoy immensely. They must have a good supply of water to drink when this is fed.

Many of the pet food manufacturers market various kinds of tinned dog foods. *Which* did an interesting analysis on this some time ago with some rather revealing results. There is no doubt though that the tinned foods purchased from the reputable firms are good value, and certainly make an excellent and handy standby.

Some firms market frozen foods, usually minced cooked udder, tripe liver cereals. Again many people feed these with good results.

There are also many dried meats and pellets (similar to calf nuts) which claim to contain all the nutrition required by the dog. Again many breeders use these and find them very satisfactory.

It may well be that all such foods have their place in the diet for the dog, and perhaps they all help to allow the owner to vary his dog's diet more now than he would have done some years ago. Certainly one sees more well-fed dogs around today than ever before, some far too well fed.

Some useful additions are Vetzyme tablets, Calcidee tablets, halibut liver oil capsules, cod liver oil, olive oil, Neo Ferrum, Collocal 'D', Stress, Vionate or Vivomin and Cytacon (excellent in cases of loss of appetite and nerves).


*Invalid Diets*

When a dog or a bitch has been seriously ill one of the most difficult things is to get it to start eating properly. Most breeders will at one time or another have gone to great expense buying tempting morsels and then are more often than not disappointed because the dog will rarely touch them.

Some of the items we have found accepted when all else has failed are tinned soup, especially cream of tomato. Then Complan and of course Bengers Food are also extremely good.

The addition of glucose to the drinking water is of great help and in itself can assist a dog over the worst part of his illness.

After anaesthesia a dog requires vitamin B and Cytacon, one dessertspoonful per day, is very beneficial.

### Exercise

At first the young puppy requires no formal exercise and a romp in a well fenced garden is quite enough until he is about three to four months old. This area must be secure and free from any infection as far as you know until the dog had been fully inoculated. All he needs is a hard ball which he cannot chew pieces of rubber off to swallow, and/or a knitted woollen scarf knotted once or twice. This latter is a great favourite.

Apart from these 'adventures' in the garden the young puppy will spend most of his time sleeping.

As he grows older the periods of play will gradually be extended. When you can see he has had enough it is wise in his interest to curtail it. In a Labrador it is quite easy to detect when he has had enough. His face becomes creased and he does look tired and strained.

After three months and his inoculations he can be taken out on short walks. About five to ten minutes are enough at first, gradually increasing to about thirty minutes when he is six months. During the first year of his life he is growing rapidly and great demands are made on his constitution in the production of bone, muscle, change of teeth, etc., and it is important that he is not overtaxed.

When the dog is fully grown his main exercise should be extended to one hour or more. If your dog lives indoors he must have at least a short period of exercise on rising, a short period at midday and a long period in the evening or some similar arrangement. Whatever happens do not keep him too long waiting to relieve himself – this is cruel and quite unforgivable. So too would be simply opening the door and letting him wander the streets a danger to himself and traffic.

During these exercise periods part can be devoted to some form of training (see later chapter) i.e. lead training or training him to become accustomed to traffic. *Never let him anywhere near a road or traffic unless he is held firmly on a leash.*

### Grooming

Grooming forms another essential part of the pattern of your dog's life. He loves to sit and be combed and brushed. A steel comb with fairly wide teeth at one end, and finer ones at the other, is the main piece of equipment. Being a short-coated dog it does not take very long to run a comb through, to take out the loose hair, then give him a good brush with a fairly stiff brush. A hound glove is also very useful for removing loose hair and imparting a shine to the coat.

The blacks score in this respect. A few minutes' work and their coat can gleam like black satin. You will find a piece of rolled-up newspaper excellent for giving that final 'polish'. When he is casting his coat in the spring and the autumn, grooming does take longer but the reward comes with the new coat. Never cut a Labradors' coat.

EARS: Once a week the grooming session should be extended by a few minutes to check ears and their cleanliness. Some dogs tend to get 'waxy' ears fairly quickly. We have found that a piece of cotton wool rolled round a cocktail stick (with the point removed) is ideal for cleaning the crevices in and around the ear. When clean, a pinch of boracic powder in each ear will help to keep them clean.

Should your dog shake his head a lot, or rub his ears along the ground and be in obvious distress, consult your veterinary surgeon. Although there are many proprietary ear remedies on sale, some of which are excellent, it is always far better to seek skilled profession advice from the outset.

NAILS: These should not cause you much trouble if your dog is spending a fair amount of his time on hard ground such as roads, or pavements, etc. If they do need cutting, it is quite simple to do. The main requirement is the correct type of strong cutters, for scissors and the like are quite useless. One of the most popular cutters is the 'guillotine' type which is made in various sizes. With this you can trim off the surplus nail, being careful not to cut too short as this may cause bleeding and discomfort to the dog. We find the black's nails more difficult in this respect because the quick cannot be seen so clearly as in the nails of the yellow. Caution, therefore, is necessary.

After cutting, the nails should be filed and here we find a sharp 4 to 6 inch medium steel file to be ideal. Although it does take a little longer, the nail can be completely filed instead of cut and filed. This produces the best results but, if the nail is long, it can be a rather tedious process for both dog and owner. Alternatively, it can be done in two sessions, front feet one day and rear feet another.

BATHING: Unless you live in an industrial area, bathing usually is unnecessary. Should you decide that for some reason or other your dog does need a bath it is better in warm weather, to take him on the lawn or some similar place. Have a large bowl or bath filled with lukewarm water nearby, and a jug to pour the water over him. Have your shampoo, specially purchased for the occasion, ready made up and to hand. Wet the coat thoroughly, and then pour some of the shampoo over him and work it into a lather, rinse off and repeat. When you are sure you have rinsed all the shampoo out of his coat, dry him thoroughly paying particular attention to his back just above the tail. Do not let him lie around in draughts after his bath, because you have washed all the protective grease out of his coat and left him susceptible to cold. Under no circumstances should ordinary household soap be used.

## The Season

Before we leave this section on the care of your pet, there remains the all important consideration of the season, heat or oestrum of the bitch. In Labradors this can start at any time after six months of age. It can be as late as fifteen months of age, but the usual time for the commencement of the first season is between seven to ten months. The signs to watch for are:

1 A fairly heavy coat cast, which usually appears about four to six weeks before the season.

2 Nearer the season she will display signs of restlessness, nervousness, and excitement. She may be unusually coy when meeting strangers – people or dogs.

3 Swelling of the vulva.

As soon as your bitch starts her season, give her one of the proprietary preparations (we have always found Amplex to be excellent) but be careful to give the correct dosage. Continue this throughout the entire season which will last twenty-one days. In addition to these tablets for internal use, a solution can be made up which you sponge on to the coat around the vulva and the surrounding area. This helps to prevent the attentions of unwelcomed dogs. For this sponging some breeders consider oil of eucalyptus to be the best.

During the three weeks that she is in season, and despite all the precautions you may have taken, you must be extremely careful during her periods of exercise. On no account let her outside your garden or some other enclosed and secure area. When she is taken out for her longer exercise each day, it is a good idea to back your car to the door and take her out to some common land where she can be exercised properly, but on a lead. Always try to ensure that she does not leave the scent of her season outside your garden gate. The danger period, when the greatest care is required, is between the ninth and the eighteenth day, and during this time she must be under supervision.

One final point. Please make some allowances for your bitch during this period. She is not fully herself, and may do things which are completely foreign to her. Try to be understanding; the time will soon pass and she will be back to normal and her own endearing self again.

## Ill-health

No section on the care of your pet would be complete without a few words on some of the more common complaints which may affect your dog, and cause you concern. When your dog is off-colour he largely has to depend upon your understanding of him and his moods. He cannot tell you what he is feeling, and this is what makes the veterinary surgeon's job so difficult. So when you consult your veterinary surgeon it is always advisable to go over the preceding few days in your mind, so that you can give him a clear picture of the events. He will want to know about food, appetite, motions and whether the dog has been listless or displayed any other symptoms.

The danger signals to watch for are a marked loss of appetite accompanied by listlessness or severe diarrhoea. In both cases check the temperature by inserting the thermometer, gently, into the rectum. When normal it should be 101.5°F(38.6°C); if it should be more than 102.2°F(39°C) it is wise to consult your veterinary surgeon fairly early.

Do not, under any circumstances, experiment with your dog if he is sick and you are not sure what the trouble is. The delay may only increase the danger to his life, and something quite simple – which could have been cured quickly and easily – may well become complicated and involved. This golden rule is, 'when in doubt consult your veterinary surgeon at once'. (See Chapter 12 on The Labrador in Sickness).


*Kennelling*

The Englishman's home is his castle, and as far as possible this principle should be applied to your dog or dogs. They must feel from a very early age that their kennel is a place in which they are warm, cosy and above all secure. That is, secure from any outside interference, secure in that they can sleep if they wish, or gnaw their bone in peace and quietness without some other dog trying to take it away.

It matters little if this 'kennel' is in fact a warm spot in the kitchen and takes the form of a folded blanket, or if it is a more formal type of kennel in a run. The main issue is it must be clear to the dog from a very early age that here he is safe, and this is his castle.

Perhaps we might dwell a little on the types of 'kennel' available for the Labrador, dealing first with the one or two dogs in a household. There are many proprietary dog beds, folding and otherwise which are suitable for use in the home. These, in

Am. Ch. Shamrock Acres Light Brigade had a very impressive
record of wins in the USA (*Earl Graham*)

Bermuda and Am. Ch. Rupert John Glenn

Danish Ch. Kale of Oakshaw (*Vedels Reklame*)

Swedish Ch. Kamrats Hulda (*Lars Söderbom*)

Int. Ch. Kamrats Jeanny, Swedish and Fin Ch. and Sw. Ob. Ch.
Kamratts Buse, and Nordic Ch. Kamrats Angel (*Lars Söderbom*)

Norwegian Sh. Ch. Sandylands Be Gentle

Ch. Lawnwoods Hot Chocolate

Ch. Follytower Merrybrook Black Stormer (*C. M. Cooke*)

my opinion are superior to putting a folded blanket or similar on the floor because:

1 They are raised 4 to 6 inches off the ground.
2 They have sides which prevent draughts.

Usually these are made out of a very strong canvas material, sewn on to a metal frame (see Figure 9). They are ideal in that they are light, will fold flat, and therefore can easily be moved or taken away on holiday if you so wish.

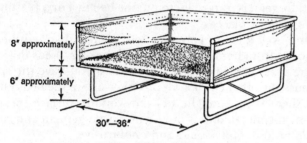

8″ approximately

6″ approximately

30″–36″

*Figure 9* Collapsible or fold-away bed

Cleaning this type of bed presents little or no problem because it is a simple matter (if done regularly) to brush and/or scrub them, and they dry relatively quickly. This ensures that any grease out of the dog's coat doesn't become too bad on the sides of the bed and of course it avoids any offensive doggy odour.

Similar beds can be made of wood, and whilst these are equally satisfactory they are not so light and easily transportable as the metal variety, and quite honestly they do seem to lack the finish of their purpose-built metal counterpart. In their favour they are a little less expensive but here again it is only marginal.

On balance therefore the metal folding-type bed is to be recommended. If you wish to avoid the chore of washing the bed, a loose piece of blanket thrown over it will keep it clean and help keep the dog warm. It is then a matter of changing the blanket rather than washing the bed and this is perhaps more convenient.

A word of warning here; be very careful that when you buy such a bed your dog is ready for it. In other words, he should have finished his teething process and not be likely to tear it to shreds in your absence. Until he is ready as has been recommended earlier a cardboard box will be fine.

If you see that any part of a bed you purchase is painted, do ensure that a non-lead-based paint has been used. Otherwise if he does chew the paint off you may well have a very sick dog on your hands, to say nothing of veterinary bills, etc.

Before leaving the subject of beds for dogs inside the house, don't forget it is important to put the bed in a dry, reasonably draughtproof place.

One well-known Labrador owner has had cupboards removed from her fitted kitchen and the dogs' beds fit snugly in the space. This is an ideal solution if you have the space, because the other cupboards on either side of the beds ensure that there is no draught and the working surface traps the warm air generated. It is quite a neat arrangement and can be made to look quite smart and unobtrusive.

### Outdoor Kennels

Like the folding beds for indoors there are many variations in type size and construction of outdoor kennels.

Perhaps the most popular of these is a light and airy wooden building of 1 inch tongued and grooved timber, shiplap or matchboard mounted on a 2 by 2 inch frame with a flat roof made weatherproof with roofing felt. It must be built so as to be snug and warm and draught free.

The inside of the building should be lined either completely or around the dog's bed. This can be done with either hardboard or some similar material. The bed should be raised approximately 8 to 9 inches off the floor.

These kennels can be made or purchased as single units or multiple units to house up to say ten in one such building. Figure 10 shows a plan view of a three compartment building which is quite large enough to house up to six dogs.

There are so many adaptations and variations that it would be impossible to describe them all but figures 10 and 11 should be sufficient to give the reader a general idea from which he can decide on a type which will suit his particular purpose.

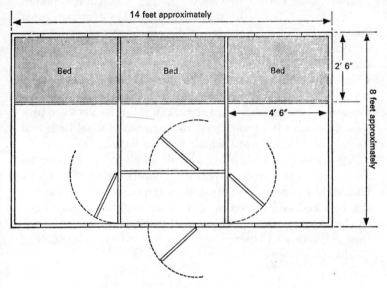

*Figure 10* Plan of kennel: not to scale

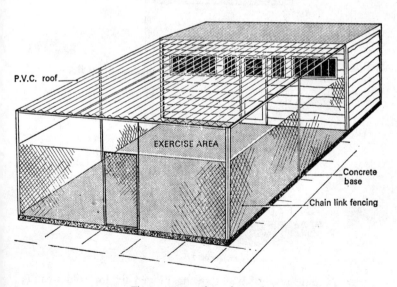

*Figure 11* Outdoor kennel

There is of course one grave danger with these wooden buildings and that is the very high fire risk. Great care must therefore be taken if any form of heating is introduced. I cannot emphasize this too much. Far too many breeders have lost valuable stock, the result of many years painstaking breeding which is literally irreplaceable, because there has been an electrical fault, or a paraffin heater has 'gone wrong' and caused a fire with all the resultant heartbreak. It is far, far better to provide the dogs with good, deep straw or wood wool beds and forget altogether heaters which may go wrong.

A good idea is to fit a hinged lid about 2½ to 3 feet above the dog's bed so that in cold weather it can be lowered to trap a layer of warm air around the dog. When the weather is warm it can be lifted and bolted up out of the way (see Figure 12).

The best type of kennelling is of brick or similar construction. It is costly and therefore the amount of use to be made of

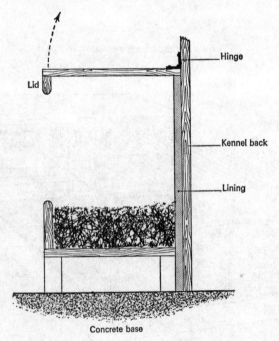

*Figure 12* Side view of bed showing hinged lid for cold weather use

the building must be assessed to see whether it is a viable proposition. Here again the variety is immense and the final item will depend on the personal whim of the would-be purchaser. It does of course have the advantage of not being such a fire hazard as a wooden building, and presumably electricity would be properly installed and be readily available if required.

Outhouses or similar can also be adapted as kennels using either concrete blocks, bricks or Weldmesh to subdivide the space available.

The golden rules for any kennels are:

1 They should be dry and draughtproof.

2 They should be light and airy.

3 The beds must be raised 9 inches approximately from the floor.

If you have decided on a wooden kennel it is a good scheme and saves considerable time and expense in replacement to cover all wooden projections with some sheet metal. Examples are door jambs, bed fronts, or the bottom half of the door. When the dogs 'try' their teeth on these they will then do little or no damage, and, more important, you will be spared the perhaps exasperating task of replacing some part which you only installed the previous day.

Siting your outdoor kennel is often of great importance, Obviously it should not be sited in the teeth of the prevailing wind, nor should it face north or east. Try to have it in as sheltered a spot as possible facing south. Do not put the kennel under trees where it will be constantly wet during winter months.

There is then the question of some freedom of movement for the dog around his 'home'. The easy way to do this is to enclose the kennel in some fencing either chain link or similar. It should be sufficiently strong and secure so that you can be certain he cannot roam.

Adequate area must be given remembering that a healthy Labrador is a vigorous dog and needs a fair area to be contented. A *minimum* of ten square yards per dog must be achieved, and if there are only one or two dogs it must be more.

A typical layout suitable for say six dogs is shown in Figure

11. Note the concrete base and here be careful with your levels remembering that you want any slope away from the dogs' bed, and away from the kennel. When you hose the kennel out the water will then drain off the area fairly quickly. Note also that some or all of the 'area' can be covered with translucent P.V.C. corrugated sheeting. This is relatively cheap and it is a great advantage to have this outside area covered in case of bad weather.

Some breeders put one or two pallets or tables in the run for the dogs to lie on. Whenever I have seen these they are always used.

One small point: don't forget drinking water in the run. Here again an old stone kitchen sink is ideal.

# 10
# Showing

This has become an increasingly popular pastime of late perhaps because of the publicity some of the bigger shows gain by way of wide television coverage in addition to coverage in the national press. Over the last ten years attendances at most of the big shows have trebled and now it is commonplace to see more than five thousand exhibits at any one show.

There are of course several different types of dog shows held under Kennel Club rules. They are:

THE MEMBERS' SHOW: As the name implies this is a show confined to members of a particular canine society. The number of exhibits at such a show will be generally in the region of 200 to 300.

THE OPEN SHOW: This is open to all exhibitors whether they are members of the society organizing the show or not. There is a wide variation here in the number of exhibits from say 200 to, in some cases, 2000.

THE CHAMPIONSHIP SHOW: Again this is open to all exhibitors and here of course Kennel Club Challenge Certificates are on offer and are awarded to the best dog and best bitch as listed in the show schedule. The number of exhibits at these shows will be in the order of 5000, some slightly more, others less.

Should you therefore decide that you would like to show your dog, it would most likely be better from your point of view to go to a local show as a spectator so that you can study the general procedure.

You could then join your local canine society and try your
hand at one of the smaller shows before you travel further
afield to the championship shows. If you are keenly interested
in dogs you will find that, win or lose, most dog shows are
thoroughly enjoyable affairs with a lot of dogs of all types and,
for want of a better description, the doggie crowd. A unique
fraternity, usually good company, good friends and dog mad.
I can think of many worse, but few better.

Obviously everyone goes to a dog show to win, the main
object being to make the dog into a champion. This can only
be done at either the general championship shows or the
breed championship shows where challenge Certificates are
being awarded. A dog becomes a champion after having been
awarded three Challenge Certificates under different judges.
That is, he has been the best dog or bitch in his breed present
at the show and the judge considers he is worthy of the title of
champion. Having won these three awards, and after the Kennel Club has confirmed them then the coveted 'Champion'
goes before the dog's name. In the case of gundogs it is Show
Champion until your dog has qualified in the field.

The Kennel Club lay down all the rules governing such
shows and these must be strictly adhered to by the society
organizing the show. This ensures uniformity of dog shows
and showing throughout the UK. The Kennel Club also makes
absolutely certain that a society running a show is financially
viable and is able to meet all incurred expenses, e.g. prize
money.

Before your dog can be exhibited at any show held under
Kennel Club rules he must be on the K.C. active register.

On entering for the show a declaration must be signed on
the entry form to the effect that the exhibitor agrees to abide by
the Kennel Club rules and that the exhibit has not been
exposed to the risk of distemper or other contagious disease
within a given period. This entry form is obtained together
with a schedule of classes from the secretary of the society
concerned.

The schedule will give all the details of the eligibility, venue,
name of judge(s), time of judging and any other information.

At the show itself catalogues showing the entries in each class are on sale.

A copy of this catalogue with all results shown must be sent to the Kennel Club immediately after the show for checking. Any errors on the part of the exhibitor or others, e.g. entering a dog in a class for which he is not eligible are then penalized by the Kennel Club and other awards adjusted.

Countess Howe writes on this subject as follows:

It can be classified under three headings, the judge, the exhibit, the exhibitor. We will deal with the judge first. A judge is born, not made, though as he or she goes on knowledge is increased. There are really two classes – the specialist and the all-rounder. The latter has to have a knowledge of all breeds of dogs which he or she will have to adjudicate on in variety classes or in judging Best in Show. The specialist judge should have a really intimate knowledge of the breed to be judged. All breeds have a standard of points agreed upon by the Kennel Club. I do not think any judge should attempt to judge a breed without first studying this standard; after all, it is the standard agreed upon by clubs which promote the study of various breeds.

The Labrador has several points entirely different from other breeds and to judge the breed well the judge should be well acquainted with those points. I have dealt with the points elsewhere but I cannot too strongly emphasize the importance of the coat, the tail, the intelligent, kindly hazel eye, the wide skull not cheeky, and the powerful hindquarters. All these points help him in his natural work as a gundog and therefore should not be neglected in the show ring. All judges should handle and go over each exhibit and see it moving. This should be done methodically. I well know that some dogs appear in the ring that a judge can at a glance tell that they have no earthly chance of getting anywhere in the awards. Nevertheless these dogs should be gone over as carefully as the best-looking ones in the class. The exhibitor has paid his entry fee and has come to the show to get the judge's opinion. He or she may be a complete novice to whom the show is a matter of great importance. It is therefore only common courtesy, and not a waste of time, to go over the entry carefully. If the dog is just glanced at casually it may put the exhibitor off shows for ever and, moreover, give him the idea that only the best-known exhibitors stand any chance of gaining an award. This might do infinite harm.

When dogs first come into the ring it is a good policy to let them walk round a few times to give them a chance to settle down. The class can then be halted and the dogs called out one by one for inspection.

It always appears to me to be helpful to ask an exhibitor to move his dog straight away and back again, in order that movement can be seen properly. This is best done before handling a dog which might be nervous of a complete stranger going over him from his head to his tail, but this is merely my own opinion. When going over the dog one should ask the handler to open its mouth to see if the jaw is correct and not over-shot or under-shot. The coat should be carefully felt, and – please believe me – the dense undercoat is to be found on the ribs and chest, where it is likely to get most wetness when a dog is swimming, and where it will protect the dog. It is not by feeling along the back that a judge will find the correct coat. The tail should not be carried in any way curled over the back but it is permissible for a dog to carry its tail gaily – in fact, many high-couraged dogs do, especially when in a ring with a lot of strange dogs.

The judge is always provided with a steward – and what a blessing a good one is! A steward should see that all the dogs are in the ring, and it is a great help when dogs which have been placed in previous classes are put in their correct order. All the same, a wise judge will check this and be careful not to reverse a previous decision. After the steward has seen that all the dogs are in the ring, the judge should be told that all is in order and the steward should then either go away and sit down or at least stand aside and leave the judge alone. Nothing looks worse than to see a steward continually talking to the judge. It soon gives rise to the comment that the steward is doing the judging. That is not pleasant for either judge or steward.

A dog should always be approached from in front; personally, I always offer my hand to a dog to smell. Most dogs are very

good-tempered, but of course some are shy of strangers and
one has to be very understanding with them. Few dogs are
naturally bad-tempered or savage. One has to remember,
however, that the dog is away from home and among
strangers, and can well be forgiven for any nervousness. A
judge should never move suddenly or do anything to frighten
a dog. Puppies in particular need tactful and friendly handling. I know this is sometimes very difficult, especially if one is
working against time. I once had an entry of 906 Labradors to
judge at Cruft's. The largest class was one of forty-eight entries.
The ring was by no means big and I had to take the class in two
parts and pick out the best dogs in each section but it was a job
as I had to keep my eye on the clock all the time!

When judging (and I am writing now for women) it is always
advisable to dress plainly and not wear anything in the shape
of a fur or scarf that flaps about and is liable to frighten a dog. It
is always advisable, too, to wear comfortable shoes; there is a
lot of standing and foot-work to be done, and judging is a tiring
job. The more deliberately a judge goes about the job the better.
It is never good to keep up any form of play-acting to impress
exhibitors and onlookers. It very seldom does!

Before the last war the usual custom for judging Best in
Show was for the Challenge Certificate winners in each breed
to parade in a specially large ring. This was a spectacular sight.
With so many exhibits (at big shows like Cruft's, the Kennel
Club, Birmingham and the Scottish Kennel Club) it was a
lengthy proceeding and a very tiring one for judges, exhibits
and exhibitors.

The usual procedure in these days is for the judge in each
breed to select what he or she considers the best exhibits,
regardless of sex, in their respective breeds. These are divided
into groups: Gundogs, Sporting and Non-Sporting Terriers
and Toys. The best of each group is then chosen and those
selected then go before a judge or judges to pick the absolutely
best exhibit in the show, and also best of the opposite sex. This
system has been in force in America for some time. Certainly it
is quicker and less tiring for all taking part, but I do not think it
is so spectacular. I had the privilege of judging with some of
the great all-rounders under the old system. It was an edu-

cation to judge with men like Messrs Croxton Smith, Holland Buckley, Arthur Lorraine, Chris Houlker, George Wallwork, W. Nichols and Royston Mills – now all dead, I am sorry to say. How very generous they were in imparting their infinite knowledge to one anxious to learn!

I think the late Mr Croxton Smith was an example of all a judge should be. He had an intimate knowledge of all breeds and went about his many tasks of judging in an imperturbable way that gave confidence to exhibitors and exhibits. I never saw him handle a dog roughly; he always displayed unlimited patience. His death was a great loss not only to the Kennel Club (of which he was Chairman for many years) but to dogdom as a whole.

We will now pass on to the exhibit. A lot of time and trouble must be spent on getting the dog ready to show. He should be taught to stand properly, and not allowed to pull his handlers about as he likes, as one sometimes sees happening. He should also be taught to move on a loose lead up and down the ring when asked by the judge to do so. To make the most of a dog he should be on the very best of terms with his handler. He should be alert. A good showman is of infinite value. It is always a good thing to bring a young dog 'out' at an outdoor show, where he is not so liable to be nervous. In the old days loudspeakers were unknown. We got on very well without them. Admittedly they can be of great use, but to have to show a dog in a ring which is quite close to a loudspeaker can be trying to dog and handler, and is of course liable to upset a nervous dog. A quarrelsome dog should be stopped at once; a really disagreeable fellow who growls and snarls and continually tries to attack other dogs is an abomination, and if such a dog continues to upset other exhibits, and so gain an unfair advantage, a judge is quite entitled to order him out of the ring. Fortunately most Labradors are of an amiable disposition.

The exhibitor should be ready for the class for which his dog is entered. It is unfair, not to say rude, to keep a judge waiting whilst the handler is gossiping and not paying attention to his job. An exhibitor should always remember that his or her dog is not the only entry. One should never crowd other exhibitors out of their places; all are entitled to equal consideration and it is extremely inconsiderate not to remember this. In a big class I have found with Labradors that if the judge is going methodically round the dogs, it is good to let my own dog sit down. He cannot stand at attention and be at his best all the time; therefore if he sits quietly down it rests him. Further, if the judge happens to look round suddenly he does not see the dog standing 'all anyhow'. The dog needs training to lead quietly on a loose lead and not be allowed to pull his handler all over the ring and generally make a nuisance of himself. A good many dogs may be, and often are, upset at their first show. One should do all one can to prevent this. When he is in his own kennels at home let him be handled by any visitors who may come to the kennel. This all helps to accustom the dog to strangers. It is also wise to get him out on roads, or into towns, to get used to traffic and people. He should likewise be accustomed to a car, train or any other transport likely to take him to a show.

True, this all means a good deal of effort, but if one has a good dog it is well worth it. When a judge asks for a dog to be moved and run out in a ring the dog's education should have taught him to make the most of himself. He should not be held on a tight lead or strung up in any way. An exhibitor should always be on the alert to obey the judge's instructions, and when asked to stand in any particular place should remain there and not wander off to talk to a friend. One should always watch one's judge and always try to prevent him from seeing one's dog standing in a careless way. A dog which shows naturally is invaluable, but a clever handler can get an immense amount out of a dog which does not normally show well. Some dogs will stand and 'ask for it'; one has to get the best out of others by any legitimate means one can.

The Labrador is what one can call a natural dog and has not got to have a lot of trimming; in fact there is not much one can do, beyond generally tidying him up and trying to make him look his very best.

It is essential to arrive in good time at a show – this obviates a last-minute rush and scramble. It also gives time for the dog to be exercised and to settle down and get accustomed to his surroundings.

The exhibitor should make certain in which ring his breed will be judged and when exercising his dog beforehand he should go to the space provided for exercising and not take his dog into a ring set aside for another breed.

I have noticed of recent years a habit handlers have developed of going down on their knees and holding their dog's head under the chin into the position the handler desires the head to be carried, whilst the other hand is employed in holding the dog's tail out straight. This is, I believe, termed 'topping and tailing'. I dislike this habit very much as I think a Labrador should be able to carry his own head and tail correctly. It certainly gives an advantage to a dog with a bad tail carriage. An otter-tail is one of the main characteristics of the breed; a dog which is blessed with one needs no assistance. I well remember an occasion, in days long gone by, when a Labrador of mine was left in for the final for 'Best' at a very important show. My opponent was a dog which was most ably assisted by his handler, who held his dog's head and tail in their correct positions. The two judges could not agree and finally the referee was called in, a Frenchman, who said pointing to my dog, 'I give it to the dog which can carry his own head and tail'. Those words, said thirty years ago, have always remained in my mind.

I was once showing a very well-known dog, a full champion and winner of a first and other prizes at field trials. It was in my early days of exhibiting. Quite unexpectedly the judge came up to me and said, 'I suppose you wonder why I put your dog down?' I had not time to reply, for he said at once, 'I know he has won a lot and is a champion but I never liked his mother.' I thought that was rather hard on the dog to visit the sins of his mother (who, by the way, was also a champion) upon her son!

Once when I was judging, an exhibitor came up to me with a dog which was far from my idea of what a Labrador should be, and said, 'This is a direct descendant of your beloved Bolo.' I could only reply, 'How dreadfully ashamed the poor old gentleman would be!'

## SHOWING OVERSEAS

### Eire

To become an Irish Champion a dog must have won Green Stars which total in value at least sixteen points. The points are obtained by the wins of the dog at shows where Green Star Points are on offer i.e. similar to UK championship Shows.

The number of points awarded to the dog as a result of his win depends on the number of dogs actually exhibited (not entered) and can be one, two three or four. Minimum numbers of exhibits are laid down by the Irish Kennel Club in their rules and regulations.

If a dog goes on to win the group he wins the highest points on offer in that group.

Although the system sounds complicated, it is really relatively simple and is a genuine attempt to make the award commensurate with the competition. It does mean, of course, at least four shows each with the highest number of points before a dog can claim the title of Champion.

### Australia

Many will have heard of the 'Royal' shows in Australia. They are so called because they are run by the Royal Agricultural Society in each state. These shows go on for eight to ten days and include all types of livestock, machinery, farm produce, flowers and the like. The dog show forms a part of this event.

The Sydney and Melbourne shows have 3000 to 4000 dogs attending with the other states close behind.

In general the standards of the breeds and the ring procedures follow reasonably closely those in Britain. However, the qualifications for a dog or bitch to obtain the title of champion differ in the two countries.

Championship shows are those at which Challenge Certificates may be won. Each state, including the Australian Capital Territory, is an independent controlling body which authorizes its own affiliate clubs to hold shows, parades, etc., as it sees fit. So there are far more championship shows in Australia at which challenges may be on offer for all breeds. Less than twenty years ago each state also awarded its own championship titles so that a dog might well be a champion in two or three states.

The Australian National Kennel Council tries to establish uniformity in rules and regulations throughout the country. Unlike the Kennel Club, it can only recommend to the states but its recommendations are becoming more and more generally accepted. It has established the following procedure:

When a dog (or bitch) is awarded a Challenge Certificate the points gained are entered on the 'ticket'. Five points are awarded for gaining the challenge plus one point for each dog (or bitch) actually competing. Extra points are awarded for going Best in Group or Best in Show. The maximum number of points allowed on one challenge is twenty-five. When challenges totalling 100 points have been gained the dog (or bitch) is eligible to apply for its Championship title.

The least number of points which can be gained on a challenge is six, when that is the only competitor of that breed and sex. This does happen at times with the more rare breeds and would obviously take seventeen of such challenges to apply for a championship. If it is the only dog or bitch it does not matter if in going Best of Breed it beats twenty of the opposite sex – it gets no more points.

Equally, of course, in a popular breed the challenge winner may beat thirty, forty or more, but still get only twenty-five points even if going Best in Show over several thousand entries. So, however good, it takes a minimum of four challenges to qualify for a championship. It must also be remembered that Australian judges by no means infrequently withhold challenges when they consider the entries do not attain championship standard.

Before reaching a hasty judgement on this system, consider the geographical factors influencing its introduction when country centres may be separated by several hundred miles and an owner might have to travel one or two thousand miles to get in a couple of championship shows.

## Continent

Here again Challenge Certificates C.A.C. (National C.C.) or C.A.C.I.B. (International C.C.) must be won on at least three occasions before the dog is entitled to be called Champion. In some countries, but not all, an award in the field is also a requisite.

## Scandinavia

SWEDISH SHOW CHAMPION: For a dog to qualify as a Show Champion in Sweden it requires three certificates of exhibitions in Scandinavia, of which at least one must be won in Sweden, plus a field trial award. Alternatively, it must have two certificates of Scandinavian exhibitions, one having been won in Sweden, plus a first prize in the highest class of field trial competition (in Sweden called the élite class).

SWEDISH FIELD TRIAL CHAMPION: The requirements for a field trial champion are two first prizes of élite class in a field trial competition, and the passing of the examination of a real shot under a judge (the dog is not allowed to whine; it must retrieve properly and fast), or a first prize of élite class in a scenting test plus second prize of quality in an exhibition.

FINNISH SHOW CHAMPION: To make up a Show Champion in Finland three certificates of exhibitions, of which one must be won in Finland, are required plus the passing of a field trial competition, for which either one first prize or two second prizes in a Finnish or Swedish field trial competition is demanded. However, one first prize or two second prizes of a Finnish scenting test is an alternative to the three certificates of exhibitions. The dog must be X-rayed and found clear of hip dysplasia.

INTERNATIONAL SHOW CHAMPION: An International Show Champion must gain the qualification for a Swedish Show Championship plus two international certificates, of which one has to be won in Sweden and one in another Scandinavian country.

SCANDINAVIAN SHOW CHAMPION: Three certificates won in three Scandinavian countries plus the qualifications from field trial competitions are required for a Swedish Show Championship. The dog must be clear of hip dysplasia and X-rayed in Scandinavia.

NORWEGIAN SHOW CHAMPION: To become a Norwegian Show Champion three certificates of exhibitions, of which at least one must be gained in Norway, are required. The certificate of a Norwegian exhibition must be won in an exhibition acknowledged by the Norwegian Kennel Club.

DANISH SHOW CHAMPION: All that is required for a Danish Show Champion is three certificates and a field trial award, similar to neighbouring countries.

# 11

# Field Trials

Lorna, Countess Howe was probably one of the most knowledgeable experts on this subject. She writes in *The Popular Labrador Retriever* with a rare authority and understanding as follows:

There are now a number of field trials being held; some people think too many and I am inclined to agree with this opinion. When I first ran dogs in field trials immediately after the 1914–18 war one was expected to leave, as far as possible, game finding to the dog one was handling. In fact, it was impressed upon one that field trials were run to discover dogs that possessed the most natural ability. Of course, a wild dog, or a dog out of control, was penalized, but judges paid most attention to dogs which displayed a game-finding ability greater than those which were trained to such perfection that their natural ability became subservient to reliance on their handler.

It was always impressed on one that Retrievers were not sheep dogs, that their first and most important work was to find game – particularly wounded game. This is always of the greatest importance if only for humane reasons. At the present time dogs seem to rely much more on their handler's direction than on their own nose and ability. This seems to me to be a pity, and if I were able to judge now (and many handlers must realize with relief that I am not able to!) I should heavily penalize any dog which could not find game without being placed on the absolute spot by his handler. Dogs sent into the wind should, if they have not marked their game, quarter the ground methodically until they come upon the game or, in the case of a runner, get the fall. A good marker goes straight to the fall. Very high marks should be given to a good marker, for good marking saves time and in the case of a strong runner this is important. I think marking is often under-estimated, more attention being paid to a dog that proceeds to the fall through instructions from his handler. It should always be remembered that a dog is much more easily sent out a long distance down-wind than when sent into the wind. This, I know from experience, is often not sufficiently taken into account. A dog which, when sent to collect a runner, makes good the fall, then carefully puzzles out the line and finally gets his game is invaluable. A dog should not be penalized for going slowly on plough even if he appears to potter, neither should he be on any ground, for a dog which will adjust his pace to his nose is to be admired and should not be, as I have often heard, accused of being a potterer. A retriever's first purpose is to collect game which one cannot collect oneself. A dog which faces brambles and water fearlessly is much to be desired. Many dogs display very pretty style and pace in roots and on easy ground, but some of these have a most pressing engagement elsewhere if asked to go into the thick or to face water!

A judge should always remember that after a dog has had a long hunt he cannot retrieve as clearly, or perhaps as quickly and smartly, as a dog which has had the good fortune to be sent for game which can be quickly picked up and which should clearly delivered to hand. A dog, which puts a bird down to obtain a good balance and then retrieves it cleanly to hand has done good work, but a dog which keeps on dropping his game and finally deposits it at his handler's feet should be penalized. Hard-mouth is an abomination. The hard-mouthed dog does not drop his game frequently; he gets hold of it with a determined grip, as much as to say 'Come on, I want you!', gives it a hearty nip that catches both sides of the ribs and crushes them. This is the really hard-mouthed dog. A dog which, when extricating game from a thick place, tears some of the feathers and fat flesh away is generally soft in the mouth and careful. I have seen people blowing up feathers to look for the teeth marks. The really hard-mouthed dog seldom leaves teeth marks but crushes the ribs; to disentangle a difficult bird from brambles, or such-like, he will grip it and so crush the ribs. I know some people say that even if a dog is hard in the mouth and gets a runner it means one more in the bag; in other words, it is a dinner gained. Of course this is true. There is, however, another side to the picture. Hard-mouth is hereditary – of this I am sure. There is also another consideration – the market value of the bird. Dealers are not going to pay top prices for birds that have had ribs crushed in.

Game which has fallen on the far side of water and has fallen far out is naturally much more difficult to collect than that which has fallen in rushes on the edge of the water. A dog that is obedient to his handler's commands is very useful here. Water tests are most valuable; a dog is really needed for this work as (unless there should be a convenient bridge) it would be most unpleasant to have to collect such game oneself – so it would probably be left until such time as it became possible for someone to collect it. Fortunately most Labradors are as at home in water as they are on land.

The first trials for retrieving dogs were held by permission of the late Mr B. B. Warwick at Little Green, near Havant, in 1899. A mixed assortment of breeds competed, consisting of one Irish Spaniel, two Clumbers, one Field Spaniel, five flat-coated Retrievers and one curly. There were no Labradors and the first three places went to flat-coats. In 1900 trials were again held at Little Green when only flat-coats competed. No trials were held in 1901. In 1902 two meetings were held; at both all entries were flat-coats. In 1903 there were no trials.

It was at the trials held by the International Gundog League in 1904 that the first Labrador, Munden Single, owned by the Hon. A. Holland-Hibbert, afterwards Third Viscount Knutsford, competed in a Stake of nineteen consisting of seventeem flat-coats, one Labrador and one curly. Munden Single was awarded a Certificate of Merit and so led the way to the great achievements attained by the Labrador in the years that were to come. At a meeting held by the same body in 1905, Munden Single and Satrap (the latter owned by Mr Clutterbuck) were awarded certificates. They were the only Labradors in a Stake of twenty.

In 1911 the first Champion Stake was held and it was won by Peter of Faskally. In 1912 the flat-coat Meery won the Champion Stake after a field trial season in which fourteen Stakes were held, not counting the Champion Stake, ten being won by Labradors. In 1913 a Golden Retriever owned by the late Mrs Charlesworth was the first of this breed to appear at a field trial and gained a Certificate at the Kennel Club Trials. A large majority of wins in this season was attained by Labradors and again a Labrador, Patron of Faskally (a son of Peter's) won the Champion Stake.

In 1914 trials practically closed down, only three meetings being held. These included five Stakes all won by Labradors, as were the three Stakes held at the one meeting in 1915.

So the history of field trials before World War I records the arrival and success of the Labrador as a working dog.

In 1919 trials were resumed and continued without interruption until 1938. Many new societies were formed and Labradors, Flat-coats, Goldens and Curly coated Retrievers ran trials for their respective breeds.

Handling or working one's own dog gives one a thrill beyond description. I think that most people who have handled their own dogs at trials will tell you the same. Obviously a good dog is needed, but I am quite certain that a good deal of good luck, is also required, for without the opportunity the best dog in the world cannot get to the front. An indifferent dog may have all the luck and win a trial now and again but assuredly it must be a good dog that keeps his place in the first three or four dogs at trial after trial. I think I can safely say that in the period betwen the 1914–18 and 1939–45 wars the two dogs which stood out at trials were F.T. Ch. Hiwood Chance, twice winner of the Champion Stake, and F.T. Ch. Balmuto Jock, three times winner of the Champion Stake. These two dogs had all the best qualities desired in a Retriever – each was a delight to watch at work and each had those essentials, temperament and sense combined with good noses and perfect mouths.

At a time when so many good dogs were competing it is difficult to make a choice, but if I had to take my pick, of dogs likely to win the greatest number of trials those are the two I would select.

It should always be remembered that trials were originally started to find out the best dogs for recovering game that is shot and to breed from these dogs to carry on such strains.

On all programmes for Retriever trials it is stated that 'No dog shall be asked to do anything at these trials [which means trials held by any society which holds a field trial meeting governed by these two bodies] which in the opinion of the judges might not prove to be useful work in an ordinary day's shooting.' Of course at field trials a good deal of walking up in roots in done. This is not often done on an ordinary day's shooting and I very much question if the host or the guns at such a day's shoot would be very pleased if a dog were sent out 300 yards to a mark in undisturbed roots which had not been walked up already for game and which therefore would be put up out of shot by the questing dog.

I know that it is useful to be able to send a dog across water and out beyond to gather game, but it is not useful work to disturb a lot of game for the sake of making one spectacular retrieve of game lying far out in undisturbed roots. It should always be remembered that a dog should quarter out into the wind and 'feel' and hunt and 'sink the wind' to make good his ground. Down-wind a dog should go out and quarter the ground back to make it good if he has not accurately marked the fall.

Whining is an objectionable habit and should be penalized. It is well to remember that a dog which is not keen and is listless and uninterested probably lies down and even takes a nap, but the keen dog is all attention, is out to watch and mark every bird. Personally, I think a very keen and intelligent dog that gives a small whimper occasionally is preferable to one that takes no interest at all. Of course there are degrees of whining, and the dogs I am thinking of give only a low whimper. It is quite different when they whine loudly enough for game to hear and turn back. I have even heard dogs so excited that they have barked. That is going much too far! A dog that marks well and goes straight to the fall saves valuable time. If the bird is a runner, by doing this the dog gets a chance of getting straight on to the line and therefore there is less likelihood of game being lost.

It should never be forgotten that wounded game should be collected as soon as possible. This should be done if only for humane reasons. A dog which goes quickly out to the fall makes a clean pick-up and a quick return is always a pleasure to watch. Many dogs have an unpleasant habit of dropping retrieved game at their handler's feet and sometimes even some distance away. This is a most unpleasant, unsightly habit. If the bird retrieved happens to be a runner it can again escape, which not only means loss of time but very often the loss of the bird. It is a well-known, recognized fact that birds so escaping are always more difficult to find again. Bad delivery is largely due to bad training and can be remedied. Temperament plays a great part in the make-up of any dog used for shooting, and, for that matter, for any purpose. Some dogs are very excitable, always jumping about, panting and behaving foolishly. A dog can take a keen, intelligent interest in what is going on without being so excited that it does not know what it is doing. These excitable dogs often let their excitement get the better of their training and break from heel, run wild and become quite out of control. Such dogs are a nuisance to their owner and to the owner of the shoot on which they run wild.

In trials it is always wise for a judge to examine the place where a bird has fallen, particularly if it is in a wood or rough ground, as a bird can be easily damaged in this way by falling on a stump or sharp stone. This does not take long and it is more satisfactory for all concerned, judge, handler and dog. I always think it advisable for a judge to show the handler the injured game.

Another penal fault is when a dog refuses to enter water. After all, if game is shot and falls on the other side of water it would mean, if one's dog refused to enter the water, either the loss of the game or getting extremely wet oneself, both alternatives being unpleasant.

Another bad fault is refusing to go into thick or punishing covert. This is a most annoying fault and, in my opinion, one that is also hereditary. One so often sees dogs which have brilliant style and pace, which retrieve quickly to hand and are most attractive to watch in roots, become, when asked to work in brambles or thick covert, totally different, picking and choosing their way about. These dogs always seem to be looking for an easy way into a bramble bush and if one cannot be found they seem to abandon their job altogether. This is an annoying fault and one for which there does not appear to be any cure. Some people say that a dog with a very fine coat does not face thick covert as willingly as one with the dense, true coat of the Labrador. I cannot agree with this. I think it is purely a matter of courage.

A well-trained, well-mannered Retriever should walk quickly at heel, neither ahead of his handler nor lagging behind. A dog that jumps round his handler is very apt, if the man should be shooting, to distract his attention. A dog which persists in walking ahead of his handler is a nuisance. He is always inclined to take a further yard or two and eventually breaks and runs in. He is also handicapped for marking birds that fall behind. His proper place, which should be insisted upon, is at his handler's side. I found that the cause of a dog being jumpy at heel was often the result of watching Spaniels working their ground in front of the gun. This is quite understandable; the dog at heel naturally wants to see what is going on and therefore jumps from side to side of his handler as the Spaniel quarters in front. It is a bad habit and, once started, is extremely difficult to stop. These are only my own ideas and must be valued as the reader considers proper.

I do not think that anyone could admire a well-trained, biddable dog more than I do, or one that is under control and anxious to please his handler, but I do hate to see dogs become entirely subservient to their handler, which have to have their game pointed out to them, so that they are continually turning round to look at their handler for direction as to the exact location of the game they are questing for. At the present time there is a distinct danger of this becoming prevalent and if this super-handling is carried to further extremes we shall be in very real danger of losing the natural ability which at present the Labrador so fortunately possesses. Instead of this we shall have a dog so entirely dependent on his handler's whistles, signals and other directions that he becomes an automaton. This would indeed be a pity.

Remember that a good field trial dog is one that is also good in an ordinary day's shooting. It appears to me that should this not become a generally accepted view, and the field trial dog become a thing apart from the dog welcomed as an ordinary shooting companion, a very regrettable position will arise.

With all breeds of gundogs, Retrievers, Pointers, Setters and all varieties of Spaniels, there is a Kennel Club rule that before any variety of gundog is entitled to be called by the much-coveted title of Champion it must have won three Challenge Certificates in its breed under three different judges at championship shows and also have obtained a Working or qualifying Certificate at a recognized trial. That this rule is a wise one there can be no possible doubt. To obtain such a Working Certificate the dog has to prove that it is not gun-shy, that it will retrieve and that it has a tender mouth – also that it will hunt for the game for which it is sent. With Pointers, Setters and Spaniels it is necessary that they should show ability for their natural jobs. It is not a difficult matter, nor an expensive one, to train a Retriever sufficiently to enable it to carry out these tests in a satisfactory manner. Most Labradors retrieve naturally from early youth. The dog can be very easily accustomed to the sound of a gun if a little thought is exercised.

A gun should not be fired directly over a young puppy; this would indeed be foolish. I think it is always wise to get the puppy really keen on retrieving, and the, when it has become thoroughly interested, get someone to fire a gun some little distance away so as not to frighten the puppy. It is quite a good plan to get someone to throw up a dummy a little distance off for the puppy to retrieve, and when it gets absorbed in this game, to get someone to fire a gun at the moment the dummy is thrown up, making sure that the gun is not too near the puppy at first. Very few puppies are gun-shy, but some are made so through thoughtlessness or stupidity. A puppy will quickly learn to retrieve – most Labradors are instinctive retrievers. Care should be taken that a suitable object is used for the puppy to learn on; never throw stones or pieces of wood. A stuffed rabbit skin (rabbits are rare these days!) or an old stocking stuffed with soft rags, hay or straw prove ideal. Having got a puppy on to retrieving a dummy, one should then try to introduce it to real game. I know that everyone has not opportunities for natural shooting. Let not this be an excuse for not getting to work to obtain a qualifying Certificate. Surely a dog which is sufficiently good-looking to show, and to raise its owner's hopes that it may be worthy of winning Challenge Certificates, is worth a little outlay in the shape of trouble, ingenuity and even expense. A visit to a poulterer's shop will enable the owner to buy a pheasant or a partridge, so that the puppy can be introduced to real game. The game can be thrown out and the puppy sent to retrieve, and when it becomes accustomed to this the game can be hidden in long grass or fern and the puppy sent to hunt for it.

Always remember that for a Working Certificate a Labrador must retrieve tenderly and hunt for the game – not bite or crush the bird's ribs. It is not necessary for the dog to be steady (that is, not to run in), or to retrieve precisely up to hand. Surely such a simple method, and one so inexpensive, is well worth while! A dog that has been awarded a Working Certificate which enables it to be called Champion after gaining show bench qualifications is worth considerably more money either in the home or foreign market than one which has won many awards on the show bench but is unable to add the magic word Champion to its name.

Labradors with the characteristics of either field trial or show bench promise are of considerable value, and even more so dogs with dual purpose promise as a consequence, field trials seem with some people to have become a deadly serious business and are perhaps not quite the same as they were in earlier days, when people looked on trials and shows as a form of relaxation when one could have days of enjoyment amongst friends. It seems a pity that this spirit should have been lost.

Ground on which to hold trials is becoming increasingly difficult to obtain. Many of the big shoots are broken up into syndicates and not all members of a syndicate are field trial enthusiasts. People kind enough to place ground at the disposal of field trial societies should have every consideration paid to them and their wishes should be strictly adhered to. I have heard most unfortunate and uncomplimentary remarks made about ground within hearing of the donors of the ground. When people are kind enough to go to the trouble and expense of giving their ground those attending the trials, or competing in them, should surely, out of courtesy and gratitude, refrain from disparaging criticism.

I have also heard uncomplimentary remarks made about the shooting. I always think shooting for field trials must be a nerve-racking undertaking, yet I have heard (when I have been in the line and also with the spectators) unflattering remarks passed when a gun has missed a shot, and sometimes well within the hearing of the host (and sometimes of the gun) on whose grounds the trials were being held and whose guests the guns were. Such remarks do not reflect good manners and they harm the society responsible for the meeting.

There is a rule that dogs not actually in the line should be kept on a lead. This is a very fair rule and should not be departed from, yet I have seen it most flagrantly broken and dogs allowed off the lead and even hunted by their owner on ground which has not yet been used. This is unfair to the host and to his keeper. There is usually a man who carries a flag and competitors not in the line, and under a judge, and also spectators, should keep with the flag and not wander all over the ground, perhaps disturbing game.

These may seen small points but they are important to the host and lessen his anxiety – for a host at field trials has many anxieties. Field trials are increasing and, added to actual Retriever trials, trials for Spaniels are now being run in much the same manner as those for Retrievers.

Now that rabbits have been practically wiped out those responsible for Spaniel trials are now falling back on winged game and so running them in much the same way as Retriever trials. The result is that more and more ground is being sought on which to test retrieving dogs.

The outstanding dog of all retriever breeds in field trials at the time of writing [1959] is undoubtedly Mr Laurence Taylor's Field Trial Champion Galleywood Shot, which won the

Champion Stake in 1957 and repeated this performance in 1958. These wins place him among the very great gundogs of all time. His performance equals that of the great little Field Trial Champion Hiwood Chance and has been excelled only by Field Trial Champion Balmuto Jock who won it three times. Dual Field Trial Champion Titus of Whitmore also won the Champion Stake twice, but we have to go back to 1923 and 1924 to read about his great wins.

The Champion Stake has been held many times since it was inaugurated in 1911 (it was in abeyance during both World Wars) and on no fewer than thirty-two occasions Labradors have won it. Twice it was won by Golden Retrievers, twice by the Interbreds Dazzle and Flashy, owned by the late Mr C. Alington, and once by a Flat-coat. Galleywood Shot's wins in 1957 and 1958 therefore mark him out as a really outstanding dog. Unfortunately, I have not seen him, but I understand that he won the 1958 Stake very clearly and that he never put a foot wrong in a most searching test.

In his postscript to the third edition [1961] Cliff Brown wrote:

Little need be added to the author's original work, except perhaps to record that Labradors have fully maintained their wonderful record both in the field and on the show bench, and of the many successes achieved during the last two years, the most notable are those of Champion Ruler of Blaircourt, owned by Mr and Mrs Grant Cairns. Ruler followed up his reserve best in show all breeds at the 1959 Cruft's by winning the supreme best in show at the 1960 Scottish Kennel Club show at Glasgow where the writer had the pleasure of awarding him one of his many Challenge Certificates. The latest of a long line of Champions turned out by the Sandylands Kennel of Mrs G. Broadley is Champion Sandylands Tweed of Blaircourt, who gained a total of six Challenge Certificates to become the top winner of 1960. The Loughderg Labradors owned by Mrs John Sim have come rapidly to the fore and Loughderg Strokestown Urch was twice best in show all breeds at important Championship shows during 1960–1.

In the field, the most consistent performer has undoubtedly

been the Lord Rank's Field Trial Champion Scotney Jingle. During 1959 and 1960 this good black dog, bred by Lt.-Col. Bucher, won no few than nine Open or All Aged Stakes and was placed in seven more, a truly great record which gained for his owner the Rank-Routledge Gold Cup in both years.

# 12

# The Labrador in Sickness

It is obviously impossible to cover all the ills to which an animal is prone, so this chapter is necessarily confined to the more common ailments and is extracted from the paperback, *The Family Labrador Retriever*, which I wrote with my wife. It is not suggested that the section should be regarded as anything other than a general guide. Once again I must stress that you should not experiment with your dog. If he is sick and you are not sure what the trouble is, then consult your veterinary surgeon at once.

ABSCESS: A painful swelling which usually forms very quickly. There is a corresponding rapid rise in temperature. Clip off the surrounding hair, and apply hot poultices (Kaolin or similar) every three to four hours until the abscess bursts. Keep open by bathing as often as possible until all the poison has been removed.

ACCIDENTS: As it is quite impossible to cover all accidents which could happen we will deal, very simply, with a few.

BURNS AND SCALDS: There are two main considerations here; the extent and degree of the burn, and shock. If the skin has been burned badly apply a tannic acid dressing, if one is available. If not, use a cold tea dressing or cover the area with a clean dressing to prevent infection until you can get to your veterinary surgeon. If the burn is not too deep or extensive, apply the dressing and after a few hours dust the area with a sulphonamide powder, and dress with a healing ointment. This should be repeated two or three times a day. Scalds should be treated similarly. But if the shock affect is great, your veterinary surgeon should be consulted immediately.

CUTS AND ABRASIONS: The first essential is to clean the area thoroughly; if the wound is very minor nothing further need be done as it will heal quite quickly and naturally. If it is deep and has to be stitched, clean it and see your veterinary surgeon. If an artery has been severed, apply a tourniquet above the cut if it is on a limb; or plug with a pad, to which pressure must be applied gently, if on the body. This will halt the loss of blood until you can get professional help. If you have applied a tourniquet, do make sure this is not too tight and release slightly every ten minutes or so.

ANAL GLANDS – INFLAMMATION OF: Swelling of the gland is often accompanied by an offensive smell. The dog draws himself in a sitting position along the ground, thus this condition can be mistaken for worms. Once the condition is apparent skilled squeezing of the anal glands is necessary and this is a job for your veterinary surgeon.

APPETITE (VARIABLE OR VORACIOUS): When several dogs are living together there is always a certain amount of rivalry in clearing the dish first, to see whether those who were not quite so fast have left any pickings. In the case of single dogs this does not apply, and the dog may pick at his food for a long time before finally finishing. Bearing such points in mind, any serious variations in your dog's appetite should be watched carefully and, if possible. the reason found. Should your dog have a variable and voracious appetite, check for worms and treat accordingly. It may be necessary to titillate your dog's appetite after an illness; apart from all the more usual items, do try tinned tomato soup. We have found this to be successful where other foods have failed.

BAD BREATH: First the cause must be traced; it can be either the result of bad teeth, kidney disorder or mouth ulcers. It can also be the effect of an upset stomach. A deodorant tablet (e.g. Amplex) could be tried if the condition is not too advanced and as a first measure.

BALDNESS: (See Skin diseases.)

BILIOUSNESS: Symptoms are vomiting, thirst and diarrhoea, and little interest in food. Curtail the water intake and do not press the dog with food. Calomel or similar should be given. The following day give Bengers Food or Complan. This will give the stomach a chance to settle before going back to normal diet.

BOWELS INFLAMMATION: Painful distended stomach, thirst, possible vomiting and rise in temperature which could be accompanied by either constipation or diarrhoea. If the dog is constipated, some such laxative as Milk of Magnesia should be given. If diarrhoea, mix approximately one tablespoonful of arrowroot into a smooth paste, add a small quantity of milk and glucose to make it more palatable, and feed this to the dog. If the symptoms do not abate within twenty-four hours consult your veterinary surgeon; your dog may have a bone or similar obstruction.

BRONCHITIS: Symptoms are a cough – difficulty in breathing – and wheezy chest. Keep your dog warm. In bad cases wrap his chest with cotton wool or similar warm material. His diet should be reasonably light and care should be taken to see that his bowels are free. A bronchitis kettle using Friar's Balsam or similar is often a great help. Watch his temperature; if it does go high consult your veterinary surgeon.

BURNS: (See Accidents.)

CANINE PARVOVIRUS: This is a virus giving symptoms similar to feline enteritis against which cat lovers have had their pets inoculated for some considerable time. It has been suggested that a mutuation has occurred in the feline virus and that it is this mutuation which is causing so much concern in dog circles today.

The virus seems to be capable of producing different symptoms:

(1) In very young puppies – heart disease (cardio myopathy). An apparently healthy puppy dies suddenly from heart failure after some very mild exercise, such as play, or even after feeding. Fortunately this is now becoming rare due to the immunity carried by the bitches from their own inoculations.

(2) In weaned puppies and older dogs – severe gastro enteritis. Early signs are vomiting and diarrhoea, the vomit being a frothy yellow and the diarrhoea being particularly evil-smelling with varying amounts of blood. The affected animal will be very dull and quickly become dehydrated.

Obviously skilled help is needed as soon as possible and your veterinary surgeon must be consulted without delay. Alas, there is not a great deal he can do with cardio myopathy so the prognosis here is not good, but fortunately with the gastro enteritis syndrome there is every reason to hope for the best.

It must be stressed that the disease is highly contagious, and, if you do suspect its presence, every effort must be made to confine it by isolation, liberal use of disinfectant, etc. It is important to burn faeces and any vomit. So far the highest mortality rate is probably in expectant and nursing bitches and great care in cleanliness of feeding utensils, and in ensuring that any clothes you are wearing have not been 'in contact', is essential.

Vaccines are now in use; they are commonly called 'live' and 'dead' vaccines. The decision concerning which one should be used is obviously one for the veterinary surgeon and the owner. In many cases the decision requires very careful consideration, particularly with bitches in whelp.

Careful consideration must also be given to the right time to administer the first inoculation, normally at 12 weeks but it could be earlier depending on the circumstances. How soon the initial inoculation is boosted and whether one boost or two are required will depend on the environment and whether parvovirus has been prevalent therein. The generally accepted dosage in normal circumstances is first inoculation at 12 weeks and a second one at 16 weeks.

CANKER OF THE EAR: Usual signs are shaking of the head, rubbing the ears along the ground and an offensive discharge. There are so many possible different causes of ear troubles that it is usually beyond a layman to diagnose the ill correctly. Consult your veterinary surgeon without delay, do *not* try all kinds of proprietary preparations which may do more harm than good.

CONSTIPATION: A correctly fed and exercised dog is rarely troubled by this, so if it does occur check the diet first. A mild laxative such as Milk of Magnesia can be given by the diet must be checked to ensure a lasting cure.

COUGHS: Ordinary cough mixture is excellent in such cases and usually gives quick results. Do watch a dog with a cough very carefully, especially if he is under twelve months old, and if there is any rise in temperature or diarrhoea consult your veterinary surgeon. It could be distemper.

CYSTS: Swellings usually between the toes called interdigital cysts which cause the dog considerable trouble if not treated. Apply hot poultices as frequently as possible until the cyst bursts then keep open by continual bathing until you are quite sure all the poison has been removed. Then allow to heal with a little Veterinary Ointment.

DIARRHOEA: First, if possible, establish the cause. In a young puppy it could be a completely unsuitable diet or too rapid a change of diet. It could be worms, a chill, bones or distemper. If the diet is normal, have all dishes, etc., been thoroughly cleaned? If a puppy, which has been satisfactorily wormed and the cause cannot be established, consult your veterinary surgeon. If you are reasonably certain it is a chill or wrong diet, in the latter case starve for twenty-four hours administering kaolin chlorodyne every six hours and giving a little water with some glucose. In the former case keep the dog warm and feed with arrowroot gruel or cornflour. Again if there is no rapid improvement consult your veterinary surgeon.

DISTEMPER AND HARDPAD: The symptoms are dullness, vomiting, cough and diarrhoea. This is followed by watering and 'made-up' eyes and a rise in temperature to above 103°F-(39.5°C). In hardpad there is a characteristic hardening of the dog's pads so that you can hear him walking. There is then a period when he apparently had rid himself of his ills (usually after about forty-eight hours) and he appears reasonably well. Do not be misled. If you suspect distemper or hardpad you must consult your veterinary surgeon at once.

ECZEMA: (See skin diseases.)

EYE TROUBLES: If you dog suffers from watery eyes which often become covered with a film, bathe frequently with a warm boracic lotion. Dry off with cotton wool and smear preferably Golden Eye Ointment or Vaseline round the eyelids. Injuries to the eyes as a result of fighting or thorn scratches must be treated on their merits. Very minor cases may be treated by frequent bathing and anointing as above, the serious cases must receive rapid veterinary attention.

FAINTING: This usually occurs in older dogs or dogs suffering from a heart disease. Care must be taken not to over-excite such dogs and heavy meals should be avoided. In place of the one main meal a day, therefore, substitute three small ones roughly equivalent. When the faint does occur, lay the dog on his side keeping his head lower than his body. When he comes round he will be dazed, so do your best to soothe and comfort him.

FEET SORENESS: (see also Cysts.) Lameness caused by cracked pads often the result of the salt and grit put down to keep roads and footpaths clear in icy weather. Rub Friar's Balsam gently into the pads until it is dry. If the condition was slight the dog will be all right almost at once.

FITS (EPILEPTIC): Here the dog, quite normal one minute, will suddenly fall to the ground, convulsing, limbs held out stiffly and twitching furiously. He will normally foam at the mouth caused by the furious champing of his mouth whilst in the fit. Take great care on two counts: (1) that the dog on coming out of the fit does not turn on you in his dazed condition; (2) that he cannot do himself harm by either running amok if indoors or running away if outdoors. Therefore he must be secured properly, but not so tightly as to stop the blood flow. While in the fit, which may last several minutes, apply cold compresses to the back of his head. He must then be given some form of sedative tablet or powder to help him relax. Then consult your veterinary surgeon for a course of treatment to prevent a recurrence if at all possible.

GASTRITIS: Symptoms are vomiting, dullness and thirst. Starve for twenty-four hours unless the dog is very weak, restrict the water to a few sips only; better still give either milk and soda water or barley water and milk, again in very small quantities. Glucose may be given and will be found beneficial. After twenty-four hours, if improvement is shown, feed beef essence or invalid diets such as Bengers or Complan, again little but often, and gradually over a period of a week to ten days go back to his normal diet (see chapter on diet). If no results after twenty-four hours consult your veterinary surgeon.

HARDPAD: (See Distemper.)

HYSTERIA: Treatment as for fits. Under no circumstances give white bread or potatoes. Adminster a sedative and change the diet to one which virtually excludes biscuits or similar starchy foods.

MANGE: (See Skin diseases.)

PNEUMONIA: The symptoms are shivering, feverish, breathing short and quick and the chest is painful, eyes bloodshot. Later a husky cough develops. Great care must be taken and warmth and a constant temperature are essentials. A pneumonia jacket which will completely cover his back and chest will be found particularly beneficial. Obviously your veterinary surgeon must be consulted immediately.

POISONING: This causes violent spasms of body muscles; the dog cannot stand and falls on to its side. The first thing is to adminster a strong emetic, e.g. salt and warm water or a knob of washing soda. After this a few drops of brandy. Keep your dog warm and send for the veterinary surgeon at once.

If you know the type of poison which has been taken by the dog the antidote treatment can be a little more positive while you are awaiting the arrival of the veterinary surgeon:

PHOSPHORUS: Give a copper sulphate solution (five grains dissolved in warm water) every few minutes. Keep the dog quiet and warm.

STRYCHNINE: Give a strong emetic at once followed by a few drops of olive oil or brandy.

WARFARIN: Normally this would have to be taken in large doses to affect your dog, but if you do suspect this poisoning consult your veterinary surgeon who will probably use Vitamin K as the antidote, this is of course a job for the professional.

RHEUMATISM: A good liniment rubbed into the affected part will be found beneficial (e.g. Radiol). Radiant heat is also a great help. Warmth and freedom from any draughts or damp are essential. If the pain is severe, aspirin may be given three times a day. Bowels must be kept free. A change of diet may assist.

SCALDS: (See Accidents.)

SICKNESS: If this is obviously quite mild and just a tummy upset, a course of garlic tablets will be found to be very helpful. If more serious see Gastritis.

SICKNESS (TRAVEL): This is not usually a Labrador complaint but if you are unlucky enough to encounter it I suggest that: (a) initial car journeys should be short, not longer than ten to fifteen minutes, e.g. going shopping; (b) the length of time spent on the journey should only be increased gradually; (c) if (a) and (b) are unsuccessful, try a course of travel-sickness tablets. These do have the effect of making the animal drowsy but this soon wears off.

SKIN DISEASES: There are many forms of skin disease and some defy treatment to the bitter end. Correct diagnosis of the condition is necessary and this is best done by microscopic examination of scrapings – a job for your veterinary surgeon.

SKIN PARASITES: These include fleas, harvest bugs and lice. If your dog is groomed regularly, as he should be, the presence of these unwelcomed guests will soon be discovered. This is important because they can cause serious skin troubles. The treatment nowadays is simple; a revolutionary collar is available from most good pet shops, or Boots, called a Vapona Dogband. All that is necessary is to fit it round the animal's neck and, within a few minutes, the parasites literally will stagger to the surface of the coat. They can then be plucked off and burned, and it is not necessary to leave the collar on for more than two hours. Alternatively, a powder obtainable from chemists or pet shops is combed into the coat, this is repeated in a few days, and the fleas are swiftly disposed of. But do not forget also to clean in and around the dog's bed.

Lice can be more difficult and they quickly set up a skin infection. Their usual habitat is under or around the ears and the tail, but they too are cleared fast if treated as for fleas. After an outbreak of parasites, do not forget to cleanse all grooming gear thoroughly.

SNAKE BITES: In this country the enemy is the adder, usually found on moorland, which can cause your dog very great pain. So far as is known, this snake only attacks when he thinks he is in danger, but in 'sniffing him out' your Labrador may provoke the adder, and the resultant bite will need immediate attention.

The quickest and best treatment is an injection with anti-venom serum but, as this is rarely available at such short notice the immediate steps are: (1) To stop the spread of the poison, if a limb is bitten, cut above the bite and tie a tourniquet or similar above this. (2) If you have any potassium per-manganate crystals available, rub these into the wound. (3) Treat the dog for shock. If the bite is in a place where this is not possible, e.g. in the neck or face, the area will swell very rapidly. The dog must be taken to a veterinary surgeon as soon as possible. It is, however, better to walk him slowly, rather than let him lie down or be carried.

TUMOURS: Hard lump or swelling rarely painful. The only treatment is by removal and the sooner this is done the better, particularly if you see that the swelling is enlarging.

WORMS: (1) Roundworms: pointed at both ends, usually a pinky grey in colour, and varying in length from about ½ in. They are not normally serious in older dogs but they do affect the dog's condition. His coat will not be as good as it might be and he will have a tendency to sickness and occasionally loose motions. His appetite, too, will usually be ravenous and he will be forever scavenging. A course of round-worm tablets which you get from your veterinary surgeon will soon put it right. Nowadays it is quite a simple matter to rid the dogs of these pests. The tablets are given without prior starving and there is little aftermath. It is advisable to treat your dog again after two to three weeks if he has been badly affected by them.

Bitches in whelp should always be wormed before they have their puppies, this can be done quite safely with modern worm tablets within the period six weeks to four weeks before she has the puppies. This will allow for the puppies having a reason-able start. The puppies should then be treated for worms at the age of six weeks whether they show signs or not. Should the lit-ter become infested, you will see this either by the puppies passing them, or vomiting them, or you may suspect it when the puppy's appetite is variable (do not forget puppies are always or nearly always hungry – so make due allowances). It is advisable to worm them at any time from three weeks onwards but use medicine prepared specially for the early worming of puppies.

(2) Tapeworm: These are normally the type which affect older dogs and cause, amongst other things, bad breath, uncertain motions either loose or constipated, bad coat, variable appetite. They can usually be seen as small 'pieces of tape' protruding from or around the anus. A course of modern tapeworm tablets will be found to be completely effective.

*In all cases of worms the excrement should be burned.*

Finally, if the time has come when you have to make the dreadful decision whether to have your dog put to sleep, try not to let your own selfishness prolong his pain. Most of us, if we are honest, have done this at some time and while we admit afterwards we were wrong, nevertheless we have possibly caused unnecessary suffering to the dog. So face up to the decision squarely for one who has served you well and let him be put to sleep painlessly in his own home by the veterinary surgeon.

APPENDIX A

# POST-WAR REGISTRATION TOTALS
## AT THE KENNEL CLUB

| | | | |
|---|---|---|---|
| 1946 | 4,839 | 1965 | 9,531 |
| 1947 | 5,221 | 1966 | 9,284 |
| 1948 | 4,244 | 1967 | 11,756 |
| 1949 | 4,690 | 1968 | 12,544 |
| 1950 | 4,189 | 1969 | 14,498 |
| 1951 | 3,859 | 1970 | 14,827 |
| 1952 | 3,196 | 1971 | 11,967 |
| 1953 | 3,488 | 1972 | 13,880 |
| 1954 | 3,374 | 1973 | 13,505 |
| 1955 | 3,575 | 1974 | 12,849 |
| 1956 | 4,041 | 1975 | 10,939 |
| 1957 | 4,409 | 1976 | 4,632* |
| 1958 | 4,672 | 1977 | 2,479* |
| 1959 | 5,577 | 1978 | 8,619† |
| 1960 | 6,098 | 1979 | 15,002 |
| 1961 | 6,964 | 1980 | 15,629 |
| 1962 | 8,139 | 1981 | 12,543 |
| 1963 | 8,453 | 1982 | 13,488 |
| 1964 | 8,673 | 1983 | 14,016†† |

*This figure is not really comparable with figures for previous years because it is the result of the new registration system introduced by the Kennel Club. It will perhaps put it more into perspective if I say that it is the highest in the gundog group and is beaten overall only by German Shepherd Dogs (Alsatians) and Yorkshire Terriers.

†A further amendment to the registration system was introduced this year.

††It is interesting to note that the Labrador Retriever is now second only to the GSD (Alsatian) in the number of registrations.

## CHAMPIONS, FIELD TRIAL CHAMPIONS, WORKING TRIAL CHAMPIONS, SHOW CHAMPIONS, AND OBEDIENCE CHAMPIONS. 1947–1983

Y—yellow   B—black   C—cream   G—golden

| Name | Sex | Born | Colour | Sire | Dam | Breeder | Owner |
|------|-----|------|--------|------|-----|---------|-------|
| **1947** | | | | | | | |
| F.T. Ch. Folkingham Seeker | D | 10.5.42 | Y | Rauceby Dan | Folkingham Susan | Owner | Dr T. W. Stanton |
| F.T. Ch. Kneveton Caen | D | 26.7.44 | B | Staindrop Rancher | Kneveton Busy | Owner | C. J. Neale |
| Ch. Poppleton Golden Flight | D | 5.4.44 | Y | Poppleton Golden Russet | Modney Crocus | E. Parker | Mrs B.M. Outhwaite |
| Ch. & F.T. Ch. Staindrop Saighdear | D | 22.2.44 | Y | Glenhead Jimmy | Our Lil | J. J. Murray Dewar | E. Winter |
| F.T. Ch. Braeroy Fudge | B | 24.10.44 | Y | Banchory Jack | Braeroy Chips | Mrs M. K. Macpherson | G. Hallett |
| Ch. Golden Gleam of Glengour | B | 21.3.44 | Y | Knaith Boboy | Golden Dot of Glengour | Owner | J. M. Hanson |
| Ch. Sandylands Blackberry | B | 20.5.44 | B | Ch. Durley Beech | Ch. June of Sandylands | Owner | Mrs G. Broadley |
| Ch. Sandylands Harley Princess | B | 4.6.44 | B | Ir. Ch. Prince of Mountpanther | Banker Bess | G. Bell | Mrs G. Broadley |
| **1948** | | | | | | | |
| Ch. Banchory Cottager | D | 17.10.44 | B | Countryman of Chrishall | Philippine Daphne | Hon. Mrs Philipps | Lorna, Countess Howe |
| Ch. Blacksmith of Ide | D | 29.5.46 | B | Jackie of Crossgar | Ch. Sandylands Harley Princess | S. F. Topott | J. H. J. Braddon |

| Name | Sex | Born | Colour | Sire | Dam | Breeder | Owner |
|---|---|---|---|---|---|---|---|
| F.T. Ch. Crudenby Sweep Whiskey | D | 9.4.44 | B | Crudenby Black Diamond | Crudenby Little Wonder | Owner | W. A. J. Mackie |
| F.T. Ch. Fordham Whiskey | D | 14.1.46 | Y | Scaltback Dan | Knownowt | H. Wragg | A. E. Newport |
| F.T. Ch. Greatford Nylon | D | 12.3.44 | B | Apethorpe Scoter | Greatford Netta | Owner | Maj H. Peacock |
| Ch. & F.T. Ch. Knaith Banjo | D | 29.3.46 | Y | Poppleton Golden Russet | Knaith Brilliantine | Owner | Mrs A. Wormald |
| Ch. Landyke Patrick | D | 5.2.46 | Y | Pat of Podington | Badgery Honey Jaala | Owner | J. Hart |
| Ch. & F.T. Ch. Rockstead Footspark | D | 26.6.45 | B | Ludford Razor | | Maj J. Benson | R. MacDonald |
| F.T. Ch. Scotney Kinsman | D | 10.4.44 | B | Countryman of Chrishall | Scotney Sadie | Owner | J. A. Rank |
| F.T. Ch. Trevelyr Swift | D | 22.5.46 | B | Penlan Don | Trevelyr Starlight | Owner | Mrs L. Williams-Owen |
| F.T. Ch. Hockham Victoria | B | 8.6.46 | Y | Knaith Bovril | Zelstone Darter | Mrs M. Radclyffe | Brig T. B. Trappes-Lomax |
| Ch. Honey of Whatstandwell | B | 8.10.44 | Y | Honey Badger | Bracken of Whatstandwell | Owners | Mr & Mrs H. Taylor |
| Ch. Lady Juliet of Hamdere | B | 13.8.43 | B | Rockstead Footprint | Trixie of Keewatin | Miss W. E. Hipworth | H. J. Easthaugh |
| Ch. Sandylands Harley Superb 1949 | B | 26.5.42 | B | Dalmas Jewel | Clatter Bridge Mimosa | T. Jackson | Mrs G. Broadley |
| F.T. Ch. Brackenbank Trigger | D | 23.6.46 | B | Brackenbank Sam | Brackenbank Judy | Owner | R. N. Burton |
| Ch. Damstead Stingo | D | 1.5.46 | B | Damstead Skipper | Damstead Secret | W. Woodhouse | J. E. Jones |
| Ch. Danny of Tobarmhuire | D | 5.5.46 | Y | Jackie of Crossgar | Heather's Pride | J. Patterson, Jnr | Mr & Mrs H. Taylor |
| F.T. Ch. Glenhead Zuider | D | 16.3.48 | B | Glenhead Jimmy | Ariston Jet | A.A. Howie | J. Annand |

| Name | Sex | Date | Colour | Sire | Dam | Breeder | Owner |
|---|---|---|---|---|---|---|---|
| Ch. Gold Rand of Glengour | D | 9.5.47 | Y | Knaith Boboy | Golden Dot of Glengour | Owner | J. M. Hanson |
| F.T. Ch. L'Ile Go Gettem | D | 19.4.43 | B | L'Ile Gameboy | Isla Susan | W. Farquharson | D. McDonald |
| Ch. Louvil of Tibshelf | D | 6.5.44 | B | Danpru of Tibshelf | Jessimont of Tibshelf | Owner | J. G. Severn |
| Ch. Sandylands Beau | D | 11.12.47 | B | Sandylands Ben | Ch. Sandylands Harley Princess | Owner | Mrs G. Broadley |
| Ch. Annette of Staithes | B | 7.12.44 | B | John of Sandylands | Black Emblem of Glengour | Miss A. R. Todd | J. S. Potter |
| Ch. Barrowy Fern of Ide | B | 16.2.44 | B | Harbood of Tibshelf | Lock House Bess | J. Topps | J. H. J. Braddon |
| F.T. Ch. Rough Justice | B | 25.4.47 | B | Ch. Rockstead Footspark | Pont Du Fah | Owner | A. C. Higgs |
| Ch. Treat of Treesholme | B | 26.12.46 | Y | Lochar Gold Flake | Poppleton Golden Sherry | Owner | H. Smith, Jnr |
| F.T. Ch. Zelstone Darter | B | 21.10.44 | Y | Durley Bracken | Glenmorag Parella of Podington | Owner | Mrs A. M. Radclyffe |

**1950**

| Name | Sex | Date | Colour | Sire | Dam | Breeder | Owner |
|---|---|---|---|---|---|---|---|
| F.T. Ch. Brackenbank Jasper | D | 18.6.47 | B | Sudborough Ben | Banchory Murton Mystic | G. Smith | R. N. Burton |
| Ch. Braeroy Reiver of Drum Corrie | D | 20.6.44 | G | Conquest of Hayton | Lady Sunshine | J. P. Wilson | Miss M. De Beaumont |
| Ch. British Justice | D | 24.4.48 | B | Banchory Jack | Pont Du Fahs | P-Sgt A. C. Higgs | Lorna, Countess Howe |
| Ch. Donnybrook Thunder | D | 10.7.46 | B | Black Eagle of Glengour | Donnybrook Wendy | Owner | Mrs P. F. Morris |
| F.T. Ch. Hallingbury Sweep | D | 5.3.47 | B | Scotney Sprite | Hallingbury Quail | V. Routledge | J. A. Rank |
| Ch. Kim of Balvie | D | 14.1.49 | Y | Golden Glint of Glengour | Amber Gypsy | Owner | Mrs G. W. Tait |
| F.T. Ch. Staindrop Ray | D | 5.5.48 | Y | Ch. & F.T. Staindrop Saighdear | Cheverells Sally | Mrs R. Heaton | E. Winter |
| Ch. Ballyduff Whatstandwell Rowena | B | 6.2.48 | B | Whatstandwell Ballyduff Robin | Sandylands Juny | Mr & Mrs H. Taylor | Dr T. S. Acheson |

| Name | Sex | Born | Colour | Sire | Dam | Breeder | Owner |
|---|---|---|---|---|---|---|---|
| Ch. Colleen of Blaircourt | B | 27.3.48 | B | Jr Ch. Prince of Mountpanther | Mourne View Queenie | D. Orr | Mr & Mrs G. Cairns |
| Ch. Cookridge Blimbo | B | 17.6.44 | B | Keewatin Big Ben | Trixie of Keewatin | Miss W. Hipworth | Mrs M. Y. Pauling |
| Ch. Durley Blossom of Bonython | B | 1.2.46 | B | Durley Bracken | Durley Blackout | W. Watchman | Mrs D. & Miss J. Lee |
| W.T. Ch. Frenchcourt Ripple | B | 11.5.46 | B | Donnybrook Ben | Donnybrook Secuta | Miss E. Titterton | J. Simpson |
| F.T. Ch. Greatford Uffington Brandysnap | B | 6.11.47 | B | F.T. Ch. Greatford Nylon | Greatford Sherry | A. G. Teesdale | Maj H. Peacock |
| Ch. Liddly Coffee | Y | 1.9.47 | Y | Durley Cider | Liddly Tulip of Haymax | Owner | H. A. Saunders |
| Ch. Sandylands Belle of Helenspring 1951 | B | 11.12.47 | B | Sandylands Ben | Ch. Sandylands Harley Princess | Owner | Mrs G. Broadley |
| Ch. Ballyduff Orangeman | D | 12.7.47 | Y | Ballyduff Major | Ballyduff Venus | Owner | Dr T. S. Acheson |
| F.T. Ch. Corbridge Drake | D | 2.2.47 | B | Riding Rajah | Brackenbank Dainty | Miss G. B. Short | Maj C. Douglas Blackett |
| F.T. Ch. Halingbury Snipe | D | 5.3.47 | B | Scotney Sprite | Halingbury Quail | Owner | V. Routledge |
| Ch. Hilldown Jet of Ethie | D | 22.4.46 | B | Ch. Durley Beech | Gyppie of Ethie | Earl & Countess of Northesk | M. L. Rapley |
| Ch. Poppleton Lieutenant | D | 19.3.49 | Y | Poppleton Beech Flight | Poppleton Golden Sunray | Owner | Mrs B. M. Outhwaite |
| Ch. Poppleton Lucky Boy | D | 19.3.49 | Y | Poppleton Beech Flight | Poppleton Golden Sunray | Owner | Mrs B. M. Outhwaite |
| F.T. Ch. Shavington Bob | D | 2.5.47 | B | Shavington Ben | Draysal Beauty | J. Dickin | Mrs A. Heywood Lonsdale |
| Ch. Baric Russette | B | 1.1.49 | Y | Ch. Poppleton Golden Flight | Baric Jill | Dr R. F. Paget | V. Thompson |

| Name | Sex | Date | Sire | Dam | Breeder | Owner |
|---|---|---|---|---|---|---|
| Ch. Greatford Churchfield Jet | B | 23.2.49 | Greatford Pettistree Shadow | Mackland Honeysuckle | R. W. B. Newton | Maj H. Peacock |
| Ch. Holton Pipit | B | 24.5.49 | Holton Canter | Holton Gleaner | Owner | M. C. W. Gilliat |
| Ch. Landyke Sheba | B | 9.3.43 | Pasha of Podington | Badgery Honey | Owner | J. Hart |
| Ch. Pussy Willow | B | 23.6.48 | Inveravon Scamp | Amber Glint | Owner | W. B. Maclaren |
| Ch. Spurstow Scawfell Sniff | B | 4.5.48 | Grouse of Spurstow | Langnore Jane | G. F. Kite | Mrs M. V. A. Byrd |
| Ch. Wendover Topsy 1952 | B | 1.1.48 | Ch. Blacksmith of Ide | Sandylands Busybody | Owners | Mr & Mrs L. C. James |
| F.T. Ch. Hiwood Don | D | 23.1.51 | F.T. Ch. Glenhead Zuider | Hiwood Peggy | Owner | Hon. Lady Hill-Wood |
| F.T. Ch. Skip of Cromlix | D | 10.5.47 | Kirrie Kim | Lunan Una | R. Hunter | Hon. Mrs E. V. Eden |
| F.T. Ch. Whatstandwell Hiwood Brand | D | 28.3.49 | Ch. & F.T. Ch. Staindrop Saighdear | Staindrop Carnation | E. Winter | Mr & Mrs H. Taylor |
| F.T. Ch. Ballyduff Jassie | B | 23.5.48 | Greatford Pettistree Shadow | Ballyduff Jane | Owner | Dr T. S. Acheson |
| Ch. Black Bess of Ide | B | 21.7.50 | Ch. Blacksmith of Ide | Ch. Barrowby Fern of Ide | Owner | J. H. J. Braddon |
| Ch. Shadow of Creation of Ide 1953 | B | 18.4.47 | Bruce of Sholebroke | Janet of Hollowbrooks | F. N. Gee | J. H. J. Braddon |
| F.T. Ch. Brackenbank Merry | B | 26.3.51 | F.T. Ch. Brackenbank Jasper | Brackenbank Gyrn Chuillin | Owner | R. N. Burton |
| Ch. Cookridge Intelligence | D | 24.10.50 | Cookridge Roamer | Cookridge Patience | Owner | Mrs M. Y. Pauling |
| Ch. Craigluscar Emperor of Blaircourt | D | 23.3.49 | Darky of Elmbank | Craigluscar Black Gem | D. Reid | Mr & Mrs Grant Cairns |
| F.T. Ch. Galleywood Swift | D | 13.7.49 | F.T. Ch. Treveilyr Swift | Staindrop Winkie | Owner | W. L. Taylor |
| F.T. Ch. Hilldyke Simon | D | 26.6.49 | F.T. Ch. Trevilyr Swift | Laureate Bess | E. E. Smith | T. C. Hardy |

| Name | Sex | Born | Colour | Sire | Dam | Breeder | Owner |
|---|---|---|---|---|---|---|---|
| Ch. Holton Baron | D | 26.4.51 | B | Sandylands Bob | Holton Whimbrel | Owner | M. C. W. Gilliat |
| F.T. Ch. Kale of Chrishall | D | 23.6.50 | B | Pinehawk Black Tarquin of Glaven | Walden Lass | A. R. Heasman | J. Kent |
| F.T. Ch. Oxendon Dan | D | 11.5.51 | B | Greatford Pettistree Shadow | Mackland Honeysuckle | R. W. B. Newton | Dr J. Hurndall Gann |
| F.T. Ch. Shavington Rip | D | 10.3.50 | B | Pinehawk Black Tarquin of Glaven | Shavington Bess | C. Cartledge | Mrs A. Heywood Lonsdale |
| Ch. Whatstandwell Ballyduff Robin | D | 28.7.46 | B | Sudborough Ben | Lady Juliet of Hamdere | H. J. Easthaugh | Mr & Mrs H. Taylor |
| F.T. Ch. Blackhambleton Starlight | B | 17.2.48 | B | Knepp Bill | F.T. Ch. Blackhambleton Skell | G. Richards | Capt F. G. B. Stephens |
| Ch. Corsican Quest | B | 8.3.50 | Y | Landyke Shot of Goodhope | Bran of Callow | Owners | Lt-Col & Mrs C. B. Venn |
| F.T. Ch. Dinah of Cromlix | B | 10.4.47 | B | Janefield Don | Remony Hula | A. Duncan Millar | Hon Mrs E. V. Eden |
| Ch. Hilldown Sylver | B | 9.1.48 | Y | Kirkby Brandy | Whiphill Sheila | M. L. Rapley | Mrs B. Eustace-Duckett |
| Ch. Sandylands Jilly | B | 7.5.51 | B | Ch. British Justice | Ch. Sandylands Belle of Helenspring | Owner | Mrs G. Broadley |
| **1954** | | | | | | | |
| Ch. Diant Swandyke Cream Cracker | D | 8.10.50 | Y | Ch. Poppleton Golden Flight | Lassie of Freiston | W. Tillson | Mrs L. Wilson-Jones |
| Ch. General of Garshangan | D | 26.6.51 | C | Ch. Poppleton Lieutenant | Gigha of Garshanghan | Owners | Lt-Col & Mrs M. H. L. Hill |
| F.T. Ch. Greatford Teal | D | 12.6.52 | B | Greatford Pettistree Shadow | Mackland Honeysuckle | R. W. B. Newton | Maj H. Peacock |
| F.T. Ch. Grouseadee | D | 1.5.50 | B | F.T. Ch. Scotney Kinsman | Westelm Black Princess | J. Stephens | F. Bell |

| Name | Sex | Date | Colour | Sire | Dam | Owner | Breeder |
|---|---|---|---|---|---|---|---|
| F.T. Ch. Minstrel of Glenmorag | D | 27.3.50 | Y | Braedrop Bruce | Glenmorag Parella of Podington | Owner | Maj K. J. Malcolm |
| Ch. Sandylands Justice | D | 7.5.51 | B | Ch. British Justice | Ch. Sandylands Belle of Helenspring | Mrs G. Broadley | Lorna, Countess Howe, & Mrs G. Broadley |
| F.T. Ch. Staindrop Sweep | D | 11.6.53 | B | Staindrop Murton Marksman | Hiwood Dee | Lady J. Hill-Wood | E. Winter |
| Ch. Wendover Soloman | D | 10.6.52 | B | Sh. Ch. Sandylands Justice | Ch. Wendover Topsy | Owners | Mr & Mrs L. C. James |
| Ob. Ch. Amber Sunlight | B | 29.4.48 | Y | Sporting Piper | Beautiful Dreamer | Owner | W. R. Lord |
| Ch. Carena of Heatheridge | B | 25.7.50 | B | Cornblade of Metesford | Susan of Heatheredge | Owner | Miss M. Ward |
| Ch. Creedypark Solo Fitch | B | 31.5.50 | B | F.T. Ch. Scotney Kinsman | Quest of Clarendon Park | Owner | Col H. C. Kingsford Lethbridge |
| Ch. Eaglet of Ulphathwaite | B | 12.5.48 | Y | Braeroy Rumple | Tarnhow's Golden Amy | Owner | Mrs J. C. Cooper |
| Ch. Imp of Blaircourt | B | 22.2.52 | B | Ch. Craigluscar Emperor of Blaircourt | Sandra of Blaircourt | Mr & Mrs Grant Cairns | T. Campbell |
| Ch. Landyke Poppy | B | 8.10.50 | Y | Ch. Poppleton Golden Flight | Lassie of Frieston | W. Tillson | J. Hart |
| Ch. Landyke Velour | B | 17.2.50 | Y | Landyke Ottery Boomerang | Landyke Sally | S. A. Lloyd | Lorna, Countess Howe |
| F.T. Ch. Roffey Gay Time 1955 | B | 12.4.51 | B | Ch. Staindrop Saighdear | Staindrop Glenhead Wren | E. Winter | D. F. Cock |
| F.T. Ch. Crudenbay Bob | D | 11.6.50 | B | Greatford Petitstree Shadow | Crudenbay Jean | Owner | W. A. J. Mackie |
| Ch. Brandy Honey | B | 17.9.50 | Y | Liddly Honey | Jill of Ballinomona | Mrs J. Fox | L. W. Lees |
| Ch. Craigluscar Echo of Lisnamallard | B | 23.3.49 | B | Darky of Elmbank | Craigluscar Black Gem | D. Reid | Mrs A. Hayes |
| F.T. Ch. Hiwood Gypsey | B | 17.5.52 | B | F.T. Ch. Glenhead Zuider | Hiwood Peggy | Owner | Lady J. Hill-Wood |

| Name | Sex | Born | Colour | Sire | Dam | Breeder | Owner |
|---|---|---|---|---|---|---|---|
| Ch. Judith Aikshaw | B | 25.12.51 | Y | Woodlands Major | Woodlands Queen | Miss H. M. Dennis | Dr G. E. & Master / D. R. C. McVitie |
| Ch. Lady of Tring | B | 21.5.50 | Y | Ch. Ballyduff Orangeman | Queene of Battlersgreen | A. Hill | F. Marland |
| F.T. Ch. Sophronia | B | 1.9.51 | B | Balmuto Burns | Balmuto Biddy | D. Black | J. Milne |
| Ob. Ch. Wanda of Tankersley | B | 5.10.50 | C | Haygreen Milk Punch | Haygreen Tawny | Miss V. Hay | Miss U. Ogle |

**1956**

| Name | Sex | Born | Colour | Sire | Dam | Breeder | Owner |
|---|---|---|---|---|---|---|---|
| F.T. Ch. Eastwalton Blackberry | D | 26.2.53 | B | F.T. Ch. Hiwood Dan | Eastwalton Pimpernel | Owner | Lt-Col E. H. M. Unwin |
| F.T. Ch. Galleywood Shot | D | 10.2.54 | B | F.T. Ch. Staindrop Murton Marksman | Hiwood Peggy | Lady J. Hill-Wood | W. Lawrence Taylor |
| F.T. Ch. Hanlye Bobby | D | 3.3.53 | B | F.T. Ch. Hiwood Dan | Hanlye Topsy | Sir Robert Black, Bt | Mrs F. Fairfax Ross |
| F.T. Ch. Harpersbrook Poacher | D | 12.10.53 | B | Oxendon Mick | Princess Sheba | R. J. Ryley | F. George |
| F.T. Ch. Roffey Gamble | D | 3.3.52 | B | Greatford Pettistree Shadow | Galleywood Swallow | Owner | D. F. Cock |
| Ch. Tibshelf Joyful | D | 22.3.50 | B | Ch. Louvil of Tibshelf | Sandmar of Tibshelf | Owner | J. G. Severn |
| Ch. Whatstandwell Coronet | D | 3.12.51 | Y | F.T. Ch. Whatstandwell Hiwood Brand | Ch. Honey of Whatstandwell | Mr & Mrs H. Taylor | Mrs E. Salisbury |
| F.T. Ch. Corndean Sherry | B | 26.5.53 | B | Shavington Ted | Brackenbank Jessie | G. Smith | T. J. Greatorex |
| F.T. Ch. Greatford Seal | B | 19.2.52 | B | Greatford Pettistree Shadow | F.T. Ch. Greatford Uffington Brandysnap | Owner | Maj H. M. Peacock |
| F.T. Ch. Hiwood Amber | B | 10.2.54 | Y | F.T. Ch. Staindrop Murton Marksman | Hiwood Peggy | Owner | Lady J. Hill-Wood |
| F.T. Ch. Norham Blackie | B | 6.12.53 | B | F.T. Ch. Glenhead Zuider | Venny Queen | T. Davidson | W. Campbell |
| Ch. Roberta of Coohoy | B | 11.9.51 | B | Ch. Whatstandwell Ballyduff Robin | Wanda of Coohoy | Mrs D. Cliffe & Miss J. Hoyland | Mrs D. Cliffe |

| Name | | Date | Sire | Dam | Breeder | Owner |
|---|---|---|---|---|---|---|
| Ch. Tiny of Cromlix | B | 14.3.53 | F.T. Ch. Glenhead Zuider | Dinah of Cromlix | Owner | Hon Mrs Drummond of Cromlix |
| **1957** | | | | | | |
| F.T. Ch. Tittenley Jimmy | D | 27.5.53 | Shavington Ted | Staindrop Winkie | W. Laurence Taylor | Miss K. Eason |
| F.T. Ch. Creedypark Stella | B | 8.2.55 | F.T. Ch. Galleywood Swift | Creedypark Slipper | Col H. C. Kingsford-Lethbridge | Mrs G. M. Benson |
| F.T. Ch. Heathside Roots | B | 24.7.52 | Heathside Stubble | Redeal Gipsy | H. C. Leader | Mrs B. Harcourt Wood |
| Ch. Zelstone Leap Year Lass | B | 29.2.52 | Braedrop Bruce | F.T. Ch. Zelstone Darter | Owner | Mrs A. M. Radclyffe |
| Ch. Artistry Laffah | D | 15.11.53 | Ladybower Musketeer | Artistry Gleam | Owner | Lt-Col L. H. Morris |
| F.T. Ch. Avenham Dictator | D | 22.4.54 | Shavington, Ted | Sandylands Judetta | Owner | F. K. Atkinson |
| F.T. Ch. Brackenbank Tanner | D | 30.1.54 | F.T. Ch. Brackenbank Jasper | Brackenbank Gym Chuillinn | Owner | R. N. Burton |
| Ch. Cedar Woodland | D | 27.4.52 | Sandalwood | Susan of Hayward | Mrs E. White | Mrs F. B. Morton Ball |
| Cornlands Peter So Gay | D | 22.5.53 | Ch. Diant Swandyke Cream Cracker | Flush of Cornlands | Owner | Mrs D. P. Rae |
| F.T. Ch. Galleywood Shot | D | 10.2.54 | F.T. Ch. Staindrop Murton Marksman | Hiwood Peggy | Lady J. Hill-Wood | W. L. Taylor |
| Ch. Laird of Lochaber | D | 23.7.53 | Treesholme Trigger | Thrill of Treesholme | H. Smith, Jnr | J. W. Alexander |
| F.T. Ch. Peteradee | D | 24.6.53 | F.T. Ch. Grouseadee | Shelcot Sue | J. D. Blyth | R. S. Wilkins |
| F.T. Ch. Sheena's Mist | D | 9.1.53 | Dan O'Hattie | Amber Glint | W. B. MacLaren | J. Tait |
| **1958** | | | | | | |
| F.T. Ch. Hiwood Dipper | D | 28.1.56 | F.T. Ch. Greatford Teal | F.T. Ch. Hiwood Gypsey | Owner | Lady J. Hill-Wood |
| F.T. Ch. Johnlaw Pip | D | 29.1.56 | Staindrop Ringleader | Shrivenham Susan | C. Wroe | J. A. Taylor |
| F.T. Ch. Roffey Dunlop | D | 22.5.55 | F.T. Ch. Glenhead Zuider | Roffey Sally | Owner | D. F. Cock |
| Ch. Ruler of Blaircourt | D | 21.4.56 | Forbes of Blaircourt | Olivia of Blaircourt | Owners | Mr & Mrs Grant Cairns |
| F.T. Ch. Strattonley Raven | D | 6.7.54 | Dullingham Danger | Strattonley Rita | J. Purbrick | Lord Rank |

| Name | Sex | Born | Colour | Sire | Dam | Breeder | Owner |
|---|---|---|---|---|---|---|---|
| Ch. Charlotte Queen | B | 15.4.52 | Y | Cornblade of Metesford | Cornhill Queen | Mrs L. C. Coulder | C. E. R. Mellor |
| F.T. Ch. Churn Jet | B | 1.5.54 | B | Dullingham Danger | Wisper | Col A. Scrope | Sir Charles Colston |
| Ch. Diant Juliet | B | 27.5.47 | Y | Diant Swandyke Cream Cracker | Diant Reflection | Mrs J. M. Steeds | Mrs L. Wilson Jones |
| Ch. Jasmin of Heatheredge | B | 28.4.55 | Y | Whatstandwell Seeker | Bliss of Heatheredge | Owner | Miss M. Ward |
| F.T. Ch. Zelstone Moss | B | 29.1.56 | Y | Bench | Ch. Zelstone Leap Year Lass | Owner | Mrs A. Radclyffe |
| **1959** | | | | | | | |
| Ch. Cookridge Otter | D | 22.8.52 | B | Cookridge Roamer | Careena of Heatheredge | Miss M. Ward | Mrs M. Y. Pauling |
| F.T. Ch. Glenfarg Brigg | D | 5.4.56 | B | F.T. Ch. Greatford Teal | F.T. Ch. Norham Blackie | Owner | Mrs B. Harcourt-Wood |
| Sh. Ch. Sam of Blaircourt | D | 11.6.57 | B | Hawk of Luscander | Olivia of Blaircourt | Mr & Mrs Grant Cairns | Mrs G. B. Lambert |
| F.T. Ch. Scotney Jingle | D | 9.5.57 | B | Scotney Dusty | Macdap Moya | Col F.M. Bucher | Lord Rank |
| Sh. Ch. Silver Stanshang | D | 5.7.56 | Y | Ch. General of Garshangan | Shelagh of Zoar | Owner | Mrs F. M. Margerison |
| Sh. Ch. Dorbrudden Debonnet | B | 28.3.54 | Y | Ch. Cookridge Intelligence | Dorbrudden Derrcaw Easter Bonnet | Owner | Mrs K. Phillips |
| Ch. Gussie of Garshangan | B | 9.8.56 | C | Ch. Gold Rand of Glengour | Grace of Garshangan | Owners | Lt-Col & Mrs M. H. L. Hill |
| Sh. Ch. Kinley Curlew of Ulphathwaite | B | 17.7.55 | Y | Kinley Comet | Oriole of Ulphathwaite | Mrs J. C. Cooper | F. G. Wrigley |
| Ch. Kinley Melody | B | 27.3.56 | Y | Ch. Whatstandwell Coronet | Kinley Charm | Owner | F. G. Wrigley |
| F.T. Ch. Nazeing Soot | B | 21.9.52 | B | Nazeing Butch | Nazeing Nigger | Owner | Mrs R. Crawshay |
| Ch. Romantic of Coohoy | B | 11.9.51 | B | Ch. Whatstandwell Ballyduff Robin | Wanda of Coohoy | Mrs D. Cliffe & Miss J. Hoyland | Mrs A. Hardy |

| Name | Sex | Date | Sire | Dam | Breeder | Owner |
| --- | --- | --- | --- | --- | --- | --- |
| Ch. Rookwood Honeysuckle 1960 | B | 28.6.55 | Ch. Diant Swandyke Cream Cracker | Mandy of Breakneck Farm | Owner | Mrs M. E. Saffell |
| F.T. Ch. Glenfarg Ben | D | 5.4.56 | F.T. Ch. Greatford Teal | F.T. Ch. Norham Blackie | Owner | Mrs B. Harcourt-Wood |
| Ch. Holton Lancelot | D | 14.4.56 | Ch. Holton Baron | Ch. Holton Pipit | Owners | Mr C. W. & Miss D. L. T. Gilliat |
| F.T. Ch. Lambdale Simon | D | 4.4.56 | F.T. Ch. Glenhead Zuider | Glennewton Wisp | Owner | Mrs C. C. Lamb |
| Ch. Landyke Lancer | D | 5.2.57 | Nokeener Novelcracker | Ch. Landyke Poppy | Owner | J. Hart |
| Sh. Ch. Landyke Stormer | Y | 5.2.57 | Nokeener Novelcracker | Ch. Landyke Poppy | Owner | J. Hart |
| Ch. Loughderg Ket | D | 13.4.58 | Loughderg Strokestown Urch | Beau Regard | J. C. Denning | Mrs J. Sim |
| Ch. Midnight of Mansergh | D | 24.4.54 | Hallbroom Sportsman | Cora of Mansergh | Owner | Mrs M. Roslin-Williams |
| F.T. Ch. Nazeing Mick | D | 1.5.56 | Greatford Kip | Nazeing Soot | Mr & Mrs C. F. Crawshay | Mrs C. Crawshay |
| Ch. Sandylands Tweed of Blaircourt | D | 25.6.58 | Ch. Ruler of Blaircourt | Sh. Ch. Tessa of Blaircourt | Mr & Mrs Grant Cairns | Mrs G. Broadley |
| F.T. Ch. Sendhurst Zelstone Tinker | D | 3.3.59 | F.T. Ch. Galleywood Shot | Galleywood Pigeon | Mrs A. Radclyffe | R. S. Wilkins |
| F.T. Ch. Sendhurst Galleywood Monty | D | 6.4.57 | F.T. Ch. Galleywood Shot | Strattonley Ruff | Sir Charles Colston | R. S. Wilkins |
| Ch. Corsican Corona | B | 20.2.56 | Ch. Whatstandwell Coronet | Ch. Corsican Quest | Owners | Lt-Col & Mrs C. B. Venn |
| Ch. Guildown Wagtail | B | 16.5.57 | Wendover Daniel | Guildown Ecru | Owner | Miss M. Tomkins |
| Ch. Hollybank Beauty | B | 10.12.58 | Bickerton Salmon Prince | Cookridge Gay Princess | Mrs M. Y. Pauling | Mrs M. Wilkinson |
| F.T. Ch. Ruro Snipe | B | 10.8.56 | F.T. Ch. Greatford Teal | Ruro Black Diamond | A. P. J. Fairfax | R. Grant |

| Name | Sex | Born | Colour | Sire | Dam | Breeder | Owner |
|---|---|---|---|---|---|---|---|
| Ch. Sandylands Cora | B | 6.7.56 | B | Ch. Whatstandwell Coronet | Sandylands Belle of Helenspring | Mrs G. Broadley | Miss M. Thorp |
| Sh. Ch. Tessa of Blaircourt | B | 24.1.57 | Y | Ch. Laird of Lochaber | Ch. Imp of Blaircourt | T. Campbell, Jnr | Mr & Mrs Grant Cairns |

### 1961

| Name | Sex | Born | Colour | Sire | Dam | Breeder | Owner |
|---|---|---|---|---|---|---|---|
| F.T. Ch. Alreoch Skipper | D | 28.11.57 | B | Alreoch Clyde | Wheatrig Tiny | Owners | Mr & Mrs A. Lockhart |
| Sh. Ch. Boyranch Merlin | D | 16.7.56 | B | Strokestown Duke of Blaircourt | Wendover Rachel | Mr & Mrs J. B. Pielow | Mrs D. E. Tucker |
| F.T. Ch. Cornbury Regent | D | 11.3.58 | B | F.T. Ch. Galleywood Shot | Polebrooke Garlenick Smog | Owner | O. P. Watney |
| Ch. Cornlands Westelm Flight | D | 29.6.54 | Y | Ch. Poppleton Lieutenant | Westelm Whisper | Mr & Mrs P. Fountain | Mrs D. P. Rae |
| Ch. Kinley Skipper | D | 27.2.59 | Y | Sh. Ch. Kinley Matador | Kinley Mantilla | G. W. Stevenson | F. G. Wrigley |
| Ch. Loughderg Strokestown Urch | D | 1.7.56 | B | Strokestown Duke of Blaircourt | Lisroyan Lady | Maj S. Hales-Pakenham-Mahon | Mrs J. Sim |
| Ch. Neil of Tomorven | D | 15.8.59 | B | Ch. Ruler of Blaircourt | Wendover Bathsheba | G. C. Neil | T. Cambell |
| F.T. Ch. Rivington Braeroy Swift | D | 2.5.57 | B | Braeroy Bruar | Braeroy Dale | Mrs M. K. Macpherson | Mrs E. K. Thomson |
| Sh. Ch. Sandylands Sam | D | 1.3.59 | B | Sh. Ch. Sam of Blaircourt | Diant Pride | Mrs J. Owen | Mrs G. Broadley |
| Ch. Sandylands Showman of Landrow | D | 1.3.59 | B | Sh. Ch. Sam of Blaircourt | Diant Pride | Mrs J. Owen | E. A. Rowland & Miss K. McCallum |
| F.T. Ch. Shavington Templegrove Trigger | D | 3.8.58 | B | F.T. Ch. Galleywood Shot | Galleywood Tess | W. D. Bell | Mrs A. Heywood-Lonsdale |
| Ch. Ballad of Barra | B | 3.4.57 | Y | Sh. Ch. Kinley Matador | Lady Copper | Owner | Mrs N. Underwood |
| Ch. Bumblikite of Mansergh | B | 20.7.59 | B | Ch. Midnight of Mansergh | Lace of Mansergh | Capt R. Gaisford, R.N. | Mrs M. Roslin Williams |

| Name | Colour | D.O.B. | Sire | Dam | Breeder | Owner |
|---|---|---|---|---|---|---|
| F.T. Ch. Castlemore Black Gem | B | 12.1.57 | Strokesdown Duke of Blaircourt | Ch. Hilldown Sylver | Owner | Mrs B. Eustace Duckett |
| Ch. Dobrudden Miss Debutante | B | 15.4.57 | Ch. Poppleton Lucky Boy | Dobrudden Derrycaw Easter Bonnet | Mrs K. Phillips | Mrs R. M. Chadwick |
| W.T. Ch. Foxhanger Maize | B | 29.5.57 | Copperhill Chearful | Foxhanger Lass | Lady Simpson | Miss D. M. Gowland |
| F.T. Ch. Hallingbury Blackbird | B | 15.2.57 | F.T. Ch. Strattonley Raven | Scotney Char | Owner | V. Routledge |
| F.T. Ch. Mischievous Maid | B (white blaze on chest) | 6.6.54 | F.T. Ch. Brackenbank Jasper | Leighton Lovely | Owner | Col F. M. Bucher |
| F.T. Ch. Scaltback Nell of Glenmorag | B | 17.6.56 | Pinehawk Samuel | Scaltback Bess | E. E. Smith | Maj K. J. Malcolm |
| F.T. Ch. Staindrop Woodstain Tern | B | 9.3.58 | Hiwood Scoter | Staindrop Nipsy | J. Donaldson | Mrs E. Winter |

1962

| Name | Colour | D.O.B. | Sire | Dam | Breeder | Owner |
|---|---|---|---|---|---|---|
| Ch. Ardler Mac | D | 8.7.55 | Ch. Holton Baron | Ardler Jet | Owners | Mr & Mrs D. Hendry |
| Ch. Braeduke Joyful | D | 14.2.59 | Sh. Ch. Landyke Stormer | Diant Joy of Braeduke | Owner | Mrs E. Wynyard |
| Ch. Cornlands Landy | D | 1.1.60 | Ch. Cornlands Westelm Flight | Linda of the Leys | Mrs D. P. Rae | R. L. Rayment |
| Ch. Glenarvey Brand | D | 6.9.57 | Cookridge Otter | Hillside Lady | Owner | Mrs J. Harvey |
| F.T. Ch. Glenfarg Rivertay Ranter | D | 28.5.59 | F.T. Ch. Glenfarg Ben | Newburgh Caution | J. Ross | Mrs B. Harcourt Wood |
| Ch. Rookwood Petergold | D | 4.5.60 | Nokeener Newcracker | Rookwood Honeygold | Owner | Mrs M. E. Saffell |
| F.T. Ch. Scotney Crickleybarrow Pebble | D | 22.3.59 | Shelcot Punch | Creedypark Gay | Mrs H. J. Colburn | Lord Rank |
| F.T. Ch. Wincote Sam | D | 5.11.57 | Hiwood Reeve | East Roy Flight | Mrs E. P. WIlson | A. W. C. Thursby |
| F.T. Ch. Glenfarg Bunting | B | 6.3.58 | Oxendon Shadow | F.T. Ch. Norham Blackie | Owner | Mrs B. Harcourt Wood |

| Name | Sex | Born | Colour | Sire | Dam | Breeder | Owner |
| --- | --- | --- | --- | --- | --- | --- | --- |
| F.T. Ch. Glenfarg Bunting | B | 6.3.58 | B | Oxendon Shadow | F.T. Ch. Norham Blackie | Owner | Mrs B. Harcourt Wood |
| F.T. Ch. Mycur Kate | B | 14.3.57 | B | Emperor of Balbrogie | Gairie | Lord Douglas-Gordon | D. I. Walker |
| Ch. Rookwood Honeyblonde | B | 3.11.59 | C | Ch. Diant Swandyke Cream Cracker | Mandy of Breakneck Farm | Owner | Mrs M. E. Saffell |
| Sh. Ch. Sandylands Tanna | B | 30.5.61 | Y | Sandylands Tan | Sandylands Shadow | Owner | Mrs G. Broadley |
| Ch. Sandylands Truth 1963 | B | 7.10.60 | B | Sandylands Tan | Sandylands Shadow | Owner | Mrs G. Broadley |
| Ch. Ballyduff Hollybranch of Keithray | D | 6.1.62 | B | Ch. Sandylands Tweed of Blaircourt | Ch. Hollybank Beauty | Mrs M. Wilkinson | Dr T. S. Acheson |
| Sh. Ch. Dykewell Clarion of Gorsedale | D | 27.9.59 | Y | Ch. Landyke Lancer | Bergamot Honey-Be | Mrs S. Walker | Mr & Mrs K. T. Freer |
| F.T. Ch. Glenfarg Skid | D | 4.1.57 | B | F.T. Ch. Glenhead Zuider | Ballyduff Eastwalton Sloe | Mrs B. Harcourt Wood | W. G. Meldrum |
| F. T. Ch. Greatford Park | D | 13.2.59 | B | Greatford Glenfarg Brent | Greatford Gerda | V. R. Paravicini | F. George |
| F.T. Ch. Hedenhampark Shot | D | 1.6.60 | B | F.T. Ch. Galleywood Shot | Soda of Sudbourne | J. Cuthbert | F. Clitheroe |
| F.T. Ch. Holdgate Boffin | D | 6.4.59 | B | F.T. Ch. Galleywood Shot | F.T. Ch. Creedypark Stella | Owner | Mrs G. Benson |
| Ch. Brentchase Pompadour | B | 30.10.59 | Y | Cornlands Peter So Gay | Brentchase Polly Flinders | Owner | Mrs L. G. Kinsella |
| Ch. Kinley Copper | B | 8.4.62 | Y | Ch. Kinley Skipper | Kinley Tango | Owner | F. G. Wrigley |
| F.T. Ch. Little Wonder | B | 9.6.60 | B | Ruro Weasel | Dunphail Sue | Owner | Maj F. H. Foster |
| Sh. Ch. Rookwood Silver Dew | B | 18.1.61 | C | Roncott Shandy | Ch. Rookwood Honeysuckle | Owner | Mrs M. E. Saffell |
| Ch. Threepears Sandylands Tania | B | 7.10.60 | Y | Sandylands Tan | Sandylands Shadow | Mrs G. Broadley | Mrs E. Raymond |

| Name | Sex | Date | Sire | Dam | Breeder | Owner |
| --- | --- | --- | --- | --- | --- | --- |
| F.T. Ch. Berrystead Bee | B | 8.8.61 | F.T. Ch. Roffey Dunlop | Glenbruar Beauty | B. Death | W. Charles Williams |
| Ch. Cookridge Tango | B | 23.6.61 | Ch. Sandylands Tweed of Blaircourt | Cookridge Gay Princess | Owner | Mrs M. Y. Pauling |
| Ch. Courtcolman Jess of Glynwood | B | 22.11.61 | Zelstone Tramp | Courtcolman Honey | Mrs V. Wood | Maj A. W. Jones |
| F.T. Ch. Holdgate Vesta | B | 31.3.61 | F.T. Ch. Hiwood Dipper | Holdgate Bramble | Owner | Mrs G. M. Benson |
| W.T. Ch. Karadoc Zanella | B | 28.2.58 | Whatstandwell Andrew | Whatstandwell Janice | Miss J. Horridge | Mr & Mrs J. S. Mason |
| Ch. Odessa of Heatheredge | B | 18.6.61 | Ch. Cookridge Otter | Ch. Jasmin of Heatheredge | Owner | Miss M. Ward |
| F.T. Ch. Zelstone Bonnie | B | 13.5.61 | F.T. Ch. Galleywood Shot | Ch. Zelstone Moss | Owner | Mrs Radclyffe |
| F.T. Ch. Berrystead Bob | D | 29.5.60 | F.T. Ch. Roffey Dunlop | F.T. Ch. Staindrop Woodstain Tern | J. Donaldson | W. C. Williams |
| F.T. Ch. Creedypark Digger | D | 26.2.60 | F.T. Ch. Hiwood Dipper | Creedypark Sapphira | Col H. C. Kingsford-Lethbridge | F. George |
| F.T. Ch. Dacre Hiwood Frank | D | 24.5.62 | F.T. Ch. Hiwood Dipper | Dacre Doll | Lady J. Hill-Wood | Miss A. Hill-Wood |
| F.T. Ch. Hiwood Glenfarg Dirk | D | 6.5.61 | F.T. Ch. Hiwood Dipper | F.T. Ch. Norham Blackie | W. Darling | Lady J. Hill-Wood |
| F.T. Ch. Jensuedee Flash | D | 2.4.59 | Avenham Kneveton Alva | Avenham Beautie | T. Southward | F. Haworth |
| Sh. Ch. Landyke Teal | D | 18.2.60 | Ch. Landyke Lancer | Landyke Bran | Owner | J. k. Hart |
| Ch. Reanacre Mallardhurn Thunder | D | 7.2.60 | Ch. Sandylands Tweed of Blaircourt | Mallardhurn Pat | N. D. Robinson | Mr & Mrs J. Johnson |
| Ch. Roncott Toppa | D | 14.12.61 | Roncott Shandy | Black Jane | Mrs T. Goulder | Miss R. L. Norcott |
| F.T. Ch. Sandringham Ranger | D | 5.2.60 | F.T. Ch. Roffey Dunlop | Sandringham Mask | Owner | H.M. The Queen |
| F.T. Ch. Yoxvale Black Knight | D | 4.4.60 | F.T. Ch. Roffey Dunlop | Black Nell | R. R. Shelley | J. Longhurst |

| Name | Sex | Born | Colour | Sire | Dam | Breeder | Owner |
|---|---|---|---|---|---|---|---|
| **1965** | | | | | | | |
| Ch. Big Brother of Old Forge | D | 15.5.62 | B | Sh. Ch. Sandylands Sam | Black Princess of Old Forge | Owners | Ft-Lt & Mrs R. A. McCosh |
| Sh. Ch. Hollybunch of Keithray | D | 6.1.62 | Y | Ch. Sandylands Tweed of Blaircourt | Ch. Hollybank Beauty | Owner | Mrs M. Wilkinson |
| F.T. Ch. Margerywing Stag | D | 1.1.61 | B | F.T. Ch. Peteradee | Holdgate Beetle | Mr & Mrs J. G. Richards | Mr E. Hill |
| Ch. Sandylands Tandy | D | 30.5.61 | Y | Sandylands Tan | Sandylands Shadow | Owner | Mrs G. Broadley |
| F.T. Ch. Sendhurst Sweep | D | 16.3.61 | B | Scotney Dusk | F.T. Ch. Hallingbury Blackbird | V. Routledge | R. S. Wilkins |
| Ch. Wanderer of Blaircourt | D | 28.8.59 | B | Ch. Ruler of Blaircourt | Snipe of Luscander | Owners | Mr & Mrs Grant Cairns |
| Sh. Ch. Brentchase Pistachio | B | 30.10.59 | Y | Ch. Cornlands Peter So Gay | Brentchase Polly Flinders | Owner | Mrs L. G. Kinsella |
| Sh. Ch. Danecote Delila | B | 15.10.63 | Y | Danecote Risque Duff | Nympton Sue | Owner | Mrs F. Coates |
| F.T. Ch. Gifford Jet | B | 30.8.61 | B | | Beam Betty | P. Martin | Col G. C. Graham |
| Sh. Ch. Hollybeaut of Keithray | B | 6.1.62 | B | Ch. Sandylands Tweed of Blaircourt | Ch. Hollybank Beauty | Owner | Mrs H. Wilkinson |
| Sh. Ch. Landyke Magic | B | 22.2.61 | B | Ch. Landyke Lancer | Tessa of Wittering | Mrs V. M. Hurn | A. N. Wilcox |
| Ch. Poolstead Kinley Willow | B | 18.9.60 | Y | Ch. Kinley Skipper | Sh. Ch. Kinley Curlew of Ulphathwaite | F. G. Wrigley | Mr & Mrs R. V. Hepworth |
| Ch. Sandylands Truth | B | 7.10.60 | B | Sandylands Tan | Sandylands Shadow | Owner | Mrs G. Broadley |
| Sh. Ch. Skelbrook Vanity | B | 21.10.62 | Y | Halsinger Madford March | Reethwood Jan | E. J. Stead | Mr & Mrs E. J. Stead |
| **1966** | | | | | | | |
| F.T. Ch. Avenham Pat | B | 20.2.63 | B | Scotney Dusty | Avenham Roughtor Dido | Owner | F. Atkinson |
| Ch. Follytower Silsdale Old Chelsea | B | 24.6.63 | B | Ch. Braeduke Joyful | Silsdale Glenarvey Quita | Mr & Mrs Dodgson | Mrs H. B. Woolley |

| Name | | Date | Sire | | Dam | Breeder | Owner |
|---|---|---|---|---|---|---|---|
| Ch. Poolstead Powder Puff | B | 27.2.64 | Ch. Reanacre Mallardhurn Thunder | Y | Braeduke Julia of Poolstead | Owners | Mr & Mrs R. V. Hepworth |
| Sh. Ch. Sandylands Katrinka of Keithray | B | 24.3.64 | Ch. Sandylands Tandy | Y | Sh. Ch. Hollybeaut of Keithray | Mrs M. Wilkinson | Mrs G. Broadley |
| Ch. Renacre Tracer | B | 14.8.63 | Ch. Reanacre Mallardhurn Thunder | Y | Reanacre Copperhill Charm | Owners | Mr & Mrs J. Johnson |
| Sh. Ch. Sandylands Troubella | B | 16.11.64 | Ch. Sandylands Tandy | Y | Antonia of Rugby | Mrs Allsop | Mrs G. Broadley |
| F.T. Ch. Staindrop Doune | B | 14.3.63 | F.T. Ch. Templegrafton Jason | B | Staindrop Cindy | Owner | Mrs E. Winter |
| Ch. Baron of Beadles | D | 2.12.61 | Ch. Midnight of Mansergh | B | Teak of Heatheredge | Owners | Mr & Mrs G. A. Jenkin |
| F.T. Ch. Berrystead Berry | D | 22.3.63 | F.T. Ch. Sendhurst Zelstone Sweep | B | F.T. Ch. Berrystead Bee | Owner | W. Williams |
| Ch. Cookridge Cormorant | D | 15.9.62 | Cookridge Jasper | B | Cookridge Olga | Mrs J. Pickles | Mrs M. Y. Pauling |
| Sh. Ch. Garvel of Garshangan | D | 26.1.60 | Ch. General of Garshangan | Y | Ch. Gussie of Garshangan | Lt-Col & Mrs H. H. L. Hill | Mr & Mrs F. Whitbread |
| F.T. Ch. Glenfarg Winterwell Shot | D | 5.6.60 | F.T. Ch. Glenfarg Brigg | B | Winterwell Staindrop Jill | I. Martin | G. Meldrum |
| F.T. Ch. Hallingbury Wild Duck | D | 25.4.63 | F.T. Ch. Scotney Jingle | B | F.T. Ch. Hallingbury Blackbird | Owner | G. T. Routledge |
| Sh. Ch. Landyke Beech | D | 18.9.60 | Ch. Landyke Lancer | Y | Landyke Bran | J. K. Hart | E. Gill |
| F.T. Ch. Ruro Swagman | D | 27.2.63 | F.T. Ch. Cornbury Regent | B | F.T. Ch. Ruro Snipe | Owner | R. Grant |
| F.T. Ch. Strokestown Derry 1967 | D | 18.8.60 | F.T. Ch. Galleywood Shot | Y | Hiwood Widgeon of Strokestown | Owner | Maj S. Hales-Pakenham-Mahon |
| F.T. Ch. Annan of Lanfine | D | 11.3.63 | F.T. Ch. Cornbury Regent | B | Pinkie of Lanfine | Lord Rotherwick | Capt P. Mackinnon |
| Am. & Eng. Ch. Ballyduff Seaman | D | 25.5.66 | Ch. Ballyduff Hollybranch of Keithray | B | Cookridge Negra | Mrs R. Harrison | Mrs B. M. Docking |

| Name | Sex | Born | Colour | Sire | Dam | Breeder | Owner |
| --- | --- | --- | --- | --- | --- | --- | --- |
| F.T. Ch. Coppicewood Ben | D | 11.11.63 | Y | Jerry Jason | Juno of Catlee | Mrs Telfer | Mr & Mrs J. Johnson |
| Ch. Cornlands Kimvalley Crofter | D | 24.12.63 | Y | Ch. Sandylands Tandy | Kimvalley Guildown Cassandra | Mr & Mrs Beckett | Mrs D. P. Rae |
| Sh. Ch. Cornlands Nokeener Highlight | D | 25.2.65 | Y | Cliveruth Harvester | Nokeener Night Light | Mrs R. Williams | Mrs D. P. Rae |
| Sh. Ch. Glenarvey Balbriggan | D | 22.1.65 | Y | Glenarvey Barrister | Warilda Alexis | G. A. Wallace | Mrs J. Harvey |
| Ch. Kimbo of Ardmargha | D | 28.5.66 | Y | Diant Jaysgreen Jasper | Sandylands Komely of Ardmargha | Owners | Mr & Mrs H. W. Clayton |
| Sh. Ch. Ramah Rampant | D | 2.6.62 | Y | Ramah Newgit of Veray | Ramah Sunrise | Mrs J. C. Waring | K. J. Thorne |
| Ch. Sandylands Mark | D | 5.7.65 | B | Ch. Reanacre Mallardhurn Thunder | Ch. Sandylands Truth | Owner | Mrs G. Broadley |
| Sh. Ch. Sandylands Midas | D | 5.2.65 | Y | Ch. Reanacre Mallardhurn Thunder | Ch. Sandylands Truth | Owner | Mrs G. Broadley |
| Ch. Cornlands My Fair Lady | B | 31.7.65 | Y | Ch. Cornlands Kimvalley Crofter | Cornlands Lady Be Good | Owner | Mrs D. P. Rae |
| F.T. Ch. Joys Scamp | B | 14.2.63 | B | Barry of Tarfside | Ruro Blue Bell | A. Inglis | G. Black |
| Ch. Liddly Cornflower | B | 22.4.65 | Y | Liddly Chrysanthemum | Furzeholt Pale Moonlight | Mr D. E. Mann | Mrs E. R. Boyer |
| Sh. Ch. Poolstead Personality of Lawnwood | B | 21.3.65 | Y | Ch. Reanacre Mallardhurn Thunder | Braeduke Julia of Poolstead | Mr & Mrs A. Hepworth | Mrs M. I. Satterthwaite |
| F.T. Ch. Shavington Jericho Jane | B | 13.3.63 | B | Tittenley Simon | Juney for Fame | Mrs R. Monkton | Mrs A. Heywood-Lonsdale |
| F.T. Ch. Sherry of Biteabout | B | 9.4.64 | B | F.T. Ch. Glenfarg Skid | Moorhen of Biteabout | W. Davidson | H.M. The Queen |

| Name | Sex | Date | Sire | Dam | Breeder | Owner |
|---|---|---|---|---|---|---|
| Ch. Staxigoe Stiletto | B | 16.6.64 | F.T. Ch. Glenfarg Skid | Staxigoe Sylph | J. Grant | D. Mackenzie |
| Sh. Ch. Tanya of Keithray 1968 | B | 27.3.65 | Ch. Sandylands Tweed of Blaircourt | Ch. Hollybank Beauty | Mrs M. Wilkinson | Mr J. Boothroyd |
| Sh. Ch. Danecote County Squire | D | 5.4.66 | Reanacre Skeldyke Bo'sun | Lawnhollow Daphne | Mrs Bean | Mrs F. Coates |
| Ch. Lowna Suffolk Gem | D | 23.4.66 | Ch. Reanacre Mallardhurn Thunder | Sh. Ch. Rookwood Silver Dew | Mmes Lamming & Saffel | C. L. Lamming |
| F.T. Ch. Mycur Magnus | D | 13.5.65 | F.T. Ch. Glenfarg Skid | Kate of Carmyllie | J. S. Sharp | D. I. Walker |
| Ch. Reanacre Twister | D | 14.8.63 | Ch. Reanacre Mallardhurn Thunder | Reanacre Copperhill Charm | Owners | Mr & Mrs J. Johnson |
| Sh. Ch. Tadfield Black Shadow | D | 22.1.62 | Ch. Ruler of Blaircourt | Millstone Mockbeetle | Owner | Mrs Morrison-Jones |
| Ch. Wishwood Winston | D | 24.11.64 | Cornlands Cedar | Cornlands Copper Rose | Owners | Mr & Mrs C. R. Rayment |
| F.T. Ch. Cornbury Ruro Teal | B | 27.2.63 | F.T. Ch. Cornbury Regent | F.T. Ch. Ruro Snipe | R. Grant | H. C. Henderson |
| F.T. Ch. Corsican Bellewarde Tessa | B | 18.5.66 | F.T. Ch. Creedypark Digger | Waitenhill Quail | Mrs H. Wiley | Mrs C. B. Venn |
| Ch. Damson of Mansergh | B | 6.3.65 | Reanacre Sandylands Tarmac | Ch. Bumblikite of Mansergh | Owner | Mrs Roslin Williams |
| Sh. Ch. Kenbara Jill | B | 15.1.65 | Halsinger Madford March | Sandyland Kaprice | Owner | Mrs B. M. Vipond |
| W.T. Ch. Linnifold Blarney | B | 25.6.62 | Linnifold Loughderg Churchman | Karadoc Zanella | Owners | Mr & Mrs J.S. Mason |
| F.T. Ch. Sandringham Slipper | B | 18.4.66 | F.T. Ch. Glenfarg Skid | Sandringham Juniper | Owner | H.M. The Queen |
| Sh. Ch. Sandylands Dancer | B | 20.3.66 | Diant Jaysgreen Jasper | Trewinnard Sandylands Tanita | Owner | Mrs G. Broadley |

| Name | Sex | Born | Colour | Sire | Dam | Breeder | Owner |
|---|---|---|---|---|---|---|---|
| **1969** | | | | | | | |
| F.T. Ch. Wolviston Bob | D | 12.4.63 | B | F.T. Ch. Sendhurst Zelstone Tinker | Irbymarsh Tide | P. Sinclair | D. Townsend |
| F.T. Ch. Beinhmhor Tide | B | 24.3.67 | B | Beinhmhor Venom | F.T. Ch. Cornbury Ruro Teal | H. Henderson | Capt D. Mackinnon |
| F.T. Ch. Berrystead Bramble | B | 7.5.66 | B | F.T. Ch. Creedypark Digger | F.T. Ch. Berrystead Bee | Owner | W.C. Williams |
| F.T. Ch. Burnhatch Linn of Dee | B | 3.2.66 | B | Burnhatch Comptondene Sam | Burnhatch Dee | Owner | Hon. Mrs N. Hopkinson |
| Sh. Ch. Glenarem Wilkamaur Cascade | B | 2.5.67 | Y | Glenarem Gay Fallow | Shan of Westelnz | Mr & Mrs Wilkinson | Mr & Mrs A. Greenhalgh |
| Ch. Glendale Penny | B | 10.6.66 | Y | Braejoy Nightingale | Glenalton Sheila | Mrs A. Thomson | Mrs J. Nolan |
| Sh. Ch. Kinley Spruce | B | 3.6.66 | Y | Kinley Sandylands Kricketer | Kinley Fantasy | Owner | F. G. Wrigley |
| Ch. Liddly Buddleia | B | 6.4.66 | B | Liddly Chrysanthemum | Rhodina Wendy | Mrs E. A. K. Small | H. A. Saunders |
| Sh. Ch. Sandylands Star of Jayncourt | B | 13.9.67 | Y | Sh. Ch. Sandylands Midas | Jayncourt Michelle | Mr & Mrs P. H. Palmer | Mrs G. Broadley |
| F.T. Ch. Sarumvale Amy | B | 21.12.63 | B | F.T. Ch. Scotney Jingle | Sarum Wendy | Owner | Lt-Cdr P. A. Whitehead |
| Sh. Ch. Stanwood Leda | B | 6.7.64 | Y | Ch. Kinley Skipper | Stanwood Solomans Queen | Owner | Mrs J. M. Hurley |
| **1969** | | | | | | | |
| F.T. Ch. Ballyfrema Moonshot of Triple Crown | D | 1.6.66 | B | Ballyfrema Sammy of Sean Baile | Ballyfrema Ranee | Mrs R. Tenison | R. C. O'Farrell |
| Sh. Ch. Brentville Daniel | D | 16.11.65 | Y | Ch. Sandylands Tandy | Manorroy Marchioness | Owner | Mrs B. M. Taylor |
| Ch. Candlemas Rookwood Silver Moonlight | D | 28.4.64 | Y | Ch. Sandylands Tweed of Blaircourt | Sh. Ch. Rookwood Silver Dew | Mrs Saffell | Mrs J. Kneller |

| Name | Sex | Date | | Sire | Dam | Owner | Owner |
|---|---|---|---|---|---|---|---|
| Ch. Gay Piccolo of Lawnwood | D | 9.7.65 | C | Bradyke Silsdale Music Man | Spinneyhill Lilac of Lawnwood | of Owner | Mrs M. I. Satterthwaite |
| F.T. Ch. Glenfarg Dante | D | 6.5.61 | B | F.T. Ch. Hiwood Dipper | F.T. Ch. Norham Blackie | Mrs B. Harcourt-Wood | G. Meldrum |
| Ch. Kingsbury Nokeener Moonstar | D | 30.3.68 | Y | Sh. Ch. Nokeener Moonrocket | Nokeener Nightlight | Mrs R. Williams | Mrs G. M. Preston |
| Sh. Ch. Poolstead President | D | 2.4.66 | Y | Sh. Ch. Hollybunch of Keithray | Braeduke Julia of Poolstead | Owners | Mr & Mrs R. V. Hepworth |
| Sh. Ch. Skelbrook Swift | D | 1.11.65 | Y | Plainsman of Skelbrook | Kimvalley Carousel | Owners | Mr & Mrs E. J. Stead |
| F.T. Ch. Staxigoe Snap | D | 2.2.67 | B | Staxigoe Shackle | Larkhall Sheila | C. Milne | D. Mackenzie |
| Sh. Ch. Trewinnard Vagabond 1970 | D | 29.9.66 | Y | Trewinnard Skiff | Bramble of Trentdene | C. W. Scott | T. R. Pasco |
| F.T. Ch. Baldovie Barrister | D | 23.3.68 | Y | Baldovie Banker | Milltimber Jill | Mrs A. Glashen | W. W. Blair |
| F.T. Ch. Brampton Dipper | D | 27.5.66 | B | F.T. Ch. Creedypark Digger | Stella of Brampton | L. Wilson | F. George |
| Ch. Cornlands Young Emperor | D | 3.3.66 | Y | Rookwood Silver Tweed | Cornlands Cream Susan | Owner | Mrs D. P. Rae |
| Ch. Dale of Tarmac | D | 8.4.66 | B | Reanacre Sandylands Tarmac | Ellerthwaites Polly Cinders | Miss A. G. Rogers | E. G. Holyoake |
| Sh. Nokeener Moonrocket | D | 15.3.67 | Y | Ch. Candlemas Rockwood Silver Moonlight | Nokeener New Novel | Owner | Mrs R. Williams |
| Ch. Othamcourt Shane of Suddie | D | 30.1.69 | Y | Kimvalley Kenbarra Mr Softee | Minivet of Suddie | Miss Simmonds | Mr & Mrs E. H. Climpson |
| Sh. Ch. Rebma Byng | D | 18.11.64 | B | Ch. Ballyduff Hollybranch of Keithray | Rebma Sweet Fairy | Owners | Mr & Mrs V. Lewis |
| Sh. Ch. Tadfield Kirbyhall Sherpa | D | 29.10.65 | B | Tadfield Black Shadow | Kirbyhall Muffin | Mrs P. Hoar | Mrs M. Morrison Jones |
| F.T. Ch. Tendring Sam | D | 23.3.64 | Y | Red Masterpiece | Vain Lady | J. Currah | Sir Joshua Rowley |

| Name | Sex | Born | Colour | Sire | Dam | Breeder | Owner |
| --- | --- | --- | --- | --- | --- | --- | --- |
| F.T. Ch. Avenham Jenny | B | 18.5.65 | B | Staindrop Talent | Avenham Roughter Dido | F. Atkinson | J. A. Kersley |
| Sh. Ch. Brentchase Kimvalley Rosanna | B | 13.8.67 | Y | Ch. Sandylands Mark | Kimvalley Brentchase Anita | Mr & Mrs D. Beckett | Mrs L. G. Kinsella |
| F.T. Ch. Burnhatch Leader | B | 3.2.66 | B | Burnhatch Comptondene Sam | Burnhatch Dee | Hon. Mrs Hopkinson | R. D. Methuen |
| Sh. Ch. Glenarem Caprice | B | 16.7.67 | Y | Ch. Sandylands Tandy | Glenarem Saucy Sheba | Owners | Mr & Mrs A. Greenhalgh |
| F.T. Ch. Hedenhampark Halcot Fay | B | 14.3.67 | B | F.T. Ch. Hallingbury Wild Duck | Holcot Brackenbank Heidi | F. Howlett | F. Clitheroe |
| Ch. Leyward Magic | B | 8.4.67 | Y | Sh. Ch. Sandylands Midas | Leyward Little Wonder | Mrs R. V. Woodward | Mr & Mrs R. A. Jelley |
| Sh. Ch. Roydwood Right On Time | B | 6.7.68 | Y | Roydwood Reveller | Brentchase Kilkee | K. Mathews | M. J. Boothroyd |
| F.T. Ch. Seal of Glenmorag | B | 23.5.66 | B | F.T. Ch. Dacre Hiwood Frank | Polly of Glenmorag | Owner | Maj Malcolm |
| Ch. Tamstar Glenfield Mischief | B | 13.6.66 | Y | Braeduke Star Worthy | Wendover Crocus | Mr & Mrs L. C. James | Mr & Mrs F. W. Crisp |
| **1971** | | | | | | | |
| F.T. Ch. Trentlock Beat | B | 1.6.66 | B | F.T. Ch. Margerywing Stag | Burghwood Gay | E. Hill | Mrs P. J. Cunningham |
| F.T. Ch. Black Meg of Albury | B | 5.4.68 | B | F.T. Ch. Berrystead Berry | Tiny Tiche of Albury | A. Mitchell-Innes | A. L. Gibb |
| F.T. Ch. Holdgate Willie | D | 6.6.69 | B | Holdgate Steven | Wing of Ruckley | R. Baxter | Mrs D. Benson |
| F.T. Ch. Strattonley Plover | B | 9.6.64 | B | Glenbruar Ranger | Strattonley Eider | Mrs D. Purbrick | B. Death |
| Sh. Ch. Ramah Benedictus | D | 18.9.67 | Y | Ramah Newgit of Veray | Tadfield Black Charm | J. W. R. Swayne | Mrs J. Waring |
| Ch. Follytower Poolstead Pinafore | B | 7.68 | B | Ch. Reanacre Mallardhurn Thunder | Poolstead Pincushion | Mr & Mrs V. Hepworth | Mrs M. Woolley |

| Name | Sex | Date | | Sire | Dam | Breeder | Owner |
|---|---|---|---|---|---|---|---|
| W.T. Ch. Manymills Tanne | B | 7.3.65 | Y | Ch. Sandylands Tandy | Manymills Lucky Charm | Owner | Mrs S. G. Pickup |
| Sh. Ch. Colinwood Fern | B | 12.9.68 | Y | Ch. Sandylands Tandy | Redgame Liz's Daughter | P. C. Woolf | Mr & Mrs P. Woolf |
| Sh. Ch. Sandylands Garry | D | 28.4.68 | Y | Sandylands General | Sandylands Memory | Owner | Mrs G. Broadley |
| Ch. Timspring Mace | D | 23.9.69 | Y | Timspring Martin | Ch. Timspring Jubilant | Owner | Mrs J. Macan |
| Sh. Ch. Sandylands Holly | B | 12.1.69 | B | Pinchbeck Nokeener Harvest Home | Ch. Sandylands Truth | Mrs G. Broadley | Mrs R. V. Clark |
| Sh. Ch. Strinesdale Showman | D | 9.9.69 | B | Ch. Sandylands Mark | Contesa of Keithray | Owner | F. Belshaw |
| Ch. Timspring Jubilant | B | 20.7.67 | Y | Ch. Braeduke Joyful | Timspring Landyke Venus | Owner | Mr J. Macan |
| Sh. Ch. Sandylands Honour | B | 12.1.69 | Y | Pinchbeck Nokeener Harvest Home | Ch. Sandylands Truth | Owner | Mrs G. Broadley |
| Sh. Ch. & Ir. Ch. Kinky of Keithray | D | 29.1.69 | B | Am. & Eng. Ch. Ballyduff Seaman | Sh. Ch. Hollybeaut of Keithray | Mr & Mrs J. Wilkinson | Mrs M. Haffey |
| Ch. Kilree of Ardmargha | B | 18.10.65 | Y | Diant Jaysgreen Jasper | Sandylands Komely of Ardmargha | Owners | Mr & Mrs H. W. Clayton |
| Sh. Ch. Lawnwoods Fame and Fortune | D | 15.11.67 | Y | Rockabee Tobin | Spinneyhill Lilac of Lawnwood | Owner | Mrs H. I. Satterthwaite |
| F.T. Ch. Wheatrig Irrepressible 1972 | D | 17.6.67 | B | Wheatrig Commodore | Wheatrig Attractive | Owner | T. Ramsey |
| Ch. Deeside Sultan | D | 13.6.68 | B | Ch. Sandylands Tandy | Deeside Lunar Velvet | Owner | Miss M. H. Abell |
| Ch. Ballyduff Marina | B | 18.5.69 | B | Am. & Eng. Ch. Ballyduff Seaman | Electron of Ardmargha | Mrs E. M. Butchart | Mrs B. M. Docking |
| Sh. Ch. Sandylands My Lad | D | 31.5.70 | Y | Ch. Sandylands Mark | Sandylands Good Gracious | Owner | Mrs G. Broadley |
| Ch. Mansergh Antonia | B | 27.5.70 | B | Ch. Sandylands Mark | Ch. Damson of Mansergh | Owner | Mrs M. Roslin-Williams |

| Name | Sex | Born | Colour | Sire | Dam | Breeder | Owner |
| --- | --- | --- | --- | --- | --- | --- | --- |
| Sh. Ch. Kimvalley Picklewitch | B | 16.7.70 | B | Ch. Sandylands Mark | Shanbally Sapphire | R. H. & A. M. Shorbrook | Mmes Beckett & Clark |
| Ch. Faith of Ardmargha | B | 31.10.69 | Y | Ch. Sandylands Tandy | Ch. Kilree of Ardmargha | Owners | Mr & Mrs H. W. Clayton |
| F.T. Ch. Lambdale Shaun | D | 4.3.68 | Y | F.T. Ch. Lambdale Simon | Glenfarg Belle | Mr & Mrs E. Lamb | Mrs M. Lamb |
| F.T. Ch. Jericho Jingo 1973 | D | 31.5.67 | B | Rockstead Footswish | Jericho Jet | Owner | Mrs S. Monkton |
| Ch. Follytower Merrybrook Black Stormer | D | 7.6.69 | B | Ch. Sandylands Tandy | Follytower Old Black Magic | Mrs J. I. & Mr D. J. R. Hoare | Mrs M. Woolley |
| Ch. Mansergh Moleskin | B | 11.2.70 | B | Ch. Dale of Tarmac | Musquash of Mansergh | Owner | Mrs Roslin-Williams |
| Sh. Ch. Othamcourt Sinead | B | 9.5.71 | Y | Sh. Ch. Othamcourt Shane of Suddie | Grainne of Suddie | Mr & Mrs E. H. Climpson | T. A. Salaman |
| Ch. Sam of Suddie | D | 30.1.69 | Y | Kimvalley Kenbara Mr Softee | Minivet of Suddie | Owner | Miss F. H. Simmonds |
| Sh. Ch. Linershwood Sentinal | D | 15.2.70 | Y | Sh. Ch. Tadfield Kirbyhall Sherpa | Linershwood Crystal of Keithray | Owner | Mrs D. H. Coulson |
| Ch. Powhatan Solo | D | 15.6.68 | Y | Powhatan Percy | Powhatan Tonic | Owners | Maj & Mrs R. C. Aikenhead |
| Sh. Ch. Roydwood Royal Tara | B | 1.10.68 | Y | Ch. Sandylands Tandy | Sh. Ch. Tanya of Keithray | Owner | Mr M. J. Boothroyd |
| Ch. Oakhouse Glenarem Classic | D | 30.3.70 | Y | Sh. Ch. Sandylands Garry | Sh. Ch. Glenarm Wilkamaur Cascade | Mr & Mrs A. Greenhalgh | Mrs L. Litherland |
| F.T. Ch. Craighorn Dirk | D | 17.2.69 | B | F.T. Ch. Glenfarg Dante | Trentlock Jet | D. Stewart | Mr J. Moffat |
| F.T. Ch. Hedenhampark Bonnie | B | 9.6.68 | B | F.T. Ch. Palgrave Edward | Bedinham Hall Jet | H. N. Hanmer | J. W. Farrow |
| Sh. Ch. Ardmargha Sandylands Giselle | B | 26.9.70 | Y | Sh. Ch. Sandylands Garry | Sh. Ch. Sandylands Dancer | Mrs G. Broadley | Mr & Mrs H. W. Clayton |

| Name | Sex | Date | Sire | Breeder | Dam | Owner |
|---|---|---|---|---|---|---|
| F.T. Ch. Swinbrook Tan | D | 25.4.70 | F.T. Ch. Palgrave Edward | Owner | F.T. Ch. Beinnmhor Tide | D. Mackinnon |
| F.T. Ch. Berrystead Glenbruar Beau | D | 28.8.67 | Berrystead Fenfarm Barley | B. Death | Strattonley Plover | W. C. Williams |
| Ch. Groucho of Mansergh | D | 12.9.69 | Ch. Sandylands Mark | Owner | Sardonyx of Mansergh | Mrs Roslin-Williams |
| F.T. Ch. Angeltown's Black Sapphire | B | 6.6.68 | Jericho Joker | Owner | Little Angel | Mrs Townsend |
| F.T. Ch. Beinnmhor Tithe | B | 24.3.67 | Beinnmhor Venom | H. C. Henderson | Cornbury Ruro Teal | J. A. Wilson |
| Ch. Curnafane Seamansal | B | 24.5.69 | Am. & Eng. Ch. Ballyduff Seaman | Mrs E. M. Butchart | Electron of Ardmargha | Mrs R. Harrison |
| Sh. Ch. Sandylands Blaze | D | 10.5.71 | Sandylands Charlie Boy | Owner | Sandylands Gojo | Mrs G. Broadley |
| Sh. Ch. Sandylands Midnight Magic | B | 3.1.71 | Ch. Sandylands Mark | Owner | Sh. Ch. Sandylands Katrinka of Keithray | Mrs G. Broadley |
| Ch. Roseacre Siani | B | 19.3.70 | Ch. Kingsbury Nokeener Moonstar | Owner | Honeysuckle of Roseacre | Miss N. Hudson |
| Sh. Ch. Nokeener May Blossom of Lasgarn 1974 | B | 22.5.71 | Ch. Sandylands Mark | Mrs R. Williams | Firholme Tania | Messrs E. G. & R. L. Edwards |
| Sh. Ch. Heatherbourne Lawnwoods Laughing Cavalier | D | 19.8.69 | Ch. Gay Piccolo of Lawnwood | Mrs M. I. Sattherthwaite | Ch. Poolstead Personality of Lawnwood | Mrs H. G. Wiles |
| Ch. Sandylands Geannie | B | 26.9.70 | Sh. Ch. Sandylands Garry | Mrs G. Broadley | Sh. Ch. Sandylands Dancer | Mrs Chapman |
| Sh. Ch. Tidesreach Neptune | D | 16.8.70 | Ch. Candlemas Rookwood Silver Moonlight | Mr & Mrs H. F. Lewis | Tidesreach Shenandoa | Mrs M. I. Satterthwaite |
| Sh. Ch. Sandylands Girl Friday | B | 27.3.70 | Sh. Ch. Sandylands Garry | Owners | Trewinnards Sandylands Tanita | Mrs G. Broadley & G. Anthony |

| Name | Sex | Born | Colour | Sire | Dam | Breeder | Owner |
|---|---|---|---|---|---|---|---|
| Sh. Ch. Sandylands Waghorn Honesty | B | 7.11.71 | Y | Ch. Sandylands Tandy | Sh. Ch. Sandylands Honour | Mrs C. Y. Lewis | Mrs G. Broadley & G. Anthony |
| Sh. Ch. Sandylands Strinsdale O'Malley | D | 3.10.71 | B | Eng. & Aus. Ch. Sandylands My Lad | Contessa of Keithray | F. Belshaw | Mrs G. Broadley & G. Anthony |
| Sh. Ch. Poolstead Popularity | B | 21.5.70 | Y | Ch. Sandylands Tandy | Poolstead Pussywillow | Owners | Mr & Mrs R. V. Hepworth |
| Sh. Ch. Poolstead Problem | D | 18.6.72 | Y | Eng. & Aus. Ch. Sandylands My Lad | Poolstead Pussywillow | Owners | Mr & Mrs R. V. Hepworth |
| Sh. Ch. Poolstead Porcelain | B | 10.3.69 | Y | Rockabee Tobin | Ch. Poolstead Powder Puff | Owners | Mr & Mrs R. V. Hepworth |
| Sh. Ch. Follytower Merry Go Round of Brentville | B | 20.1.72 | C | Ch. Follytower Merrybrook Black Stormer | Follytower Artemis | Mrs M. Woolley | Mrs B. M. Taylor |
| Sh. Ch. Nokeener Taffy | D | 11.1.70 | Y | Ch. Reanacre Twister | Birdrock Nokeener New Moon | Mrs Rogan | Mrs R. Williams |
| Sh. Ch. Longley Count On | D | 6.5.71 | Y | Sandylands Chalrie Boy | Sandylands Co Lightly of Longley | Owner | Mr & Mrs G. Kenningley |
| Sh. Ch. Lowna Suffolk Rhus | B | 23.12.69 | Y | Ch. Lowna Suffolk Gem | Lowna Candlemas Sigurd | Owner | Mr & Mrs C. L. Lamming |
| F.T. Ch. Sandringham Sydney | D | 14.5.70 | Y | F.T. Ch. Creedypark Digger | F.T. Ch. Sherry of Biteabout | Owner | H.M. The Queen |
| F.T. Ch. Strathfieldsaye Calcot Crossbow | D | 3.6.70 | Y | Calcot Blaise | Persian Pride | W. Rice Adams | The Duke of Wellington |
| F.T. Ch. Barnavara May Fly | B | 10.5.71 | Y | Stonner Point Nathaniel | Sapperton Dawn | Owner | Mrs P. T. Ryan |
| F.T. Ch. Belway Della | B | 12.7.71 | B | Wilby David | Belway Rosa | Owner | P. Singleton |
| F.T. Ch. Clint Sally | B | ?.2.71 | B | F.T. Ch. Glenfarg Dante | Mares Craig Susie | W. F. Welburn | R. S. Hill |
| F.T. Ch. Flightline Jaffa | B | 18.4.69 | B | F.T. Ch. Sendhurst Sweep | Bushypark Panda | F. W. Hills | P. Sinclair |

| Name | Sex | Date | Colour | Sire | Dam | Owner | Breeder |
|---|---|---|---|---|---|---|---|
| F.T. Ch. Nazeing Zelstone Lively Lady | B | 13.4.68 | Y | Zelstone Brandysnap | Meggernie Lady Sheagh | Lt. Col. Sir E. Wills | Mrs Montgomerie-Charrington |
| F.T. Ch. Tripwire Mona | B | 17.4.70 | B | Tripwire Jason | F.T. Ch. Staindrop Doune | Mrs J. M. Hayes | M. J. Carter |
| **1975** | | | | | | | |
| Sh. Ch. Keithray Marcus | D | 12.10.71 | B | Ch. Sandyland Mark | Kikia of Keithray | Owner | Mr & Mrs J. Wilkinson |
| Sh. Ch. Melfin Half Guinea | D | 29.6.70 | Y | Melfin Lowna Silver Guinea | Melfin Silver Sixpence | Mrs B. Finch | Rev. M. Parsons |
| Sh. Ch. Follytower Augusta | B | 24.8.72 | B | Ch. Follytower Merrybrook Black Stormer | Follytower Artemis | Owner | Mrs M. Woolley |
| Sh. Ch. Sandylands Longley Colour Print | B | 26.10.72 | Y | Sandylands Thomas | Longley Colouring Book | Mr & Mrs G. Kenningley | Mrs G. Broadley & G. Anthony |
| Sh. Ch. Sandylands Mercy | B | 4.2.74 | Y | Ch. Sandylands Mark | Sh. Ch. Sandylands Waghorn Honesty | Owner | Mrs G. Broadley & G. Anthony |
| Ch. Timpsring Sirius | D | 13.4.73 | B | Eng. & Am. Ch. Ballyduff Seaman | Timpsring Myrtle | Owner | Mrs J. Macan |
| Sh. Ch. Lasgarn Ludovic | D | 1.8.72 | B | Ch. Sandylands Mark | Lasgarn Louisianna | Owners | E. G. & R. L. Edwards |
| Ir. & Eng. Ch. Sandylands Magic Moment | B | 3.1.71 | Y | Ch. Sandylands Mark | Sh. Ch. Sandylands Katrinka of Keithray | Mrs G. Broadley | Miss P. Horgan |
| Sh. Ch. Sandylands Clarence of Rossbank | D | 4.4.73 | Y | Sandylands Charlie Boy | Sh. Ch. Sandylands Dancer | Mrs G. Broadley | Mr & Mrs Steven |
| Sh. Ch. Goldentone Crissandra | B | 28.8.73 | Y | Roydwood Royal Tan | Goldentone Princess | Owner | C. G. Morley |
| F.T. Ch. Eyebrook Rory | D | 30.3.72 | B | Rouser of Essendene | Eyebrook Josephine | Owner | The Lady Allerton |
| F.T. Ch. Lambdale Jammy | D | 16.9.69 | B | Lamdale Softly | Glenfarg Belle | Mr & Mrs C. C. Lamb | Mrs C. C. Lamb |
| F.T. Ch. Hynford Blue Belle | B | 11.7.72 | B | Wheatrig Impressible | Hynford Black Gem | Mr & Mrs H. Paterson | M. J. Coleman |
| F.T. Ch. Ludgwardine Jade | B | 13.6.68 | B | Jericho Rocket | Holdgate Vesta | Mrs D. Wordworth | G. Meldrum |

| Name | Sex | Born | Colour | Sire | Dam | Breeder | Owner |
|---|---|---|---|---|---|---|---|
| F.T. Ch. Palgrave Swinbrook Fern | B | 25.4.70 | B | Palgrave Edward | Biennmhor Tide | D. Mackinnon | G. D. Baldwin |
| F.T. Ch. Sandringham Magpie | B | 8.4.72 | B | Sandringham Skid | Sandringham Pippit | H.M. The Queen | D. Garbutt |
| F.T. Ch. Trentlock Bluey 1976 | B | 6.7.69 | B | Racedale Dusk | Glenfarg Skye | J. G. Craig | E. Hill |
| Ch. Navacroft Jayncourt Truly Fair | B | 24.8.72 | Y | Ch. Sandylands Tandy | Jayncourt Star Misty | Mr & Mrs P. Palmer | Mrs D. Gardner |
| Sh. Ch. Sorn Sandpiper of Follytower | D | 1.12.72 | Y | Ch. Follytower Merrybrook Black Stormer | Sandylands Be Glorianna of Sorn | J. Barbour | Mrs M. Woolley |
| Sh. Ch. Keysun Teko of Blondella | D | 3.3.74 | B | Ch. Sandylands Mark | Keysun June Rose | Mrs M. Spencer | Mrs H. Burton |
| Ch. Croftspa Charlotte of Foxrush | B | 10.2.73 | Y | Sandylands Charlie Boy | Ch. Sandylands Geannie | Mr & Mrs A. Chapman | Mrs J. Charlton |
| Ch. Squire of Ballyduff | D | 10.10.74 | B | Ch. Ballyduff Marketeer | Sparkle of Tuddenham | Mrs E. M. Butchart | Mrs B. M. Docking |
| Ch. Ballyduff Marshall | D | 22.5.74 | B | Ch. Sandylands Mark | Ch. Ballyduff Marina | Owner | Mrs B. M. Docking |
| Ir. & Eng. Ch. Labracondel Elm | D | 16.9.72 | B | Int. Ch. Kinky of Keithray | Ir. Ch. Braeduke Babette | Owner | J. R. Haffey |
| Ch. Sandylands Newinn Colombus | D | 24.4.73 | B | Ch. Sandylands Mark | Newinn Amber | Mr & Mrs Hewitt | Mrs G. Broadley & G. Anthony |
| Sh. Ch. Sandylands Busy Liz | B | 23.10.73 | Y | Sh. Ch. Sandylands Blaze | Sh. Ch. Sandylands Dancer | Owner | Mrs G. Broadley |
| Sh. Ch. Sandylands Longley Come Rain | B | 20.8.74 | Y | Sandylands Charlston | Longley in Tune | Mr & Mrs G. Kenningley | Mrs G. Broadley & G. Anthony |
| Sh. Ch. Sandylands Storm Along | D | 16.7.74 | B | Ch. Follytower Merrybrook Black Stormer | Sh. Ch. Sandylands Girl Friday | Owner | Mrs G. Broadley & G. Anthony |

| Name | Sex | Date | | Sire | Dam | Breeder | Owner |
|---|---|---|---|---|---|---|---|
| Sh. Ch. Heatherbourne Top Tune | B | 20.12.73 | Y | Ch. Heatherbourne Lawnwoods Laughing Cavalier | Sandylands Top Twenty | Owner | Mrs H. G. Wiles |
| Ch. Mansergh Ooh La La | B | 17.8.73 | B | Am. Ch. Mansergh Merry Gentleman | Ch. Mansergh Antonia | Owner | Mrs M. Roslin-Williams |
| Sh. Ch. Heatherbourne Silver Czar | D | 29.5.74 | Y | Sandylands Charlie Boy | Sh. Ch. Heatherbourne Harefield Silver Penny | Mrs H. G. Wiles | Mrs E. Hammond |
| Sh. Ch. Milkmaid of Greenworth | B | 6.12.73 | Y | Sh. Ch. Longley Count On | Candlemas April Mist | Mrs R. Lomas & Mrs J. Kneller | Mrs M. Rooth |
| Ch. Charway Nightcap | D | 11.9.71 | B | Longley Trueman of Netherton | Charway Chiming Bells | Owner | Miss J. Charlton |
| Sh. Ch. Lidcoate Fidelity | B | 26.6.72 | Y | Candlemas Copperhill Checkmate | Lidcoate Christabel | Owner | Mrs B. Lidster |
| F.T. Ch. Derryboy Drummer | D | 26.6.73 | B | F.T. Ch. Holdgate Willie | Derryboy Blue Teal | Mrs M. Glossop | A. Rountree |
| F.T. Ch. Glyn of Eyebrook | D | 12.3.71 | B | Eyebrook Jason | Burnmatch Leader | R. Methuen | The Lady Allerton |
| F.T. Ch. Hedenhampark Dash | D | 1.7.73 | B | Dongon The Great | Hedenhampark Holcot Fay | F. Clitheroe | P. R. Elsey |
| F.T. Ch. Jensuedee Edenend Flash | D | 12.12.71 | B | Rodnor of Hutton | Edenend Otter | H. Stewart | F. Haworth |
| F.T. Ch. Ulster Shane | D | 7.4.71 | Y | Sh. Ch. Kinky of Keithray | Black Demon | R. Hanna | A. Thompson |
| F.T. Ch. Westhead Shot of Drakeshead | D | 26.7.74 | B | F.T. Ch. Swinbrook Tan | Angeltowns Malcedory Dona | A. C. Higgs | J. Halstead |
| F.T. Ch. Drakeshead Swift | B | 20.7.73 | B | F.T. Ch. Pechasi Max | Dipper of Drakeshead | Mr & Mrs J. Halstead | Mrs W. Howarth |
| F.T. Ch. Stonner Point Be Hopeful of Kenswick | B | 13.4.71 | B | Rockstead Footswish | Hedenhampark Holcot Fay | F. Clitheroe | Mrs King |
| F.T. Ch. Surprise of Triplecrown | B | 5.4.74 | B | Ir. F.T. Ch. Mr Solo | Mrs Peel | Owner | R. C. O'Farrell |

| Name | Sex | Born | Colour | Sire | Dam | Breeder | Owner |
|---|---|---|---|---|---|---|---|
| F.T. Ch. Swinbrook Bumble | B | 19.4.73 | B | F.T. Ch. Swinbrook Tan | F.T. Ch. Swinbrook Bertie | D. MacKinnon | Miss Wauchope |
| F.T. Ch. Westead Tan of Drakeshead 1977 | B | 26.6.74 | B | F.T. Ch. Swinbrook Tan | Angeltowns Chalcedory Dona | A. C. Higgs | Mrs J. Halstead |
| Sh. Ch. Crawcrook Princess | B | 12.5.74 | B | Kim Monarch of Inverness | Goldie of Knockando | S. Smith | Mr & Mrs S. L. Edwards |
| Sh. Ch. Savorna Gem of Gems of Kerlstone | B | 12.5.74 | B | Longley Trueman of Netherton | Toots of Tayfield | R. Sutcliffe | Mr & Mrs W. Livingstone |
| Sh. Ch. Ardmargha Mad Hatter | D | 13.5.75 | Y | Ch. Sandylands Mark | Hope of Ardmargha | Owner | Mr & Mrs H. W. Clayton |
| Ch. Lawnwoods Hot Chocolate | D | 30.10.73 | C | Ch. Follytower Merrybrook Black Stormer | Lawnwoods Tapestry | Owner | Mrs M. Satterthwaite |
| Sh. Ch. Thor's Lightning Boy | D | 29.6.75 | B | Ch. Follytower Merrybrook Black Stormer | Napoleons Brandy Mandy | Mrs J. M. Nicholls | C. J. Nicholls |
| Sh. Ch. Poolstead Purdey | B | 27.1.75 | Y | Ch. Sandylands Mark | Sh. Ch. Poolstead Popularity | Owner | Mr & Mrs R. V. Hepworth |
| Sh. Ch. Crosscroyde Charlotte | B | 4.12.73 | Y | Ch. Heatherbourne Lawnwoods Laughing Cavalier | Beaford Hope | Owner | Mr & Mrs R. V. Lavelle |
| Sh. Ch. Joline Bonnie of Stravaney | B | 28.2.73 | Y | Sandylands Charlie Boy | Ashton Sweet Sue | Mrs J. Upward | Mr & Mrs T. Powell |
| F.T. Ch. Polwarth Merganser | D | 21.3.75 | B | F.T. Ch. Swinbrook Tan | F.T. Ch. Trentlosk Bent | H. B. MacTier | I. Glass |
| F.T. Ch. Oday Alice of Tibea 1978 | B | 14.8.71 | B | F.T. Ch. Palgrave Edward | Beinnmhor Term | J. Newton | R. A. Watson & Capt. M. Tree |
| Sh. Ch. Sandylands Sparkle | B | 9.11.75 | Y | Ch. Sam of Suddie | Sh. Ch. Sandylands Mercy | Owner | Mrs Broadley & Mr Anthony |

| Name | Sex | Date | Colour | Sire | Dam | Breeder | Owner |
|---|---|---|---|---|---|---|---|
| Ch. Charway Little Sian | B | 11.6.75 | B | Ch. Timspring Little Tuc | Roseacre Hollyberry of Charway | Owner | Mr & Mrs Pritchard |
| Sh. Ch. Ardmargha Sandylands Mirth | B | 21.3.75 | B | Ch. Sandylands Mark | Sh. Ch. Sandylands Waghorn Honesty | Mrs Broadley & Mr Anthony | Mr & Mrs Clayton |
| Sh. Ch. Baronor Pegasus of Insley | D | 5.11.73 | B | Ch. Sandylands Mark | Baronor Vesta | Mrs J. M. Cocks | Miss D. Harris |
| Sh. Ch. Balrion King Frost | D | 22.11.76 | B | Sh. Ch. Sandylands Clarence of Rossbank | Balrion Royale Princess | Owner | Mr & Mrs Crook |
| Sh. Ch. Poolstead Past Master | D | 22.8.76 | Y | Sh. Ch. Poolstead Problem | Sh. Ch. Poolstead Porcelain | Owner | Mr & Mrs Hepworth |
| Sh. Ch. Claytonholt Highjacker of Cranspire | D | 9.1.74 | B | Ch. Sandylands Mark | Claytonholt Sharon | Mrs Dibly | Mr Hunter |
| Sh. Ch. Bradking Bonnie My Girl | B | 30.9.73 | Y | Ch. Sandylands Mark | Sandylands Carona | Owner | Mr & Mrs Kelley |
| Sh. Ch. Longley in Conference | D | 20.8.74 | Y | Sandylands Charlston | Longley in Tune | Owner | Mr & Mrs Kenningley |
| Sh. Ch. Waghorn Trust | B | 27.4.73 | B | Ch. Dale of Tarmac | Sh. Ch. Sandylands Honour | Owner | Mrs Lewis |
| Sh. Ch. Jayncourt Star Appeal | B | 20.10.75 | Y | Sh. Ch. Sandylands Garry | Jayncourt Star Attraction | Owner | Mr and Mrs Palmer |
| Sh. Ch. Sandylands Not Tonight of Trewinnard | B | 20.10.75 | Y | Ch. Sandylands Newinn Columbus | Sh. Ch. Sandylands Girl Friday | Mrs Broadley & Mr Anthony | Mr Pascoe |
| Sh. Ch. Stavarney Simon | D | 1.11.76 | B | Sh. Ch. Sandylands Stormalong | Nokeener Welsh Heritage | Owner | Mr & Mrs Powell |
| Ch. Nokeener Black Spark | D | 15.9.74 | B | Heatheredge Snipemere of Beadles | Nokeener Welsh Rose | Mrs C. Williams | Mrs M. Roslyn-Williams |
| Sh. Ch. Rockabee Gretel of Lawnwood | B | 3.8.73 | Y | Eng. Am. Ch. Lawnwood Toreador | Rockabee Pisces | Thorp & Walker | Mrs Satherthwaite |
| Sh. Ch. Rossbank Cochine | B | 10.11.75 | Y | Sh. Ch. Sandylands Clarence of Rossbank | Teviotcastle Countess of Rossbank | Owner | Mr & Mrs Steven |
| F.T. Ch. Crane of Habra | B | 10.5.73 | B | F.T. Ch. Palgrave Edward | Berrystead Bramble | Mr W. C. Williams | Mr G. T. Routledge |

| Name | Sex | Born | Colour | Sire | Dam | Breeder | Owner |
|---|---|---|---|---|---|---|---|
| F.T. Ch. Nazeing Bruin | D | 12.5.72 | B | Nazeing Brewin | F.T. Ch. Nazeing Zelstone Lively Lady | Owner | Mrs Montgomerie Charrington |
| F.T. Ch. Derryboy Daniel | D | 26.6.73 | B | F.T. Ch. Holdgate Willie | Derryboy Blue Teal | Owner | Mrs M. Glossop |
| F.T. Ch. Shot of Palgrave | D | 26.5.74 | B | F.T. Ch. Palgrave Edward | Ivyland Tessa | Mr R. Wilson | Mr E. O. Baldwin |
| F.T. Ch. Swift of Swinbrook | B | 8.4.74 | B | F.T. Ch. Swinbrook Tan | Holdgate Swallow | Mrs W. F. G. Plowden | Mr D. MacKinnon |
| F.T. Ch. Gunstock Teal | D | 16.3.74 | B | F.T. Ch. Swinbrook Tan | F.T. Ch. Angeltown Black Sapphire | Mrs Townsend | Mr & Mrs Bailey |
| F.T. Ch. Drakeshead Wisp | B | 11.6.76 | B | Gallow Mill Brig | Westend Cam of Drakeshead | Mr & Mrs Halstead | Mr R. Hill |
| F.T. Ch. Sandringham Moccasin | D | 15.5.72 | B | Rockstead Footswich | F.T. Ch. Sandringham Slipper | H.M. The Queen | Mrs Heywood-Lonsdale |
| F.T. Ch. Westelm Georgia of Mirstan 1979 | B | 4.6.76 | Y | Westead Sweep of Westelm | Angeltowns Chalcedory Dona | Mrs Fountain | Mr Harvey |
| Sh. Ch. Sarenchel Bryony | B | 6.10.74 | Y | Sh. Ch. Sandylands Blaze | Saranchel Samantha | Owner | Mrs Brittain |
| Sh. Ch. Sandylands My Rainbeau | D | 2.5.77 | Y | Ch. Sandylands Mark | Sh. Ch. Sandylands Longley Come Rain | Owner | Mrs Broadley & Mr Anthony |
| Sh. Ch. Balrion Wicked Lady | B | 22.11.76 | B | Sh. Ch. Sandylands Clarence of Rossbank | Balrion Royale Princess | Owner | Mr & Mrs Crook |
| Sh. Ch. Astonbrook Crusader | D | 4.11.74 | Y | Ch. Ballyduff Marketeer | Astonbrook Gemini | Mrs Fisk | Mr Floyd |
| Sh. Ch. Martin of Mardas | D | 11.5.75 | B | Ch. Ballyduff Squire | Mardas Vivette | Owner | Mrs Hepper |
| Sh. Ch. Poolstead Preface | B | 7.9.76 | Y | Sh. Ch. Sandylands Stormalong | Poolstead Prelude | Owner | Mr & Mrs Hepworth |

| | | | | | | | |
|---|---|---|---|---|---|---|---|
| Sh. Ch. Mansergh Sailors Beware | B | 22.8.76 | Sh. Ch. Sandylands Stormalong | B | Ch. Mansergh Ooh-La-La | Mrs Roslin-Williams | Mr Hepworth |
| Sh. Ch. Newinn Kestrel | D | 4.5.76 | Ch. Keyson Teko of Blondella | Y | Newinn Fleur | Owner | Mrs Hewitt |
| Sh. Ch. Bradking Black Charm | B | 10.12.76 | Ch. Follytower Merrybrook Black Stormer | B | Sh. Ch. Bradking Bonny My Girl | Owner | Mr & Mrs Kelley |
| Sh. Ch. Timspring Serendipity | B | 13.4.73 | Eng. & Am. Ch. Ballyduff Seaman | B | Timspring Myrtle | Owner | Mrs Macan |
| Sh. Ch. Newinn Harmony of Peradon | B | 14.9.75 | Ch. Sandylands Mark | B | Newinn Angelina | Mrs Hewitt | Mrs Wholey |
| Sh. Ch. Psalmon of Leyward | D | 10.10.74 | Leyward Sortilege | Y | Ottersett Morning Mist | Mr Watts | Mrs Woodward |
| Sh. Ch. Stanwood Puckwudgie | D | 1.12.71 | Ch. Sandylands Mark | Y | Sh. Ch. Stanwood Leda | Mrs Hurley | Mrs J. Harris |
| F.T. Ch. Carlos of Reflux | D | 6.76 | Hynford Hustler | B | Carla Cinders | Owner | Mr Booker |
| F.T. Ch. Drakeshead Tinker | D | 20.2.75 | F.T. Ch. Swinbrook Tan | B | Dipper of Drakeshead | Owner | Mr Halstead |
| F.T. Ch. Gunstock Lisleholme Black Bun | B | 2.71 | Eryri Poolstead Pirate | B | Dusky Aphrodite | Mrs T. Lisk | Mr & Mrs Bailey |
| F.T. Ch. Hogarth Sam | D | 23.3.74 | F.T. Ch. Palgrave Edward | B | Fenland Duchess | Mr Norman | Mr Herbert |
| F.T. Ch. Leacross Rinkals | D | 3.76 | F.T. Ch. Swinbrook Tan | B | F.T. Ch. Holdgate Swallow | Mrs Plowden | Mr Rowntree |
| F.T. Ch. Sarumvale Geantrees Camilla | B | 1.1.75 | F.T. Ch. Berrystead Glenbruar Beau | B | Geantrees Joanna | Mrs Richardson | Lt-Cdr. Whitehead |
| 1980 | | | | | | | |
| Sh. Ch. Strinesdale Old Spice | D | 10.10.74 | Ch. Sandylands Mark | B | Strinesdale Bianca | Owner | Mr F. Belshaw |
| Sh. Ch. Strinesdale Bianca | B | 3.10.71 | Sh. Ch. Sandylands My Lad | Y | Contessa of Keithray | Owner | Mr F. Belshaw |
| Sh. Ch. Cambremmer St. Clair | B | 2.3.77 | Sh. Ch. Glenarem Skyrocket | Y | Braunspath Simona of Cambremer | Owner | Mr D. Brabban |

| Name | Sex | Born | Colour | Sire | Dam | Breeder | Owner |
|---|---|---|---|---|---|---|---|
| Sh. Ch. Stajantors Honest John | D | 25.11.75 | Y | Sandylands Charlie Boy | Lochranza Cherry Blossom | Owner | Mrs J. Cole |
| Sh. Ch. Lasgarn Leia | B | 11.2.78 | Y | Sandylands Gay Boy | Lasgarn Linaria | Miss S. Mortimer | E. G. & R. L. Edwards |
| Sh. Ch. Friarsgarth Marrell | B | 11.7.75 | Y | Ch. Sandylands Mark | Sandylands Let's Dance | Owner | Mr & Mrs J. A. Glasse |
| Sh. Ch. Poolstead Preferential | D | 19.8.78 | Y | Sh. Ch. Poolstead Problem | Sh. Ch. Poolstead Preface | Owner | Mr & Mrs R. V. Hepworth |
| Sh. Ch. Candlemas Teal | D | 1.5.76 | B | Ch. Bally Duff Marketeer | Candlemas Marketlane Gemini | Owner | Mrs E. J. Kneller |
| Sh. Ch. Balrion Black Ice | B | 22.11.76 | B | Sandylands Clarence of Rossbank | Balrion Royale Princess | Mr & Mrs J. Crook | Mrs D. Morden |
| Sh. Ch. Cornlands Blonde Lady | B | 17.2.78 | Y | Ch. Squire of Ballyduff | Cornlands Lady Lavender | Owner | Mrs P. D. Rae |
| Sh. Ch. Mansergh Ship's Belle | B | 22.8.76 | B | Sh. Ch. Sandylands Stormalong | Mansergh Ooh-La-La | Owner | Mrs M. Roslin-Williams |
| Sh. Ch. Marbra Minstrel | D | 1.3.73 | Y | Powhatan Chief | Marbra Kalmia | Owner | Mrs N. Whitlock |
| Sh. Ch. Balrion Royale Mischief of Rodarbel | B | 23.11.76 | B | Sandylands Clarence of Rossbank | Balrion Royale Princess | Mr & Mrs J. Crook | Mrs D. Withnall |
| F.T. Ch. Palm of Eyebrook | B | 4.8.75 | B | Eyebrook Willow | Hedenhampark Medlar | F. Clitheroe | Lady Allerton |
| F.T. Ch. Mirstan Sea Breeze | D | 1.5.77 | Y | Mirstan Sea Hawk | Tibea Teal of Mirstan | P. Denny | S. Harvey |
| F.T. Ch. Raughlin Whippet | B | 12.5.75 | B | F.T. Ch. Berrystead Glenbruar Beau | Mushbrook Maize | Owner | S. J. Ennett |
| F.T. Ch. Kenswick Hamish | D | 5.7.76 | B | Danbrias Black Tern | F.T. Ch. Stonnerpoint Be Hopeful of Kenswick | Mrs M. King | R. M. L. Walker |

**1981**

| Name | Sex | Born | Colour | Sire | Dam | Breeder | Owner |
|---|---|---|---|---|---|---|---|
| Sh. Ch. Rossbank Kansas | B | 11.6.79 | Y | Sh. Ch. Balrion King Frost | Teviotcastle Countess of Rossbank | Mr & Mrs J. Steven | H. Armstrong |

| | | | | Sire | Dam | Breeder | Owner |
|---|---|---|---|---|---|---|---|
| Sh. Ch. Lasgarn Livingstone | D | 6.9.77 | Y | Ch. Sandylands Newind Columbus | Acornhill Yolande | Owner | Mr & Mrs E. G. Edwards |
| Sh. Ch. Novacroft Chorus Girl | B | 17.3.78 | Y | Sandylands Charlston | Novacroft Gay Rhapsody | Owner | Mrs D. J. Gardner |
| Sh. Ch. Ednan Friar of Glenarvey | D | 17.1.78 | Y | Heathersedge Barathea | Ednan Emma | E. Austermuhle | Mrs J. Harvey |
| Sh. Ch. Poolstead Pictorial | B | 23.10.74 | Y | Sh. Ch. Poolstead Problem | Poolstead Piccadilly | Owner | Mr & Mrs R. V. Hepworth |
| Sh. Ch. Poolstead Matchmaker | D | 8.4.79 | B | Ch. Nokeener Black Spark | Sh. Ch. Mansergh Sailors Beware | Owner | Mr & Mrs R. V. Hepworth |
| Sh. Ch. Poolstead Postal Vote | B | 15.7.77 | Y | Ch. Sandylands Mark | Poolstead Pictorial | Owner | Mr & Mrs R.V. Hepworth |
| Sh. Ch. Bradking Cassidy | D | 3.1.79 | Y | Sh. Ch. Ardmargha Mad Hatter | Sh. Ch. Bradking Black Charm | Owner | Mr & Mrs A. D. Kelley |
| Sh. Ch. Timspring Tarf | D | 5.4.78 | B | Ch. Timspring Litle Tuc | Similar of Timspring | Owner | Mrs J. Macan |
| Sh. Ch. Charway Ballywillwill | D | 30.9.78 | B | Ballyduff Spruce | Caarway Simona | Owner | Mr & Mrs L.V. & Miss J. Pritchard |
| Sh. Ch. Mornington Stormtrooper | D | 3.7.78 | B | Ch. Follytower Merrybrook Black Stormer | Mornington Tobla | Owner | M. Roberts |
| Sh. Ch. Fabracken Comedy Star | D | 20.9.79 | B | Sh. Ch. Martin of Mardas | Ch. Poolstead Pin Up of Fabracken | Owner | Miss A. Taylor |
| Sh. Ch. Copperhill Lyric of Heatherbourne | B | 28.12.77 | Y | Sh. Ch. Heatherbourne Silver Czar | Copperhill Taffeta | Miss J. Startup | Mrs H. G. Wiles |
| Sh. Ch. Heatherbourne Statesman | D | 10.9.78 | B | Ch. Follytower Merrybrook Black Stormer | Heatherbourne Moira | Owner | Mrs H. G. Wiles |
| Sh. Ch. Heatherbourne Fisherman | D | 1.10.79 | B | Sh. Ch. Balrion King Frost | Heatherbourne Moira | Owner | Mrs H. G. Wiles |
| F.T. Ch. Abbotsleigh Joshua | D | 23.2.76 | B | Angeltown Black Magic | Susan of Brackenbank | Mr & Mrs P. Hales | Miss J. D. Gill |
| F.T. Ch. Blakemere Mega of Garleton | B | 30.4.76 | B | F.T. Ch. Holdgate Willie | Blakemere Astrex | Mr & Mrs B. S. Jewitt | Mr I. Glass |

| Name | Sex | Born | Colour | Sire | Dam | Breeder | Owner |
|---|---|---|---|---|---|---|---|
| F.T. Ch. Glencoin Digger of Saddleworth | D | 9.3.78 | Y | Drakeshead Tasker | Glencoin Daffodil | Miss J. S. Hayward | Mr & Mrs J. Mayalls |
| F.T. Ch. Kelvinhead Magnum | D | 1.3.76 | B | F.T. Ch. Rumbleton Caper | Quicksilver of Kelvin Head | Owner | Mr R. J. Montgomery |
| F.T. Ch. Pocklington Glen | D | 2.6.78 | B | F.T. Ch. Swinbrook Tan | F.T. Ch. Sandringham Magpie | Owner | Mr D. Garbutt |
| F.T. Ch. Shinshail Apache 1982 | D | 12.5.78 | B | Combe Castle Chilbrook | Hollyberry Teal | Mrs Harris | Mr R. Blake |
| Sh. Ch. Squire Harvey of Allenie | D | 7.5.80 | Y | Sh. Ch. Stajantors Honest John | Stajantors Pearl | Mrs P. Crowson | Mr & Mrs Allen |
| Sh. Ch. Sandylands Rosy | B | 5.12.79 | Y | Sh. Ch. Sandylands My Rainbeau | Sh. Ch. Sandylands Longley Come Rain | Owner | Mrs Broadley & Mr Anthony |
| Sh. Ch. Trecrest Bonnie's Pride n'Joy | B | 10.1.79 | Y | Stellmara Swell Fellow | Crestlands Honeysuckle of Trecrest | Owner | Miss O. Buggs |
| Sh. Ch. Keysun Krispin of Blondella | D | 2.7.79 | B | Ch. Keysun Tako of Blondella | Bradking Bonny's Charm of Blondella | M. Spencer | Mrs H. Burton |
| Sh. Ch. Glencapel Evening Flight of Calag | B | 24.1.77 | B | Sh. Ch. Sandylands Stormalong | Sandylands Godiva of Glencapel | Mr Wilson | Mrs S. M. Butler |
| Sh. Ch. Ardmargha So Happy | B | 5.6.76 | Y | Sh. Ch. Sandylands Stormalong | Hope of Ardmargha | Owner | Mr & Mrs H. W. Clayton |
| Sh. Ch. Novacroft Charles | D | 17.3.78 | Y | Sandylands Chariston | Novacroft Gay Rhapsody | Owner | Mrs D. I. Gardner |
| Ch. Kupros Ladies' Pride | B | 26.11.77 | B | Ch. Squire of Ballyduff | Kupros My Lady | Owner | Mr & Mrs W. P. Hart |
| Sh. Ch. Newinn Oasis | B | 24.2.80 | Y | Newinn Natterjack | Poolstead Polyphoto of Newinn | Owner | Mrs M. R. Hewitt |

| Name | Sex | Date | Sire | | Dam | Owner | Breeder |
|---|---|---|---|---|---|---|---|
| Sh. Ch. Lawnwoods Midnight Folly | D | 1.6.78 | Lawnwoods Fandango | Y | Lawnwoods Starglow | Owner | Mrs M. I. Satterthwaite |
| F.T. Ch. Abbotsleigh Cossack | D | 9.7.76 | F.T. Ch. Spudtamsons Berry of Mirstan | B | Manymills Wistful | Mr & Mrs P. Hales | Miss S. Hales |
| F.T. Ch. Palgrave Kay | B | 5.5.78 | F.T. Ch. Shot of Palgrave | B | F.T. Ch. Palgrave Swinbrook Fern | E. O. Baldwin | Mr MacKinnon |
| F.T. Ch. Palgrave Kerry | B | 5.5.78 | F.T. Ch. Shot of Palgrave | B | F.T. Ch. Palgrave Swinbrook Fern | E. O. Baldwin | Mr R. S. Webb |
| F.T. Ch. Moorsdyke Logiemoor's Brig | D | 16.7.79 | Moorsdyke Angus | B | Deuce of Trentlock | A. K. Dykes | R. Keanie |
| F.T. Ch. Sandringham Salt | D | 23.1.78 | F.T. Ch. Sandringham Sydney | Y | Sandringham Mustard | Owner | H.M. The Queen |
| F.T. Ch. Leadburn Prince | D | 9.10.78 | Winston Pierpoint Sir | B | Lady Sharon of Brownrigg | B. Towler | W. L. Steel |
| F.T. Ch. Tibea Topaz | B | 14.6.78 | F.T. Ch. Hadenham Parkdash of Phildray | B | F.T. Ch. Oday Alice of Tibea | Owner | R. A. Watson |
| F.T. Ch. Blackharn Jonty | D | 12.5.79 | F.T. Ch. Swinbrook Tan | B | Blackharn Puddie | Owner | A.V. Parnell |
| F.T. Ch. Clevedale Sage | B | 4.8.77 | F.T. Ch. Westhead Shot of Drakeshead | B | Clevedale Rhoda | K. Drummond | B. Smith |
| F.T. Ch. Greenwood Timothy of Holdgate | D | 24.3.79 | F.T. Ch. Holdgate Willie | B | Greenwood Dainty | Mrs Richards | Mrs G. Benson |
| F.T. Ch. Meadow Boy Scout | D | 2.4.79 | F.T. Ch. Leacross Rinkals | B | Derramore Thatch | T. Hughes | E. Barr |
| F.T. Ch. Pocklington Ben | D | 1.6.76 | Swinbrook Mosquito | B | F.T. Ch. Sandringham Magpie | Owner | D. Garbutt |
| F.T. Ch. Kenswick Orion of Danbrias | D | 5.7.76 | Danbrias Black Tern | B | F.T. Ch. Stonnerpoint Be Hopeful of Kenswick | Mrs M. B. King | B. S. Wheatley |
| F.T. Ch. Marie of Cleary | B | 2.4.79 | F.T. Ch. Leacross Rinkals | B | Derramore Thatch | T. Hughes | A. Daly |

| Name | Sex | Born | Colour | Sire | Dam | Breeder | Owner |
| --- | --- | --- | --- | --- | --- | --- | --- |
| F.T. Ch. Veraton Viking | D | 21.4.77 | Y | F.T. Ch. Westead Shot of Drakeshead | Veraton Belinda Fair | Owner | Mrs V. Warrington |
| F.T. Ch. Brenjon Dirk of Drakeshead | D | 21.9.78 | B | F.T. Ch. Spudtamson Berry of Mirstan | F.T. Ch. Drakeshead Thorne | J. Drury | Mrs Heywood-Lonsdale |
| F.T. Ch. Kenstaff Angus of Mirstan 1983 | D | 11.6.79 | B | F.T. Ch. Drakeshead Tinker | Drakeshead April | I.F. Askew | S. Harvey |
| Sh. Ch. Sandylands Rum Baba | B | 9.10.80 | Y | Sh. Ch. Sandylands My Rainbeau | Sh. Ch. Sandylands Waghorn Honesty | Owner | Mrs Broadley & Mr Anthony |
| Sh. Ch. Balrion Miss Behave of Loxdale | B | 9.4.80 | B | Sh. Ch. Balrion King Frost | Friargarth Miss Muffet of Balrion | Mr & Mrs Crook | Mr & Mrs J. M. Charlesworth |
| Sh. Ch. Warringah Hot Favourite | B | 30.10.78 | B | Secret Song of Lawnwood | Lawnwoods Hot Pants of Warringah | Owner | Mr & Mrs D. & C.A. Coode |
| Sh. Ch. Warringah Fair n' Square | D | 11.5.80 | Y | Sh. Ch. Lawnwoods Midnight Folly | Warringah Muffin | Owner | Mr & Mrs D. & C.A. Coode |
| Sh. Ch. Sandylands Steptoe | D | 12.7.78 | Y | Sh. Ch., Sandylands Stormalong | Sh. Ch. Sandylands Busy Liz | Mrs Broadley & Mr Anthony | R. Dickinson |
| Sh. Ch. Konoboly Bunny Girl | B | 25.10.80 | Y | Konoboly Xenadu | Sandylands Sonnet of Konoboly | Owner | Mr & Mrs F. R. Ellison |
| Sh. Ch. Crawcrook Chianti of Misty Woods | B | 27.7.80 | B | Foxrush Solong of Crawcrook | Crawcrook Chintz | S. & L. Edwards | Mr & Mrs D. J. Fleming |
| Sh. Ch. Sudeo Kay Sara | B | 24.9.80 | Y | Sudeo King Pin of Vuldack | Sudeo Whisper | Owner | Mr & Mrs M. F. Givan |
| Sh. Ch. Bullion of Glenarvey | D | 15.8.80 | Y | Ch. Ednan Friar of Glenarvey | Firthorn Widgeon | Mrs Knight | Mrs J. Harvey |
| Sh. Ch. Receiver of Cranspire | D | 19.12.81 | Y | Cranspire Sicytrain | Polly's Pride of Genisval | Coddington & Shortland | Mrs R. J. Hunter |
| Sh. Ch. Angelcroft Shula | B | 20.2.80 | Y | Sh. Ch. Novacroft Charles | Elmtree Rebel | Owner | Miss O. L. Monchar |

| Name | Sex | Date | | Sire | Dam | Breeder | Owner |
|---|---|---|---|---|---|---|---|
| Sh. Ch. Trewinnard Not Likely | D | 24.7.79 | Y | Sandylands Charleston | Sh. Ch. Sandylands Not Tonight of Trewinnard | Owner | T. R. Pascoe |
| Sh. Ch. Lindal Mastercraft | D | 3.7.80 | B | Ch. Charway Ballywillwill | Morningtown Stormette | Owner | Mr & Mrs A. R. & L. M. Porter |
| Sh. Ch. Elowood Soul Singer | D | 22.9.78 | B | Secret Song of Lawnwood | Elowood Fern | Owner | Mrs J. Reader |
| Sh. Ch. Lugsmill Airs n' Graces | B | 29.3.80 | Y | Sh. Ch. Poolstead Preferential | Jayncourt Truth | Owner | Mr D. R. & Mrs J. E. Swann |
| Sh. Ch. Fabracken Dancing Shadow | B | 22.8.80 | B | Ch. Charway Ballywillwill | Ch. Poolstead PinUp of Fabracken | Owner | Miss A. Taylor |

APPENDIX C

# LABRADORS WHICH HAVE QUALIFIED FOR THE TITLE OF FIELD TRIAL AND SHOW BENCH CHAMPION, COMMONLY CALLED DUAL CHAMPIONS

*Banchory Bolo* (the first Dual Ch.)
    By Scandal of Glynn ex Caehowell Nettle
    *Owner:* Lorna, Countess Howe
*Banchory Sunspeck*
    By Ch. Ilderton Ben ex Dungavel Juniper
    *Owner:* Lorna, Countess Howe
*Titus of Whitmore*
    By Twist of Whitmore ex Teazle of Whitmore
    *Owner:* Mr T. W. Twyford
*Branshaw Bob*
    By Ch. Ingleston Ben ex Bramshaw Brimble
    *Owner:* Lorna, Countess Howe
*Lochar Nessie*
    By Lochar Peter ex Lochar Biddy
    *Owner:* Mr Morris

POST 1939

*Banchory Painter*
    By Peter the Painter ex Glenhead Bess
    *Owner:* Lorna, Countess Howe
*Staindrop Saighdear*
    By Glenhead Jimmy ex Our Lil
    *Owner:* Mr Edgar Winter
*Knaith Banjo*
    By Poppleton Golden Russet ex Knaith Brilliantine
    *Owner:* Mrs Arthur Wormald

*Rockstead Footspark*
   By Ludford Razor ex Jaala
    *Owner:* Mr R. MacDonald
*Flute of Flodden*
   By Dual Ch. Titus of Whitmore ex Wemyss Racha
    *Owner:* the late Lord Joicey

APPENDIX D

# LABRADOR CLUBS

It is with much pleasure that I can now record that there are no less than twelve Breed Clubs, as well as many Gundog Clubs.

While some of these clubs appear to be content to rest on their laurels some of the newer ones are extremely active catering for the working Labrador Retriever. By this I mean that they are striving very successfully to maintain the traditions of the breed, their main aim being to ensure the well-being of the breed by continuing to meet the high standards of breeding and working laid down by the earlier breeders. The goal is still a really good-looking Labrador who is a really good working dog, or if you will a really good working dog who is equally good-looking. Whilst dual Champions have been conspicuous by their absence for some time now I do not think this should be taken as a sign that there are two different types of Labrador, a show Labrador and a field trial Labrador. Though some fanatic on either side would probably try to convince you of this, nothing could in fact be further from the truth.

Any true Labrador breeder will say he is breeding for brains and beauty and by this he means he is endeavouring to breed good-looking working dogs. The predominantly show breeder will be just as disappointed at one of his puppies showing gun-shyness, for example, or failure to retrieve, as the predominantly field trial breeder should be at lack of success in the show ring (not necessarily championship shows).

The more 'go ahead' of the Labrador clubs have recognized this for a long time and they arrange for their members to meet as often as possible. This results in a very worthwhile exchange of ideas between the extremes.

Such things as gundog training from the beginner to the advanced dog are arranged. For the most part these are oversubscribed, if anything. They are however enjoyed by dogs and owners alike despite the fact that many owners have to travel long distances to enjoy the facility.

Then there are the rallies. At some of these a show judge and/or a field trial judge is invited to go over all the Labradors making their assessments on the show points. These assessments are not communicated to the spectators until they themselves have made their assessment. The results are then compared and the ensuing discussion is well worth while. All the arguments I have heard following these have been good natured and taken in fine spirit by the sporting owners.

Likewise at the gundog training, after a time the 'show' breeder is given the opportunity to take his class. Here again the first one or two tend to be a little chaotic as one would expect but they soon settle down and become reasonably efficient.

The resultant cross-fertilization of ideas and the welding of the club into one unit is paying great dividends. That it will go from strength to strength with the continued cooperation of the members, I am convinced.

Clubs who are not striving for this end but who appear to be paying particular attention to only one facet are not, in my opinion, and I am confident in Countess Howe's opinion, acting in the best interest of the breed.

All clubs must not only see that justice is done but they must make sure that it is seen to be done. They must give their members, all of them, a chance to compete in shows from the members' to the championship show, and a chance to compete in the working tests from the very elementary to the field trial. Classifications in these events should be so arranged as to give the newcomers some chance of success to ensure that they do not feel that they are entering but have lost before they start – this is fatal.

The newcomer, often the younger person, must be encouraged as much as possible and in the interests of the breed it is imperative that the longer serving members of the clubs should go out of their way to provide encouragement.

LIST OF ASSOCIATIONS, CLUBS AND SOCIETIES FOR THE PROMOTION OF LABRADORS, REGISTERED AT THE KENNEL CLUB

The Labrador Retriever Club
The Labrador Club of Scotland
The Midland Counties Labrador Retriever Club
The Northumberland and Durham Labrador Retriever Club
The Labrador Retriever Club of Northern Ireland
The Yellow Labrador Club
The Three Ridings Labrador Club
The East Anglian Labrador Club
The West of England Labrador Retriever Club
The Labrador Retriever Club of Wales
The North West Labrador Retriever Club
The Kent, Surrey and Sussex Labrador Retriever Club

The names of officials of the clubs have been omitted because they are subject to change. Should any reader wish to contact any club he should ascertain from the Kennel Club of 1 Clarges Street, Piccadilly, London W1Y 8AB, the name and address of the secretary.

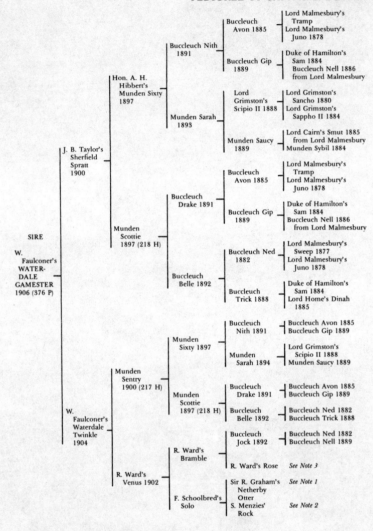

1. Sir Richard Graham could not remember Otter's breeding. He thought he was bred at Langholme Lodge, but there is no record. A. Craw, from whom he bought him, wrote that he, being very old, had forgotten, but thought he was by one of the Langholme Lodge dogs.
2. Mr S. Menzies has forgotten the breeding of Rock or Rook.
3. Mr Ward's Rose is said to have been of a mixed breed.

# PEDIGREES

## PETER OF FASKALLY 1908 (317P)

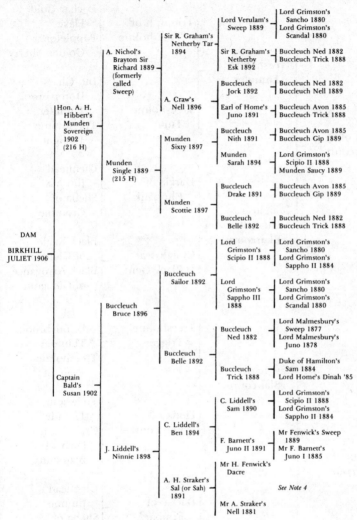

The pedigree chart reads as follows:

**DAM BIRKHILL JULIET 1906**

- **Hon. A. H. Hibbert's Munden Sovereign 1902 (216 H)**
  - **A. Nichol's Brayton Sir Richard 1889 (formerly called Sweep)**
    - **Sir R. Graham's Netherby Tar 1894**
      - **Lord Verulam's Sweep 1889**
        - Lord Grimston's Sancho 1880
        - Lord Grimston's Scandal 1880
      - **Sir R. Graham's Netherby Esk 1892**
        - Buccleuch Ned 1882
        - Buccleuch Trick 1888
    - **A. Craw's Nell 1896**
      - **Buccleuch Jock 1892**
        - Buccleuch Ned 1882
        - Buccleuch Nell 1889
      - **Earl of Home's Juno 1891**
        - Buccleuch Avon 1885
        - Buccleuch Trick 1888
  - **Munden Single 1889 (215 H)**
    - **Munden Sixty 1897**
      - **Buccleuch Nith 1891**
        - Buccleuch Avon 1885
        - Buccleuch Gip 1889
      - **Munden Sarah 1894**
        - Lord Grimston's Scipio II 1888
        - Munden Saucy 1889
    - **Munden Scottie 1897**
      - **Buccleuch Drake 1891**
        - Buccleuch Avon 1885
        - Buccleuch Gip 1889
      - **Buccleuch Belle 1892**
        - Buccleuch Ned 1882
        - Buccleuch Trick 1888

- **Captain Bald's Susan 1902**
  - **Buccleuch Bruce 1896**
    - **Buccleuch Sailor 1892**
      - **Lord Grimston's Scipio II 1888**
        - Lord Grimston's Sancho 1880
        - Lord Grimston's Sappho II 1884
      - **Lord Grimston's Sappho III 1888**
        - Lord Grimston's Sancho 1880
        - Lord Grimston's Scandal 1880
    - **Buccleuch Belle 1892**
      - **Buccleuch Ned 1882**
        - Lord Malmesbury's Sweep 1877
        - Lord Malmesbury's Juno 1878
      - **Buccleuch Trick 1888**
        - Duke of Hamilton's Sam 1884
        - Lord Home's Dinah '85
  - **J. Liddell's Ninnie 1898**
    - **C. Liddell's Ben 1894**
      - **C. Liddell's Sam 1890**
        - Lord Grimston's Scipio II 1888
        - Lord Grimston's Sappho II 1884
      - **F. Barnett's Juno II 1891**
        - Mr Fenwick's Sweep 1889
        - Mr F. Barnett's Juno I 1885
    - **A. H. Straker's Sal (or Sah) 1891**
      - **Mr H. Fenwick's Dacre**
        - *See Note 4*
      - **Mr A. Straker's Nell 1881**

4. Mr F. Barnett wrote about A. H. Straker's Sal or Sah 1891. Her sire, Hugh Fenwick's Dacre, was rather a heavy, slow, long-coated dog. Nicolas Cornish, huntsman of Tynedale 1867–81, got this dog when he was acting-keeper to Hugh Fenwick, but he had no pedigree that I could ever hear. Alfred Straker's Sah and Nell were both more like Labradors. The sire of Nell 1881 was unknown, the dam was imported by an American, Richardson, who resided in Ireland.—L.H.

# CH. RULER OF BLAIRCOURT

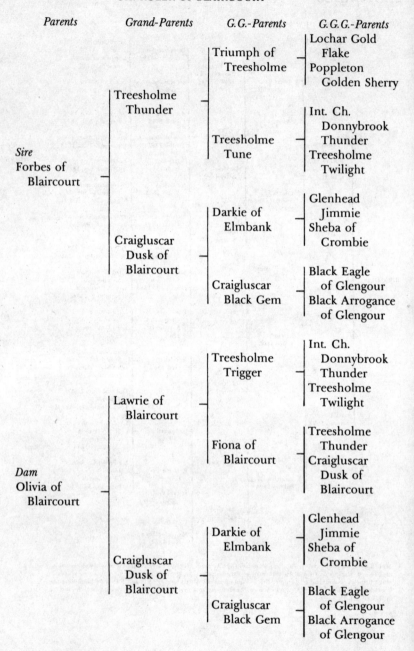

| Parents | Grand-Parents | G.G.-Parents | G.G.G.-Parents |
|---|---|---|---|
| | | Triumph of Treesholme | Lochar Gold Flake / Poppleton Golden Sherry |
| | Treesholme Thunder | | |
| | | Treesholme Tune | Int. Ch. Donnybrook Thunder / Treesholme Twilight |
| *Sire* Forbes of Blaircourt | | Darkie of Elmbank | Glenhead Jimmie / Sheba of Crombie |
| | Craigluscar Dusk of Blaircourt | | |
| | | Craigluscar Black Gem | Black Eagle of Glengour / Black Arrogance of Glengour |
| | | Treesholme Trigger | Int. Ch. Donnybrook Thunder / Treesholme Twilight |
| | Lawrie of Blaircourt | | |
| | | Fiona of Blaircourt | Treesholme Thunder / Craigluscar Dusk of Blaircourt |
| *Dam* Olivia of Blaircourt | | Darkie of Elmbank | Glenhead Jimmie / Sheba of Crombie |
| | Craigluscar Dusk of Blaircourt | | |
| | | Craigluscar Black Gem | Black Eagle of Glengour / Black Arrogance of Glengour |

## CH. WHATSTANDWELL CORONET

| Parents | Grand-Parents | G.G.-Parents | G.G.G.-Parents |
|---------|---------------|--------------|----------------|

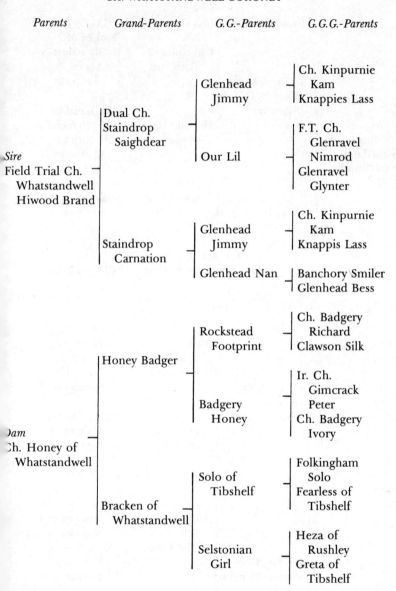

**Sire**
Field Trial Ch.
Whatstandwell
Hiwood Brand

- Dual Ch.
  Staindrop
  Saighdear
  - Glenhead
    Jimmy
    - Ch. Kinpurnie
      Kam
    - Knappies Lass
  - Our Lil
    - F.T. Ch.
      Glenravel
      Nimrod
    - Glenravel
      Glynter
- Staindrop
  Carnation
  - Glenhead
    Jimmy
    - Ch. Kinpurnie
      Kam
    - Knappis Lass
  - Glenhead Nan
    - Banchory Smiler
    - Glenhead Bess

**Dam**
Ch. Honey of
Whatstandwell

- Honey Badger
  - Rockstead
    Footprint
    - Ch. Badgery
      Richard
    - Clawson Silk
  - Badgery
    Honey
    - Ir. Ch.
      Gimcrack
      Peter
    - Ch. Badgery
      Ivory
- Bracken of
  Whatstandwell
  - Solo of
    Tibshelf
    - Folkingham
      Solo
    - Fearless of
      Tibshelf
  - Selstonian
    Girl
    - Heza of
      Rushley
    - Greta of
      Tibshelf

| Parents | Grand-Parents | G.G.-Parents | G.G.G.-Parents |
|---|---|---|---|
| | | Ch. Ruler of Blaircourt | Forbes of Blaircourt |
| | Ch. Sandylands Tweed of Blaircourt | | Olivia of Blaircourt |
| *Sire* Aust. Ch. Sandylands Tan (Imp. U.K.) | | Sh. Ch. Tessa of Blaircourt | Ch. Laird of Lochaber |
| | | | Ch. Imp of Blaircourt |
| | | Ch. Cissbury Adventure | Calcetto Carlo |
| | Sandylands Annabel | | Calcetto Brilliant |
| | | Sh. Ch. Sandylands Juno | Ch. British Justice |
| | | | Ch. Sandylands Belle of Helenspring |
| | | Aust. Ch. Stoneywood Roamer Imp | Poppleton Beech Flight |
| | Leomar Rob Roy | | Alphega Wizard of Stoneywood |
| | | Beau Glen Honey | Aust. Ch. Mahara Hara Dusty |
| *Dam* Duffton Dancer | | | Mahara Hara Goldie |
| | | Aust. Ch. Bramden Regal Scot | Aust. Ch. Stoneywood Roamer (Imp.) |
| | Aust. Ch. Duffton Bonny Sharron | | Aust. Ft. Ch. Rozavon Juliana |
| | | Pottens Jennifer (Imp.) | En. Ch. Ballyduff Orangeman |
| | | | Pottens Jill |

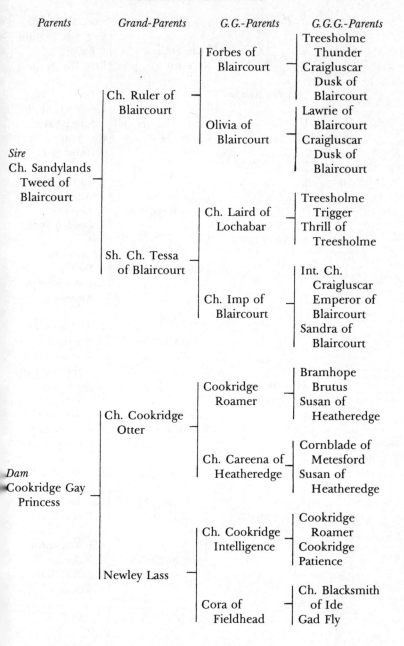

CH. COOKRIDGE TANGO

| Parents | Grand-Parents | G.G.-Parents | G.G.G.-Parents |
|---|---|---|---|
| | | Forbes of Blaircourt | Treesholme Thunder |
| | Ch. Ruler of Blaircourt | | Craigluscar Dusk of Blaircourt |
| | | Olivia of Blaircourt | Lawrie of Blaircourt |
| *Sire* Ch. Sandylands Tweed of Blaircourt | | | Craigluscar Dusk of Blaircourt |
| | | Ch. Laird of Lochabar | Treesholme Trigger |
| | | | Thrill of Treesholme |
| | Sh. Ch. Tessa of Blaircourt | Ch. Imp of Blaircourt | Int. Ch. Craigluscar Emperor of Blaircourt |
| | | | Sandra of Blaircourt |
| | | Cookridge Roamer | Bramhope Brutus |
| | | | Susan of Heatheredge |
| | Ch. Cookridge Otter | Ch. Careena of Heatheredge | Cornblade of Metesford |
| | | | Susan of Heatheredge |
| *Dam* Cookridge Gay Princess | | Ch. Cookridge Intelligence | Cookridge Roamer |
| | | | Cookridge Patience |
| | Newley Lass | Cora of Fieldhead | Ch. Blacksmith of Ide |
| | | | Gad Fly |

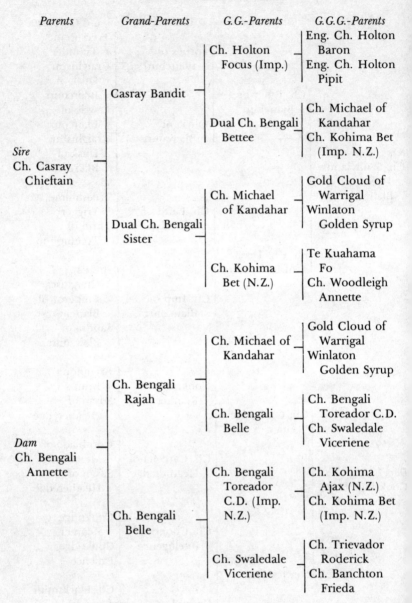

DUAL CH. BALDORRA BELLE

| Parents | Grand-Parents | G.G.-Parents | G.G.G.-Parents |
|---------|---------------|--------------|----------------|
| | | Ch. Holton Focus (Imp.) | Eng. Ch. Holton Baron |
| | | | Eng. Ch. Holton Pipit |
| | Casray Bandit | | |
| | | Dual Ch. Bengali Bettee | Ch. Michael of Kandahar |
| *Sire* | | | Ch. Kohima Bet (Imp. N.Z.) |
| Ch. Casray Chieftain | | | |
| | | Ch. Michael of Kandahar | Gold Cloud of Warrigal |
| | | | Winlaton Golden Syrup |
| | Dual Ch. Bengali Sister | | |
| | | Ch. Kohima Bet (N.Z.) | Te Kuahama Fo |
| | | | Ch. Woodleigh Annette |
| | | Ch. Michael of Kandahar | Gold Cloud of Warrigal |
| | | | Winlaton Golden Syrup |
| | Ch. Bengali Rajah | | |
| | | Ch. Bengali Belle | Ch. Bengali Toreador C.D. |
| *Dam* | | | Ch. Swaledale Viceriene |
| Ch. Bengali Annette | | | |
| | | Ch. Bengali Toreador C.D. (Imp. N.Z.) | Ch. Kohima Ajax (N.Z.) |
| | | | Ch. Kohima Bet (Imp. N.Z.) |
| | Ch. Bengali Belle | | |
| | | Ch. Swaledale Viceriene | Ch. Trievador Roderick |
| | | | Ch. Banchton Frieda |

## CH. SHAMROCK ACRES LIGHT BRIGADE

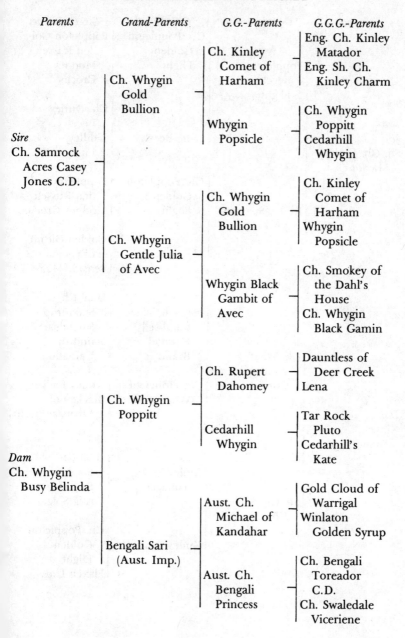

| Parents | Grand-Parents | G.G.-Parents | G.G.G.-Parents |
|---|---|---|---|
| | | Ch. Kinley Comet of Harham | Eng. Ch. Kinley Matador |
| | Ch. Whygin Gold Bullion | | Eng. Sh. Ch. Kinley Charm |
| | | Whygin Popsicle | Ch. Whygin Poppitt |
| *Sire* Ch. Samrock Acres Casey Jones C.D. | | | Cedarhill Whygin |
| | | Ch. Whygin Gold Bullion | Ch. Kinley Comet of Harham |
| | Ch. Whygin Gentle Julia of Avec | | Whygin Popsicle |
| | | Whygin Black Gambit of Avec | Ch. Smokey of the Dahl's House |
| | | | Ch. Whygin Black Gamin |
| | | Ch. Rupert Dahomey | Dauntless of Deer Creek |
| | Ch. Whygin Poppitt | | Lena |
| | | Cedarhill Whygin | Tar Rock Pluto |
| *Dam* Ch. Whygin Busy Belinda | | | Cedarhill's Kate |
| | | Aust. Ch. Michael of Kandahar | Gold Cloud of Warrigal |
| | Bengali Sari (Aust. Imp.) | | Winlaton Golden Syrup |
| | | Aust. Ch. Bengali Princess | Ch. Bengali Toreador C.D. |
| | | | Ch. Swaledale Viceriene |

## CH. KINLEY SKIPPER

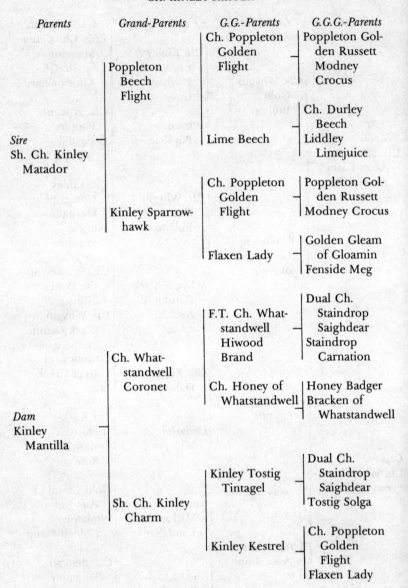

| Parents | Grand-Parents | G.G.-Parents | G.G.G.-Parents |
|---|---|---|---|
| | | Ch. Poppleton Golden Flight | Poppleton Golden Russett Modney Crocus |
| | Poppleton Beech Flight | | |
| *Sire* Sh. Ch. Kinley Matador | | Lime Beech | Ch. Durley Beech Liddley Limejuice |
| | | Ch. Poppleton Golden Flight | Poppleton Golden Russett Modney Crocus |
| | Kinley Sparrowhawk | | |
| | | Flaxen Lady | Golden Gleam of Gloamin Fenside Meg |
| | | F.T. Ch. Whatstandwell Hiwood Brand | Dual Ch. Staindrop Saighdear Staindrop Carnation |
| | Ch. Whatstandwell Coronet | | |
| *Dam* Kinley Mantilla | | Ch. Honey of Whatstandwell | Honey Badger Bracken of Whatstandwell |
| | | Kinley Tostig Tintagel | Dual Ch. Staindrop Saighdear Tostig Solga |
| | Sh. Ch. Kinley Charm | | |
| | | Kinley Kestrel | Ch. Poppleton Golden Flight Flaxen Lady |

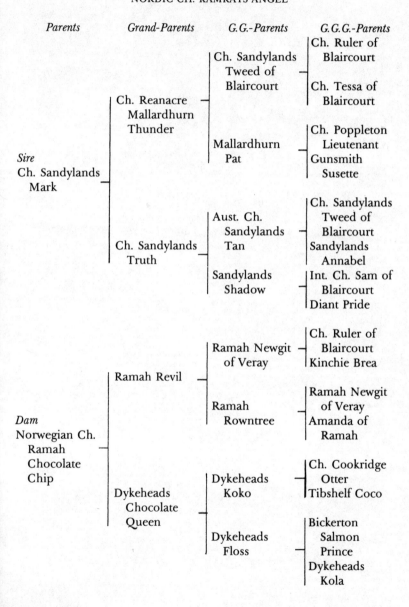

SWEDISH AND FINNISH CH. AND SWEDISH
OBEDIENCE CH. KAMRATS BUSE
INT. CH. KAMRATS JEANNY
NORDIC CH. KAMRATS ANGEL

| *Parents* | *Grand-Parents* | *G.G.-Parents* | *G.G.G.-Parents* |
|---|---|---|---|
| | | Ch. Sandylands Tweed of Blaircourt | Ch. Ruler of Blaircourt |
| | Ch. Reanacre Mallardhurn Thunder | | Ch. Tessa of Blaircourt |
| | | Mallardhurn Pat | Ch. Poppleton Lieutenant Gunsmith Susette |
| *Sire* Ch. Sandylands Mark | | Aust. Ch. Sandylands Tan | Ch. Sandylands Tweed of Blaircourt Sandylands Annabel |
| | Ch. Sandylands Truth | Sandylands Shadow | Int. Ch. Sam of Blaircourt Diant Pride |
| | Ramah Revil | Ramah Newgit of Veray | Ch. Ruler of Blaircourt Kinchie Brea |
| | | Ramah Rowntree | Ramah Newgit of Veray Amanda of Ramah |
| *Dam* Norwegian Ch. Ramah Chocolate Chip | | Dykeheads Koko | Ch. Cookridge Otter Tibshelf Coco |
| | Dykeheads Chocolate Queen | Dykeheads Floss | Bickerton Salmon Prince Dykeheads Kola |

# Index